The Evolution of
American Investigative Journalism

The Evolution of

American Investigative Journalism

James L. Aucoin

University of Missouri Press   Columbia and London

Library of Congress Cataloging-in-Publication Data

Aucoin, James, 1952–
    The evolution of American investigative journalism / James L.
Aucoin.
        p.   cm.
    Summary: "History of American investigative journalism and
the founding of the Investigative Reporters and Editors (IRE).
Discusses the murder of investigative reporter Don Bolles and
IRE's subsequent controversial Arizona Project. Applies the social-
moral development theory of Alasdair MacIntyre to explain how
the IRE contributed to the evolution of American investigative
journalism"—Provided by publisher.
    Includes bibliographical references and index.
    ISBN-13: 978-0-8262-1746-2 (pbk.: alk. paper)
    ISBN-10: 0-8262-1746-X (alk. paper)
    1. Investigative reporting—United States.   2. Investigative
Reporters and Editors, Inc.   3. Bolles, Don.   I. Title.
    PN4888.I56A83   2006
    070.4'3'0973—dc22   2005022114

    ∞™ This paper meets the requirements of the
American National Standard for Permanence of Paper
    for Printed Library Materials, Z39.48, 1984.

Designer: Jennifer Cropp
Typesetter: Phoenix Type, Inc.
Printer and binder: Thomson-Shore, Inc.
Typefaces: Minion and Goudy

*The University of Missouri Press offers its grateful acknowledgment
to an anonymous donor whose generous grant in support of the
publication of outstanding dissertations has assisted us with this volume.*

This book is dedicated to
Professor Edmund B. Lambeth

and to my wife,
Peggy A. Hansen

Contents

Acknowledgments

No book evolves from a single person. Among those who helped me with this one is Professor Edmund B. Lambeth, who introduced me to the moral theory of Alasdair MacIntyre and guided me through my dissertation at the University of Missouri–Columbia, from which this study evolves. I also thank Steve Weinberg of the University of Missouri–Columbia, former executive director of Investigative Reporters and Editors, Inc., and a superb investigative journalist and writer. He encouraged this study and generously gave of his time and knowledge. Journalists Andy Scott and Rosemary Armao, successive executive directors of IRE, generously gave me permission to research the files of the organization without restriction. Dr. Les Hansen, an outstanding teacher of composition, edited early versions of the manuscript, for which I owe him much gratitude. I, of course, am alone responsible for any mistakes that remain.

Chapter 2 originally appeared in an earlier form in *Journalism History*, Spring 1995, vol. 21, no. 1; chapter 4 includes material that originally appeared in *American Journalism*, Fall 1995, vol. 12, no. 4; and portions of chapters 5 and 7 appeared originally in the *Journal of Mass Media Ethics* in 1992, vol. 7, no. 3. All are used with permission.

Material in chapter 5 from Peter Benjaminson and David Anderson's text on investigative journalism, *Investigative Reporting*, second edition, is used with permission of the copyright holder, the University of Iowa Press.

The Evolution of
American Investigative Journalism

Introduction

The answer to the question "How healthy is investigative journalism as the practice moves into the twenty-first century?" depends on who is taking its pulse. Many investigative reporters are not optimistic about the prognosis. Because of their commitment to investigative journalism, they have been rarely satisfied with the resources allocated to such reporting by newspaper publishers and TV news managers. For example, many of the members of the national organization of investigative journalists, Investigative Reporters and Editors, Inc. (IRE), were unhappy with the quality of care publishers and station managers gave the practice in 2002. Freelance reporter Randy Dotinga, writing in the industry magazine *Editor and Publisher*, reported that investigative journalists at the IRE conference in San Diego were grim about the future of their craft: "Reporters say they face a federal government bent on keeping information to itself in the war on terror, as well as a newspaper industry more worried about profits than Pulitzers—and less likely to send someone out to file a Freedom of Information Act request in the first place." That represents a seismic shift in perspective from *Editor and Publisher*'s report on the IRE national conference held in 1998, only four years earlier. The report then carried the headline "Investigative Journalism Is Alive and Well." The subhead was even more upbeat: "A record IRE turnout in New Orleans suggests hard-boiled exposés remain newsroom staples." That year, KCOP-TV in Los Angeles announced it was expanding its commitment to investigative reporting and the recruitment boards at the conference were overflowing with job offers. But there were job offers at the 2002 conference as well, and one news organization, Knight Ridder, announced it planned to expand investigative reporting at its newspapers, though participants at the conference were skeptical. And yet, a 2002 report in the *Columbia Journalism Review*, after noting that the absolute number of investigative stories on local TV news stations had declined during the past five years, concluded honestly that "nonetheless, the figures suggest that even in the face of economic contraction, many local news stations remained committed to investigative journalism, however they defined it." Indeed, an investigative reporter at a Boston television station thought investigative journalism was thriving in 2002. "We seem to be in one of the peak periods now," Joe Bergantino told the *Kennedy School Bulletin* at Harvard University. Indeed, more investigative reporting and semi-investigative reporting is going on today than at least since the golden age of muckraking at the turn of the twentieth century, when investigative reporting became the staple of the national magazines. Moreover, today there are more journalists involved in investigative reporting than ever before.[1]

There must be a distinction drawn, however, between what some news outlets label "investigative" and what IRE and most serious investigative journalists consider "investigative." This book concerns the latter type—serious investigative journalism that takes a comprehensive, exhaustive look at issues that have significant impact on the lives of the audience. "Investigations" that use undercover cameras and other investigative techniques to examine issues of limited or negligible impact on most people are not considered by serious investigative journalists to be investigative journalism. This latter type of reporting is driven by entertainment values, not journalism values. TV journalist Bergantino, in his interview with the *Kennedy School Bulletin*, was careful to make this distinction. He said he was confident about the practice of investigative journalism, but acknowledged that much of what passes for "investigative journalism" does not meet the standards promoted by Investigative Reporters and Editors. "Investigations into the dangers of high-heel shoes or automatic doors stoop to the level of total absurdity," he noted. "Some might

1. Randy Dotinga, "News Probes Face Obstacles"; M. I. Stein, "Investigative Journalism Is Alive and Well"; Marion Just, Rosalind Levine, and Kathleen Regan, "Investigative Journalism Despite the Odds."

view the Lewinsky/Clinton or Chandra Levy scandals as investigative. I don't, and I don't think a lot of other investigative reporters do either."[2]

Bergantino was right. A wide gulf exists between serious investigative reporting as it has been practiced since at least the 1970s—the type of reporting promoted by IRE—and what some news outlets call investigative. Historically, the purpose of serious investigative journalism has been "to tell stories of wrongdoing that will stir moral outrage" and to focus on systemic problems of considerable public import. But the purpose of tabloid-styled stories erroneously labeled "investigative" is to entertain. These entertainment-oriented exposés are what Richard Parker, a senior fellow at the Shorenstein Center on the Press, Politics and Public Policy, has called "McMuck, or muckraking-lite." In contrast, serious reporters define "investigative reporting" as original reporting on an issue of significant public concern that reveals information not previously known and perhaps even hidden. The standards for documentation, context, and presentation are rigorous and have been derived from the best work of the best practitioners in the history of American journalism.[3]

But Bergantino had hit upon a major problem that confronts serious investigative journalism in the twenty-first century. Much as the serious crusades in the 1890s are overlooked because of the sensationalistic style that burst from the pages of William Randolph Hearst's and Joseph Pulitzer's New York newspapers, today's serious investigative journalism often falls into the shadows of the hyped, razzle-dazzle, scare-the-viewers reporting about minor dangers that characterize much of what is erroneously called "investigative" on local television news stations and some cable news shows. Greg Dobbs, a veteran ABC newsman and instructor at the University of Colorado, cited one egregious example from Denver's KUSA-TV, an NBC affiliate that attached the "investigative" label to a story about a Colorado teacher who was trying to locate a child to thank her for returning some money the teacher had lost. "Insufficient newsroom budgets, lean staffing and tight controls on time have relegated most investigative reporting to newspapers and magazines," *Electronic*

2. Lory Hough, "Truth Be Told."
3. Matthew C. Ehrlich, "Not Ready for Prime Time: Tabloid and Investigative TV Journalism."

Media magazine has acknowledged. Unfortunately, serious investigative journalism — in the print media, on television and cable, and on the Internet — often is tarnished with the faults of the less serious and poorly executed stories.[4]

In truth, serious investigative journalism has become nothing short of a national phenomenon. Network television and cable are awash with investigative news programs, from the sensationalistic and ethically suspect to the more journalistically sound. In addition, millions of people can easily access news Web sites to read excellent investigative reports by newspapers, television stations, and magazines throughout the United States. Local issues such as the spread of crack cocaine in Los Angeles or Iowa's child-abuse problems now achieve a national or international audience. Granted, investigative journalism in the early years of the twenty-first century seems burdened by silly McMuck stories on TV news shows, a growing threat from lawsuits, newsroom budget crunches, and tight-lipped government officials using the war on terrorism as an excuse to clamp down on information to the public. Nevertheless, serious investigative journalism has become a defining characteristic of the news media. When done well, investigative journalism sets the standard against which all news reporting is judged; when done poorly, it is a lightning rod for complaints about the news media.

Largely through the efforts of individual practitioners and IRE, serious investigative journalism has become a respectable, coveted, and distinct genre of journalism. Colleges teach courses in its practice, principles, and history. Textbooks explain how to do it. Fiction and nonfiction writers alike treat the practitioner as a modern folk hero. Popular books and television programs narrate the adventures of investigative journalists. Mass communication scholars study its techniques, its acceptance by the public, its traditions, and its role in society.

Some journalism historians trace the roots of the modern investigative journalist to America's late seventeenth and early eighteenth centuries, when Benjamin Harris and James Franklin exposed the faults of Boston officials. Other historians trace the practice's roots to the great muckrakers who worked at the turn of the twentieth cen-

---

4. Lee Hall, "Local News Must Dig Deeper Than the Hype," *Electronic Media*, October 21, 2002, 13.

tury. Still others insist that modern investigative reporters are a breed that evolved from the past but who are different from reporters of the past—they are linked to the muckraking Ida Tarbell, Lincoln Steffens, David Graham Phillips, and others of their journalistic generation, but today's reporters don't have the crusading advocacy central to the muckrakers of the Progressive era.

While much has been written on the origins, ideas, lives, and impact of the Progressive muckrakers, investigative journalism during other eras in American history, particularly since 1960, has received considerably less study. Some biographies of individual investigative journalists have been written, and more limited work has been done on their role in modern society. But there is little written about the evolution of modern investigative journalism as a practice—about how it has developed and progressed as a journalistic genre.

This book is a historical examination of investigative journalism from about 1960 to 1990, with particular emphasis on how it has evolved as a social practice and the role that IRE played in its progress since the mid-1970s. The book uses a critical historical approach suggested by moral philosopher Alasdair MacIntyre, who has described how a social practice develops and persists over time. MacIntyre uses the term "social practice" in a restricted manner, reserving it for practices that meet certain social, behavioral, and moral requirements. Moreover, I adopt MacIntyre's definition of a social practice, which he defines as a coherent, complex, cooperative human activity in a social setting. He says that members of a practice obtain goods that are specific to the practice by carrying out activities in the pursuit of standards of excellence. These are standards appropriate to and partially definitive of the practice. He argues that a social practice is sustained and, indeed, progresses through the efforts of practitioners to meet and extend the practice's standards of excellence.[5]

MacIntyre, a neo-Aristotelian, argues that "the good life" is achieved through the exercise of time-tested, fundamental virtues in a social setting, and that progress in a social practice occurs through the application of the virtues in action. He says practitioners must apply the virtues of courage, honesty, justice, and respect for tradition, as well as other virtues that may be specific to a particular practice.

5. Alasdair MacIntyre, *After Virtue: A Study in Moral Theory,* 175–82.

MacIntyre recognizes the dependence of social practices on institutions, but argues that only when virtuous people operate independent of the institutions can progress occur. To MacIntyre, it is the notion of a social practice that offers individuals the ability to separate themselves from the institutions which sustain them.

For MacIntyre, institutions offer the practitioner external goods such as power, status, money, and fame. Internal goods relative to doing the practice well and doing it better than it has ever been done before are embedded only in the practice itself, though, and are achieved only when individual practitioners, or practitioners acting in unison, apply the virtues to the tasks of the practice. MacIntyre recognizes the necessity of institutions, for institutions sustain practices by providing the external goods. But therein lies the ironic tension between the institutions and the practices, between the external and the internal goods. A practice, such as journalism, requires social power, status, and money to be effective in society, but those same goods constantly threaten the integrity of the practice. As MacIntyre explains, "the ideals and the creativity of the practice are always vulnerable to the acquisitiveness of the institution." And here the Aristotelian virtues come into play: For only when practitioners display the virtues can the practice maintain its integrity. "Without them, without justice, courage and truthfulness [and respect for tradition, at a minimum], practices could not resist the corrupting power of institutions."[6]

As the most significant force for organizing and training investigative journalists, beginning in 1975, IRE was dominant in developing the craft during the later years of the twentieth century. If investigative journalism has become a social practice, as defined by MacIntyre, IRE was the deciding factor. A MacIntyrean social practice is facilitated by some type of formal, systematic means of communication among members of the practice, and IRE fulfilled that role for investigative journalism.

Investigative journalism, as defined by IRE, has been studied, but only to a limited extent. Researcher Robert Miraldi looks at muckraking, which he sees as activist-oriented exposés by reformers, and at modern journalism, which embraces objectivity as a necessary principle. He argues that within investigative journalism, the reformist

6. Ibid., 181.

tradition of muckraking collides with the ideal of objectivity. His study contrasts the values, techniques, and ideas of the muckrakers with those of the modern investigative reporter and attempts to explain why investigative reporting is, as he sees it, ineffective in righting the wrongs of society. Miraldi's purpose, though, is to connect values to performance, not to chronicle the history of investigative reporting. Researchers Ted Glasser and James Ettema have studied the interaction between the practice of investigative journalism and society, showing that the use of narrative form injects investigative journalism with a moral dimension both in identifying, communicating, and reinforcing the American society's understanding of morality, which is usually framed in terms of good and evil. Ettema and Glasser suggest, moreover, that investigative journalism, because of the manner in which it has been practiced, has had a negative effect on American society. They argue that investigative journalists, through the subtle use of the literary device of irony, have helped create a cynical audience that is no longer interested in participating in American politics.[7]

In addition, scholar David Protess and a team of researchers adopted a social scientific approach to study the role of investigative journalism within society. Testing the agenda-setting theory of modern American journalism hypothesized by Max McCombs, Donald Shaw, and others, Protess and his team find it insufficient and propose, instead, a "consensus model." Agenda-setting theory suggests a mobilization model that assumes investigative journalism raises an issue and reports on it, stirring up public opinion, which puts pressure on public officials to respond to the social problem at issue. The consensus model as proposed by Protess and his team, on the other hand, suggests that investigative journalists do not attempt to stir the public to action. Instead, they often work hand-in-hand with public policy-makers and special interest groups from the outset of an investigation to identify the issue and orchestrate a public policy response to the published report. In this view, modern investigative journalism directly affects public policy in American society.[8]

7. Robert Miraldi, *Muckraking and Objectivity: Journalism's Colliding Traditions*; James S. Ettema and Theodore L. Glasser, *Custodians of Conscience: Investigative Journalism and Public Virtue.*

8. David L. Protess et al., *The Journalism of Outrage: Investigative Reporting and Agenda Building in America.*

Another type of study designed to quantify investigative journalism in society is the public opinion survey. The Protess, et al., study includes public opinion surveys in regards to specific investigative projects. While the results were mixed, the general conclusion by the researchers was that investigative journalism has limited impact on public opinion about specific issues under investigation. David Weaver and LeAnne Daniels reported two public opinion surveys that built on an earlier survey and compared the results to findings from a 1981 Gallup survey. They concluded that there is strong support nationally for investigative journalism. Ninety-four percent of the respondents in the national survey indicated that investigative journalism was very important or somewhat important; more than half said it was very important. However, they also found only lukewarm support for some specific, controversial techniques used by investigative reporters, including using hidden cameras or hidden microphones, failing to identify themselves as reporters, quoting unnamed sources, and posing as someone other than a reporter. Updating past work on public perceptions of investigative reporting, researchers Susan Opt and Timothy Delaney concluded that "research and polls on public opinion of investigative reporting as well as media discussions and court cases show that public support for this type of journalism varies according to the public's perceptions of the media's motives. Over time, as the findings indicate, the practice of investigative journalism has enjoyed widespread support from the public.... At the same time, though, support for the media's methods of conducting such investigations has seesawed."[9] The public wants hard-hitting investigative journalism, they contend, but it wants the media's motives to be pure and has doubt about the propriety of using hidden cameras and other ethically questionable techniques of investigation.

9. David Weaver and LeAnne Daniels, "Public Opinion on Investigative Reporting in the 1980s." The study was of 1,002 respondents to a 1984–1985 national telephone survey and 735 respondents to a 1989 statewide telephone poll conducted in Indiana. It built on a 1980 study of respondents in the Chicago area, Virginia Dodge Fielder and David H. Weaver, "Public Opinion on Investigative Reporting," and on "Investigative Reporting Has Broad Public Support." Susan K. Opt and Timothy A. Delaney, "Public Perceptions of Investigative Reporting."

That there has been little research on the evolution of modern investigative journalism and how it has developed coincides with the fact that few studies have attempted to show how the craft of journalism in general has developed. Scholar James Carey has lamented that historians' overemphasis on biography has caused media historians to miss what he calls "the central historical story"—the history of reporting. Media historians John Stevens and Hazel Dicken-Garcia agree and argue that focusing on the great men and women journalists as catalysts for the progression of the practice has led media historians to miss the history of journalism as a process that interacts with the larger culture and society. History missed, Stevens and Dicken-Garcia assert, includes specialized reporting practices wherein questions asked and answered would be "how the duties and perceived functions were understood, how the role was defined, and when the [specialized] reporter gained acceptance, following by an audience, power and status to bargain, and permanency as part of the industry."[10]

Previous studies of journalism's development have concerned journalism in general and have used to limited satisfaction a framework of professionalism to show advancement or nonadvancement of the craft. The greatest problem of the professionalization paradigm, to my mind, is that the paradigm excludes writers such as Rachel Carson, who with *Silent Spring*, which exposed the environment's contamination by pesticides, produced in 1962 perhaps the most influential muckraking work in American history. Professionalization studies, though, would exclude Carson because she was a marine scientist, not a practicing journalist. Professionalization also would exclude Ralph Nader, author of *Unsafe at Any Speed: The Designed-In Dangers of the American Automobile*, the 1965 exposé of the auto industry, because he was a consumer-rights lawyer, and not a working journalist. One notable exception to the professionalization paradigm, however, is *Journalistic Standards in Nineteenth-Century America*, by Hazel Dicken-Garcia, who concluded that journalism progresses or does not progress according to journalism's standards predominant at any given time. Because they are culturally derived, standards are a product of the social role the press fulfills at any given time in history

10. James Carey, *Communication as Culture: Essays on Media and Society.*

and set the rules that govern how reporting and writing are done and what is published.[11]

Media scholar Edmund Lambeth has suggested that historians can gain insight into the development of journalism by using the concept of a social practice as defined by MacIntyre in *After Virtue:* "The past, in this [MacIntyre's] view, is not a nostalgic montage of ill-remembered facts and chronicles. It is a living tissue that connects the best of the present with a past from which practitioners can actively learn. Because practitioner communities of the kind MacIntyre has in mind are relatively small and cohesive, a MacIntyrean history is most likely to mean an account of a specialty within the larger history of journalism."[12]

The social practice concept of MacIntyre may, in fact, be a way to meld the strategies of methodology advanced by many media historians, including those taking a Progressive, cultural, or social approach. If one is to adequately describe a social practice and how it is developing (or not developing), the historian must consider the biographies of practitioners, especially those who have influenced how journalism is done; the ideas held by practitioners about the craft; and the cultural and social setting of the practice.

The social practice paradigm has been advanced by MacIntyre, but its origin is in the ethics of Aristotle. Good work, Aristotle argued, occurs when a person acting virtuously does the work. In other words, morality is based in the actor, not in the action. The actor must act with the cardinal virtues of justice, courage, wisdom, and temperance. However, the actor develops "practical reason" only by carrying out the act over and over, always striving to do it virtuously. There is a symbiosis, then, between the practitioner and the practice. The character of the practitioner improves; that is, the practitioner gets better at what he or she does and, at the same time, the product improves.

This improving-through-acting for investigative journalism has been helped most by the establishment of IRE, an organization of practitioners that forms a buffer between the practice and the institutions that support it. The 1975 founding of IRE rode the crest of a

11. Hazel Dicken-Garcia, *Journalistic Standards in Nineteenth-Century America.*
12. Edmund Lambeth, "Waiting for a New St. Benedict: Alasdair MacIntyre and the Theory and Practice of Journalism."

reemergence of investigative journalism that began in the late 1950s. This reemergence was intimately tied to the long tradition of exposure journalism in American history that began in Boston at newspapers edited by Benjamin Harris and James Franklin. There is a direct line from Harris's *Publick Occurrences, Both Foreign and Domestick* to the reporters in the late 1950s and early 1960s who gathered their skills and talents to expose the ills of society, thereby reawakening the tradition and starting the craft on the path to becoming a vibrant social practice. Chapter 1 traces this tradition of exposure reporting in the history of American journalism.

Media historian James Baughman and *Time* editor Richard Clurman suggest that technology and new competition caused investigative journalism's emergence in the 1960s, particularly the rise of television as a news source. Many newspaper and magazine publishers saw investigative journalism as a way to counter the competition from television, which was unsuited to in-depth coverage of the news. But this explanation ignores the investigative tradition in the electronic media and fails to account for a meager amount of investigative journalism during the 1920s and 1930s, when radio challenged newspapers' dominance of the news business. Social historian Michael Schudson and former reporter James Boylan provide the added explanation of the press's break with the government's view of events, particularly over perceptions of the Vietnam War. Moreover, journalist Anthony Lewis suggests that the Supreme Court decision in *New York Times v. Sullivan* had something to do with it. Muckraking editor Carey McWilliams of *The Nation* magazine suggested that two factors spur popularity in investigative journalism—the introduction of new technology and the presence of an audience receptive to such reporting because of tensions in society.[13] Each explanation is right, as far as it goes.

MacIntyre, the moral philosopher, suggests that to understand fully

13. James L. Baughman, *The Republic of Mass Culture: Journalism, Filmmaking, and Broadcasting in America since 1941,* 120; Richard M. Clurman, *Beyond Malice: The Media's Years of Reckoning,* 202–7; James Boylan, "Declarations of Independence: A Historian Reflects on an Era in Which Reporters Rose Up to Challenge—and Change—the Rules of the Game"; Michael Schudson, *Discovering the News: A Social History of American Newspapers,* 160–94; Anthony Lewis, *Make No Law: The Sullivan Case and the First Amendment,* 158; Carey McWilliams, "Is Muckraking Coming Back?" 11.

the progression of a social practice such as investigative journalism, one must look at the development of technical skills and at the ways in which practitioners conceptualize the goals and internal values of the practice. This will always occur within the context of social and cultural circumstances. Indeed, cultural journalism historian James Carey instructs that "news is a historic reality," for it evolves at a particular time in history and is created by specific people for specific reasons. During the late 1950s and early 1960s, social and cultural developments outside of journalism, coupled with changes within journalism, refined journalism's role in American society and refocused journalism on its watchdog responsibilities.[14] Chapter 2 discusses the factors that caused the reemergence of investigative journalism during the 1960s.

Chapter 3 chronicles the development of methods and standards for modern investigative journalism from 1960 to 1975. By the mid-1970s, investigative journalism had evolved into a mature practice that built on the practice's long tradition in the United States. Individual reporters, sometimes in informal contact with other investigative journalists, had developed standards and skills within the context of their news organizations, but reporters and editors made little attempt to reach out and educate other journalists.

That outreach and a formal means of communication among practitioners appeared when IRE was founded. Chapter 4 details the founding of IRE and examines the organization's early years, from its start in 1975 to about 1980. The organization was conceived by a group of established investigative journalists called together in February 1975 by Myrta Pulliam and Harley Bierce, two reporters from the *Indianapolis Star*; Paul Williams, a journalism professor with a background in investigative journalism; and Robert Friedly, a former reporter who was then communications director for an Indianapolis church. Between 1976 and 1980, IRE established the resource center in cooperation with the University of Missouri School of Journalism, hired a permanent staff, founded a publication (*The IRE Journal*) to communicate with members, held annual and regional conferences, set up an annual awards program, and adopted a definition of investigative journalism. The central value of IRE, though, was its formation of a community composed of journalists dedicated to

14. MacIntyre, *After Virtue*, 180; Carey, *Communication as Culture*, 21.

investigating and exposing the corruption, malfeasance, and incompetence of public and private persons who wield power in America. IRE's fostering of cooperation and its encouragement of cohesion among the nation's investigative journalists were critical to the development of modern investigative journalism in the United States in the late twentieth century.

One of IRE's defining moments during its early years was the Arizona Project, the subject of chapter 5. A few days before investigative journalists gathered in Indianapolis for the first IRE national conference, one of their colleagues, Don Bolles of the *Arizona Republic*, died of injuries suffered when a bomb exploded beneath his car on June 2, 1976. His friends in IRE believed Bolles was killed to stop his exposés. IRE members viewed his killing as an assault on the practice of investigative journalism, an assault which, if left unanswered, could have meant an open season on journalists around the nation. By resolution at the first IRE conference, a team of reporters from U.S. news outlets went to Arizona under the auspices of IRE to complete the reporting that Don Bolles had started.

The growth of IRE from the late 1970s to the late 1980s into a national organization, largely because of the Arizona Project, allowed it to reach into newsrooms around the country, teaching investigative skills, promoting the practice, and emphasizing the standards that would ensure the credibility of investigative reporting. By 1990, with nearly three thousand members, IRE was a fixture in American journalism, and editors and producers at U.S. news outlets viewed investigative reporting as the standard of high-quality journalism. Chapter 6 looks at IRE's efforts that led to the institutionalization of investigative journalism in American newsrooms.

One way to better understand IRE's contribution to modern American investigative journalism is to view it through the lens of theory, specifically the sociologically grounded moral theory of philosopher Alasdair MacIntyre. Chapter 7 applies MacIntyre's blueprint to the history of IRE to show how the organization led to the progress of investigative journalism as a social practice.

All in all, this study concerns IRE's development up to about 1990. But the decade of the nineties proved to be some of the more productive years for the organization. Between 1991 and its twentieth anniversary, which the organization celebrated in 1996, IRE continued its mission to provide services to working journalists and to improve the quality of investigative journalism. Three executive directors have served the organization since Steve Weinberg announced his retirement from the job in 1990. Andy Scott began work in January 1991. When he resigned to return to newspaper work, the position was filled by reporter Rosemary Armao, who was appointed in February 1994. Three years later, Armao also resigned to return to the newsroom, and Brant Houston, director of IRE's subsidiary, the National Institute for Computer-Assisted Reporting (NICAR), was named IRE director. NICAR was founded as the Missouri Institute of Computer-Assisted Reporting, or MICAR, at the University of Missouri School of Journalism as a separate entity in 1989 under the direction of Elliot Jaspin. In late 1993, after Jaspin resigned MICAR's directorship, the institute merged with IRE, which had obtained a substantial grant from the Freedom Forum, a journalism foundation started by the Gannett Corporation, to continue the program. In February 1994, the institute's name was altered to replace "Missouri" with "National."

During the first part of the 1990s, IRE's newsletter, *IRE Journal*, was expanded from a quarterly to a bimonthly publication and was reduced from tabloid-size to an 8½-by-11-inch format to make it more attractive to libraries. A $1.1 million endowment fund was created. And IRE increased efforts to help reporters in other countries, including the former republics of the Soviet Union and Mexico, to begin similar organizations. In 1996, IRE was awarded a $540,000, three-year grant from the McCormick Tribune Foundation to fund the organization's first international effort, Periodistas de Investigacion, a computer-assisted reporting institute in Mexico. The grant also supported IRE's efforts to establish an IRE-type organization in that country.

Membership reached an all-time high of nearly four thousand in the late 1990s, and attendance at national conferences usually topped one thousand. Clearly, the organization has touched a chord in the journalism profession. It has attracted a wide variety of reporters and editors who want to learn investigative skills.

In 1996, the University of Maryland School of Journalism and three other universities invited IRE to move from the University of Missouri to their campuses. The University of Maryland's offer was particularly strong, touching off a vigorous debate among the membership about whether to abandon the nation's oldest journalism school for headquarters closer to Washington, D.C., and other political and economic power centers in the United States. After the University of Missouri journalism faculty mounted a campaign to keep IRE on their campus, IRE's board voted seven to four to reject Maryland's offer and stay at Missouri.

Communication among IRE members expanded in the mid-1990s when IRE began discussion groups on the Internet and created its own site on the World Wide Web. This was an extension of the organization's efforts to communicate with reporters. The Web site provides information about the organization, as well as practical advice and other help to journalists. Significantly, much of the Web site remains open to the public, providing education on investigative techniques to journalists who are not members and to the general public.

The organization's successful how-to publication, *The Reporter's Handbook: An Investigator's Guide to Documents and Techniques*, first published in 1983, was updated in 1991 by IRE's first executive director, John Ullmann, and Jan Colbert of the University of Missouri. It was completely revised in 1996 under the sole authorship of former IRE executive director Steve Weinberg. The book's fourth edition was published in 2002 under the editorship of Brant Houston.

In his 1996 revision of the handbook, Weinberg embraced a new definition of investigative journalism, signaling an important shift in IRE's conception of the practice that coincidentally aligns investigative journalism with the type of journalism media ethics scholar Edmund Lambeth champions in his book, *Committed Journalism*. Lambeth argues that the increasing complexity of the modern world requires a journalist to go beyond the exposure of corruption and individual wrongdoing, to embrace what *Washington Post* editor Leonard Downie has described as "expert analysis of complicated subjects and institutions" and to offer solutions to the myriad of problems uncovered by aggressive reporting. The older generation of investigative reporters who founded IRE conceived of the practice as the uncovering of information that someone or some institution wants to keep hidden. Consequently, the definition focused the practice on stories about corrupt officials. The reworked definition, however, takes the practice into a more proactive role, uncovering systemic failures and misguided policies and offering solutions.

Leading the practice of investigative journalism into new territory while retaining the practice's traditional standards and values is typical of the work IRE has undertaken from its first days in a small, crowded office in Indianapolis nearly thirty years ago. The organization has heeded the experience of the muckrakers in the early twentieth century, who saw their influence wane as shoddy workmanship among some of their brethren weakened the entire practice. In the early years of the twenty-first century, IRE continues to coax the practice to higher ground. By endorsing a vision of investigative journalism as a practice capable of blazing a perceptive path out of the muck of modern life, IRE is repositioning modern investigative reporting as an influential participant in making a better society.

The Tradition of Exposure in American Journalism

Modern investigative journalism burst upon America's collective consciousness in 1974 when *All the President's Men,* by *Washington Post* reporters Carl Bernstein and Bob Woodward, hit the bookstore shelves. The book described their dramatic exploits digging into the corruption of Watergate. Two years later, the book served as the basis for a sensationalistic, blockbuster movie starring Dustin Hoffman and Robert Redford in the lead roles. It was a heady time for U.S. journalism. In August 1974, Richard Nixon became the first American president to resign the office, driven out by a constitutional crisis that had swirled around his administration for two years. Some in the media claimed the press had brought him down, though they overstated journalism's role in the ordeal that had gripped the nation. Nevertheless, it was true that Washington journalists — Bernstein and Woodward especially — had relentlessly dug into the story, revealing illegal payoffs, dirty tricks, death threats, and other political intrigues, the reporting of which kept public pressure on Congress and other Washington institutions to eventually drive Richard Nixon from the White House. Woodward and Bernstein's book and the movie made exposé reporting sexy, and investigative journalists became America's new heroes.[1]

The sensation of Watergate, in fact, is often cited as the reason investigative journalism reemerged and became institutionalized in the American press during the latter half of the twentieth century. But that's not an accurate explanation. Watergate, despite its status as a particularly myopic myth for journalists, did not cause investigative journalism to reemerge in journalism culture. Investigative journalism had resurfaced as a strong alternative to event-focused journalism nearly two decades before the Watergate crisis. By 1962 a recognizable pattern of investigative journalism had already emerged, and by the late 1960s several newspapers, including the *Boston Globe, Newsday*, and the *Chicago Tribune*, fielded permanent investigative teams and *60 Minutes*, television's preeminent investigative newsmagazine, had debuted on CBS.[2]

This most recent revival of investigative journalism, which began in the late 1950s, grew from a historically grounded journalistic tradition of exposure that dates to the colonial era in America and undulates through the decades, always present but at differing strengths. "Exposure in the press was soon an essential part of a process that all knew must continue for as long as there was a United States," journalist Pete Hamill points out. "After the Civil War, the cycles were established: corruption, then exposure, then reform, followed by a slow drift back into corruption." Understandably, the exposés of

1. Carl Bernstein and Bob Woodward, *All the President's Men; All the President's Men*, Alan J. Pakula, director, Warner Bros. Studios, 1976; Kim McQuaid, *The Anxious Years: America in the Vietnam-Watergate Era*, 191–92. Godfrey Hodgson, *America in Our Time: From World War II to Nixon, What Happened and Why*, 381; David Halberstam, *The Powers That Be*, 606–711; the argument that the press did not play a major role in forcing Richard Nixon's resignation is made in Edward Jay Epstein, *Between Fact and Fiction: The Problem of Journalism*, 19–32; Stanley I. Kutler, *The Wars of Watergate: The Last Crisis of Richard Nixon*; and Michael Schudson, "Watergate: A Study in Mythology." On the transformation of investigative reporters into American heroes, see James H. Dygert, *The Investigative Journalist: Folk Heroes of a New Era*.

2. Protess et al., *The Journalism of Outrage*; Robert Miraldi, *Muckraking and Objectivity: Journalism's Colliding Traditions*; Michael Schudson, *Watergate in American Memory: How We Remember, Forget, and Reconstruct the Past*, 103–26. "Event-focused" journalism is distinguished by an inverted-pyramid structure, disinterested narration, concise writing, and reporting information provided by sources. Schudson, *Discovering the News*, 91.

the eighteenth and nineteenth centuries differ greatly from the carefully constructed, disinterested investigative reports found today in newspapers and magazines and on television news programs, for as Cardinal John Henry Newman has observed, long-lasting traditions—ideas, concepts, and skills handed down through generations—evolve over time as a practice's standards blend with new concepts and current social circumstances. Moreover, the editors and reporters who maintained the tradition of exposure prior to the mid–twentieth century may not have been fully aware that they were creating and nurturing what would become a recognizable tradition. Edmund Burke has explained that those who nurture a tradition often do so without appreciating the larger scheme in which they are involved. Indeed, moral philosopher Alasdair MacIntyre suggests that to fully understand the progression of a social practice (such as investigative journalism), one must look at the historical development of technical skills and ways in which practitioners conceptualize the practice's goals, standards of excellence, and internal values. In other words, to understand the emergence of a particular news form such as investigative journalism, we must look at the tradition from which it comes and the social/cultural milieu from which it emerges.[3]

The first exposé journalist was probably the first newspaperman in the Anglo-American colonies, Benjamin Harris, founder of *Publick Occurrences Both Forreign and Domestick*, the American continent's first English-language newspaper, which debuted in Boston on September 25, 1690. An accomplished London publisher, Ben Harris arrived in Boston in 1686, driven out of England under threat of imprisonment for pamphlets and broadsides that had offended British authorities. Harris had worked in an England that staggered with political upheaval in the latter half of the seventeenth century. Civil war had replaced the monarchy of Charles I with a Puritan-led republican government, which itself was overthrown eleven years later with the return of Charles II. Even with the return to monarchy, rebellion continued, and unsatisfactory kings were overthrown in 1649 and 1688. This was the world that influenced Harris's work,

3. Pete Hamill, Foreword to Bruce Shapiro, ed., *Shaking the Foundations: 200 Years of Investigative Journalism in America*, viii; John Henry Newman, *Essay on the Development of Christian Doctrine* (London: Longmans Green, 1890); Edmund Burke, *Reflections on the Revolution in France* (London: Dent, 1967); MacIntyre, *After Virtue*, 180.

and he carried that rebelliousness with him to the Massachusetts Bay Colony, establishing the colonies' first newspaper without obtaining government sanction. Harris planned to issue his paper monthly, or more frequently if "any Glut of Occurrences happen, oftener" and offered readers of the first issue a mixture of news, from the routine (the state of the harvest and reports of two fires, for example) to the scandalous. One of the more controversial pieces revealed that Britain's American Indian allies, the Iroquois ("miserable savages," he called them), had reportedly tortured French prisoners during the ongoing King William's War. The three-page publication (the fourth page, as was the practice then, was left blank) also reported political unrest in France stemming from the French king's sexual dalliances with his son's wife. While not the product of Harris's original reporting, these articles qualify as "exposés"—revealing new (to his audience) information the government did not want reported to his readers. Moreover, his reports embrace the essential qualities of investigative journalism—revelation of public wrongdoing, documentation of evidence, a challenge to established public policy, and an appeal to public opinion for reform. The reports so enraged the Massachusetts governor that he ordered Harris's "pamphlet" suppressed.[4]

Granted, exposés did not characterize the provincial newspapers that followed Harris's for the next sixty years or so. Published under government licensing, the newspapers that appeared during the next six decades deemphasized American news in favor of European news and experimented with educational or literary material, carefully avoiding government censure. But the audience was ripe for exposés. Those who settled America had fled from repressive governments and religious intolerance. They feared tyranny—of men and governments—and strongly believed in the fallibility of individuals and the governments they created. The scandalous reports of government injustices and corruption they read in their newspapers perfectly fit their shared worldview. They embraced John Calvin's vision of human depravity, in which every man is "polluted with rapine and murder" and whose "works are useless." Early Americans expected reports that revealed the failings of government, and the printers

---

4. Protess et al., *Journalism of Outrage*, 30; Charles E. Clark, "The Newspapers of Provincial America," 373–75.

who shared their vision obliged them. One such printer was James Franklin, Ben Franklin's older brother, who founded the *New England Courant* in 1721. James Franklin frequently challenged the policies of Boston's Puritan leaders and specifically criticized their failure to stem attacks by pirates in the Atlantic Ocean. Franklin, like Benjamin Harris, drew upon the investigative tradition of the British press to guide his newspaper. He republished a defense of the exposé that first appeared as one of "Cato's Letters," written by British pamphleteers, that defended "the exposing...of publick Wickedness as it is a Duty which every Man owes to his country." Indeed, the spirited exposés published by Harris and James Franklin planted the seed of journalism's tradition of exposure on American soil, a seed that flourished in the mid–eighteenth century when men turned to rebellion.[5]

The decades leading up to and during the American Revolution saw rebels using most of the colonies' thirty or so newspapers to spread dissension against the British Crown by revealing its abuses. This was a natural step, given that colonists had become avid newspaper readers. Though opinionated mixtures of fact, rumor, and exaggeration, colonial papers opposed to British rule inspired revolution by revealing corruption and abuse of power—recognizable themes among modern investigative journalists. John Peter Zenger angered authorities in 1733 for publishing scandalous stories in his *New York Weekly Journal* that exposed Governor Sir William Cosby's incompetence for allowing French warships to spy on lower-bay defenses and otherwise revealed the colonial bureaucracy's ineptitude. Later, on the eve of the revolution, Samuel Adams and his colleagues at the *Boston Gazette* stirred opposition to the British by reporting alleged atrocities by British soldiers stationed in Boston to quell rebellion. "By 1770," writes historian Thomas Leonard, "the passion for exposure was at the center of Boston political life...The marshaling of secrets and the illumination of deception was the patriots' work."[6] And colonialists read these political exposés in their newspapers, primarily through Sam Adams's "Journal of Occurrences," which

---

5. Clark, "Newspapers of Provincial America"; Edmund S. Morgan, "The American Revolution Considered as an Intellectual Movement," in Arthur M. Schlesinger, Jr., and Morton White, eds., *Paths of American Thought* (Boston: Houghton Mifflin, 1963), 11–12; Thomas C. Leonard, *The Power of the Press*, 29.

6. Leonard, *Power of the Press*, 42.

was distributed to papers up and down the Eastern Coast. Leonard explains that colonial newspapers used the political exposé to put revolutionary ideology into language ordinary people could understand, distilling the grand notions of democratic revolution into dramatic stories of corruption and abuse of power that colonialists could readily comprehend.

The press's tradition of exposing the secrets and scandals of government and powerful men continued after the American Revolution in the pages of the political party–controlled newspapers. When the Republic was formed, the press was given a privileged position as a check on the abuses of government, as a canvasser of "the merits and measures of public men of every description." Press exposés of the late eighteenth and early nineteenth centuries invariably dealt with government policies and public men, a tradition of exposure spun from press practices of the colonial era and emboldened by conceptions of a free press as envisioned by the framers of the new Republic. Consequently, as Federalists and Republicans vied for power, "the papers brimmed with charges of bribery, thievery, and treachery of every sort." Benjamin Franklin Bache, who followed his famous grandfather Ben into the newspaper business in Philadelphia, used exposure to defeat the Federalists and garner support for the Republicans. In 1795 Bache published a financial exposé of the Federalist government in Washington that may be the earliest example of investigative reporting based on a leaked government document. Bache's exposure of a government secret in a 1798 issue of the *Aurora General Advertiser* in Philadelphia galvanized the Federalists into trying to muzzle the press. Accusations of treason broiled when Bache obtained a secret, official letter seeking peace negotiations signed by Charles Maurice de Talleyrand, France's foreign affairs minister. The newspaper published the document prominently, and then accused President George Washington of keeping it from Congress "for more than a week" to stir the winds of war. The Federalists responded with the Alien and Sedition Acts of 1798, which allowed the arrest of Bache and other Republican-biased editors whom the Federalists wanted to silence. Fortunately for the press, the acts, which required congressional approval to keep them in force after 1800, were allowed to die when Republican Thomas Jefferson became president. Throughout the late eighteenth and early nineteenth centuries, the party-controlled newspapers provided weekly, then daily, accounts of personal and government secrets, vilifying their political opponents with accusations and rumors couched in the language of exposés. Independent reporting had not yet developed, but editors used opinion columns to reveal real and imagined intrigue and scandals. Included were exposés of Alexander Hamilton and his political foe, Thomas Jefferson. Jefferson was the sitting president when his alleged sexual liaison with his slave, Sally Hemings, was revealed in 1802 in the pages of a Virginia newspaper edited by scandal-monger James Callender, Jefferson's former political ally who had turned against him.[7]

Beginning in the 1830s, editors of the emerging, commercially oriented penny press—one generation past the acrimonious editors of the party press—embraced the exposure of corruption in government and other American institutions as part of their creed, while editors of abolitionist, women's rights, and other nonmainstream papers used exposés to further their various causes. In both cases, the publications expanded the terrain of press exposure.

A combination of Jacksonian democracy and new printing technology made the penny press inevitable. With the election of Andrew Jackson in 1828, Americans had explicitly rejected the elitism of the Whigs, who distrusted the "masses," and embraced an egalitarian ideal of the "common man" politicized by Jacksonian Democrats. Steam-run presses and great, continuous rolls of paper made daily circulations in the tens of thousands—a mass audience—possible. At the same time, urbanization created mass markets and consumerism, freeing publishers from reliance on political party subsidies to pursue the larger audience of the working classes. Advertising became the primary economic base for newspapers after 1833, encouraging editors to turn news into a commodity and to find human interest stories that could attract mass audiences. But America did not go quietly into the cities. Jacksonian democracy brought with it a romantic view of rural life and a complementary distrust of urban

7. James Madison, "The Danger of Tampering with Liberty of the Press," in Frank Luther Mott and Ralph D. Casey, eds., *Interpretations of Journalism: A Book of Readings* (New York: F. S. Crofts and Co., 1937), 56–57; David Paul Nord, "Newspapers and American Nationhood, 1776–1826," 401; Shapiro, ed., *Shaking the Foundations*, 3; *Aurora General Advertiser*, June 16, 1798, 1; Joseph J. Ellis, *American Sphinx: The Character of Thomas Jefferson* (New York: Alfred A. Knopf, 1997), 218–19.

morality. While Americans still distrusted government, they also grew increasingly fearful of the social changes wrought by industrialization and immigration. Newspaper exposés concerned not only politics but also social conditions, and readers were provided a symbolic world in which questions of morality and justice and social power played out. Crime news dominated penny press newspapers because it was cheap to produce and replicated a social dialogue already common to readers through the popular crime pamphlets of the day. Crime news, viewed through the rhetoric of exposés, examined broader social and spiritual issues that troubled the new urban audience. "[I]t became a public exploration of some of the hardest, most critical, most eternal questions a people must face together. It was about the possibility of justice, the privileges of power, the inequities of class, the consequences of sin, and the nature of evil; it was about the need to figure out who one was and where one fit into a community riven by change."[8] Through exposés and the editorials that commented on them, penny press editors conceived of and protected the public good, accepting a responsibility they would hand down to future editors of investigative journalism.

During this penny press era, editors James Gordon Bennett of the *New York Herald* and Benjamin Day of the *New York Sun* further extended the tradition of exposure by employing interviews with commoners and direct observation — recently introduced reportorial techniques — to enhance the credibility and allure of their stories of exposé. News reporting was becoming a practice that went beyond polemic to include independently reported accounts. During their competitive coverage of the sensational ax murder of prostitute Ellen Jewett in 1836, the *Herald* and the *Sun* went beyond the statements of police officials to add details gathered from witness interviews, visits to the scene of the crime, and coverage of courtroom testimony during the trial of Richard P. Robinson. Day, especially, investigated the machinations that led to Robinson's acquittal, citing meticulous detail gleaned from extensive interviews with court officials and jurors to document the manipulation of the justice system by Robinson and his attorneys. Focusing on the justice system, Day and other penny paper editors changed the standards of exposé, expanding the

8. Andie Tucker, *Froth and Scum: Truth, Beauty, Goodness, and the Ax Murder in America's First Mass Medium*, 3.

catalogue of possible subjects and developing detection techniques to cover crime and the courts and to promote the public good that later editors would apply to politics and social issues, changing the discourse of politics.[9]

Abolitionists, labor reformers, and women's rights advocates adopted the exposé narrative in their special-audience papers to dramatize the abuses of slavery and the repression of women and the working class in the mid–nineteenth century. Though their papers generally adopted the polemics of eighteenth- and early-nineteenth-century party papers rather than the reporting standards of the penny papers, their opinions were grounded in shocking revelations of real and perceived evils in the treatment of slaves, workers, and women. Even more than the penny papers, reform publications adopted the exposé as an instrument for promoting social change, thereby extending the reach of exposure journalism to incorporate the strategy of outraging the public so it will demand improvements.[10]

Distracted by coverage of battles, journalists during the Civil War produced few exposés of note, although the tradition was preserved through occasional revelations of military incompetence or corruption in the Northern papers (Southern papers operated under severe censorship that kept exposés from being published). Nurtured through the war, the tradition emerged vigorous and strident following the Confederacy's surrender, when the nation's attention — and journalism's attention — once again turned to politics. The focus, however, was not positive. Americans emerged from the Civil War with a general distrust of government and politicians. A particularly fertile time for investigative reporters arose during President Ulysses S. Grant's administration (1869–1877), when the newly unified nation was stained by rampant corruption reaching into the highest political offices of the federal government and filtering into state and local governments to an extent never before experienced. The press had begun separating itself from political parties before the Civil War, and after the war the press completed the break and declared

9. Ibid., 83–84; Leonard, *Power of the Press*, 58, 151.
10. Rodger Streitmatter, *Mightier than the Sword: How the News Media Have Shaped American History*, 22–23, 44–46; Jamie L. Bronstein, "Land Reform, Community-Building and the Labor Press in Antebellum America and Britain," in Michael Harris and Tom O'Malley, eds., *Studies in Newspaper and Periodical History: 1995 Annual* (Westport, Conn.: Greenwood, 1997), 69–84.

itself independent. "The result was a certain distancing from politicians, the growth of the press more or less as an autonomous institution rather than an adjunct to political parties," journalism historian Gerald Baldasty observed. With this separation, the press could more fully realize its constitutional role as a watchdog on government, and the result was a more adversarial position toward politicians. Indeed, media historian Mark Wahlgren Summers concludes that "the big story in the years after the war increasingly was one of skullduggery and corruption." A. M. Gibson of the *New York Sun*, described by Summers as "a tough investigative reporter," exposed graft, embezzlement, and corruption involving the Northern Pacific Railroad lobby, government contractors who "milked the District of Columbia's treasury," the War Department, the Post Office, and Pennsylvania politics, while Henry Van Ness Boynton of the *Cincinnati Gazette* unearthed corruption within the federal Freedmen's Bureau in connection with the construction of Howard University.[11]

In the latter half of the nineteenth century, the press "emerged as the conscience of the larger society," as both the press and the public broadened their focus on government corruption to include concerns for social problems and a demand that government become a positive force for social improvement. The ideals of liberal democracy accepted by nineteenth-century Americans rejected the laissez-faire of social Darwinism, and with that rejection came a sense of responsibility for others in society. Philosopher Lester Ward, a strong opponent of social Darwinism, argued in 1884 that "if nature progresses through the destruction of the weak, man progresses through the *protection* of the weak." Though stimulated by the potential of industrialization, social activists, intellectuals such as Ward, and the press turned their attention to the problems generated by that industrialization.[12]

This attention, for the press, was not single-minded, because newspapers in the late nineteenth century had become commercial, pro-

11. Louis Menand, *The Metaphysical Club: A Story of Ideas in America* (New York: Farrar, Straus and Giroux, 2001); Gerald J. Baldasty, "The Nineteenth-Century Origins of Modern American Journalism," 416; Mark Wahlgren Summers, *The Press Gang: Newspapers and Politics, 1865–1878*, 89–91.

12. Menand, *Metaphysical Club*, 302–3; Morton White, "Prologue: Coherence and Correspondence in American Thought," in Schlesinger and White, eds., *Paths of American Thought*, 5.

fessional operations that attended to wide audiences with multiple interests. Yet, at no time has exposure dominated the commercial newspaper or magazine industries, and it was no different during the latter half of the nineteenth century. Many publishers sought the safe — and financially rewarding — haven of boosterism, especially at the local level, but particularly during the century's last quarter editors realized the attraction of investigative reporting to readers disgusted with the social ills wrought by industrialization. *Frank Leslie's Illustrated Newspaper*, for example, exposed an unsettling tale of tainted milk, which the corrupt New York City government allowed on the market. More dramatic, though, was the nine-month crusade in 1870–1871 by *Harper's Weekly* (which unleashed the devastating comic drawings of Thomas Nast) and the *New York Times* against the stranglehold on the city held by corrupt Democratic boss William Tweed and his minions. The Tweed Ring of Tammany Hall stole millions of dollars from New York City coffers until it was exposed on the front page of the Republican-leaning *Times*. The first paragraph of an 1871 *Times* story on the corruption ended with a challenge to Tammany Hall officials to prove the newspaper wrong. Notice the editor's emphasis on the paper's documentation of the offending facts. By the mid-1800s, reliable evidence had become an investigative standard: "Reliable and incontrovertible evidence of numerous gigantic frauds on the part of the rules of the City has been given to the public from time to time in these columns.... The facts which are narrated are obtained from what we consider a good and trustworthy source, and the figures which help to explain them are transcribed literally from books in the Controller's office. If Controller Connolly can prove them to be inaccurate he is heartily welcome to do so."[13] The Tweed Ring's corruption operated in full view of the city's newspapers (many of which were bribed to stay silent), but it was difficult to prove until a disgruntled Tweed operative, former sheriff James O'Brien, provided a copy of the ring's secret account books to John Foord, a twenty-six-year-old reporter at the *Times*. The log books provided irrefutable documentation of Tweed organization payments to fake contractors for work on nonexisting buildings and other irregularities. The account book entries were

13. "More Ring Villainy, Gigantic Frauds in the Rental of Armories," reprinted in Shapiro, ed., *Shaking the Foundations*, 26–39.

published in full in the *Times*, setting a new standard for exposure reporting—the use of official documents to back up accusations.

The *Times'* success in destroying the Tweed Ring inspired other newspapers to undertake investigations of local and national corruption. Notably, the *New York Sun* and other newspapers exposed congressional corruption connected to the Credit Mobilier scandal of the early 1870s, and Joseph Pulitzer established his reputation as a crusading publisher at the *St. Louis Post-Dispatch.* Pulitzer's paper provided its readers with graphic depictions of the villainous politicians ruling the city. The paper, historian Thomas Leonard relates, "reported the high profits and poor service of the gas and streetcar monopolies, published questionable real estate deals, described fraud at the polls, and paid regular visits to the protected gambling halls and brothels."[14]

In the 1870s, publishers and editors such as Pulitzer, George Jones at the *New York Times*, Charles Dana at the *New York Sun*, Whitelaw Reid at the *New York Tribune*, William Rockhill Nelson of the *Kansas City Star*, and their counterparts on newspapers throughout the country were changing American journalism for the better. The press's social role had changed as it grew into a mass medium with the power to educate and persuade the American public, and press leaders accepted a social responsibility that included exposing corruption, injustice, and abuse of power.[15] Moreover, the press had been affected by the nation's growing appreciation for rationalism and science. The public wanted facts from their newspapers, and journalism was evolving into a profession based on social science with the expertise to deliver objective, unbiased reports. While the coming era of sensationalism in the press may have distorted the importance of individual news stories, it was not contradictory to the press's new role as a provider of facts.

When Pulitzer moved to New York to take over the *New York World*, where he launched the age of press sensationalism, he took his sense of outrage against political and social abuses with him, and it served the sensationalistic press well. Pulitzer counseled that exposés protected democracy and uplifted the moral fiber of society, for corruption and vice thrives in secrecy. "Some people try and make

14. Leonard, *Power of the Press*, 177.
15. Dicken-Garcia, *Journalistic Standards in Nineteenth-Century America*, 62.

you believe that a newspaper should not devote its space to long and dramatic accounts of murders, railroad wrecks, fires, lynchings, political corruption, embezzlements, frauds, graft, divorces, what you will," Pulitzer told his secretary, Alleyne Ireland. "I tell you they are wrong.... We are a democracy, and there is only one way to get a democracy on its feet... and that is by keeping the public informed about what is going on."[16] In fact, the World's blazing headlines and large drawings and photographs of sensationalism, which demanded a "big story" every day of the week to display on the front page, was particularly suited to the press's tradition of exposure. The sensationalistic papers of Pulitzer and his cross-town rival, William Randolph Hearst of the New York Journal, treated exposés as naturally lurid, astounding, and fascinating, and therefore a sure way to thrill their readers. One of the more remarkable stories in Pulitzer's World appeared in 1887 under the byline of Nellie Bly, who solidified undercover reporting as a weapon in the investigative reporter's arsenal. Born Elizabeth Cochrane in western Pennsylvania, Bly broke into New York journalism by begging for a job at the World and accepting editor-in-chief John Cockerill's challenge to infiltrate the notorious Blackwell's Island Insane Asylum for Women. Undaunted, Nellie Bly feigned a nervous breakdown and posed as the homeless "Nellie Brown." Authorities found her wandering the streets of New York and committed her to the asylum, where she stayed ten days, eating spoiled food, enduring ice-cold baths, and observing the staff's cruelty. Cockerill got her out, and she wrote a first-person account of her experiences that stunned the World's readers. "They inject so much morphine and chloral that the patients are made crazy," Bly quoted a patient, Bridget McGuinness. "I have seen the patients wild for water from the effect of the drugs, and the nurses would refuse it to them. I have heard women beg for a whole night for one drop and it was not give to them [sic]." Then she brought her personal observations to bear as witness and documentation: "I saw the same thing myself in hall 7," Bly reported. "The patients would beg for a drink before retiring, but the nurses—Miss Hart and the others refused to unlock the bathroom that they might quench their thirst."[17]

16. Alleyne Ireland, "Joseph Pulitzer on Practical Newspaper Ethics," 463.
17. Nellie Bly's report is reprinted in William David Sloan and Cheryl S. Wray, eds., Masterpieces of Reporting, vol. 1, 306–19.

Her report led to extensive changes at the hospital and made her a celebrity. She followed up with undercover reports of fraudulent employment agencies, unbearable working conditions in factories, lobbyist payoffs to legislators, and harsh prison conditions for women. Since Bly's reporting, undercover investigations have become an established method for rooting out misdeeds and malfeasance. Her work contributed to a form of reporting referred to in the profession of the time as "detective" journalism, and which we call "investigative reporting" today.

Undercover reporting and dramatic escapades were Bly's forte, but her contemporary in New York exposure journalism, police reporter Jacob Riis, perfected the camera as a tool of exposure. Committed for most of his professional life to a crusade against the "public neglect and private greed" that bred the city's rambling, crime- and rat-infested slums, Riis held a lens to New York's East End, providing visual documentation of the deplorable conditions. Though his photos of immigrant workers and the criminal underclass were not printed in newspapers or magazines (illustrations dominated journalism until 1887), he presented his photographs as slides during popular lectures, and the *New York Sun* printed line drawings of some of his photos in 1888. Riis published ten books about housing conditions for the poor. His most famous, *How the Other Half Lives*, was published in 1890 and included seventeen halftones and nineteen drawings, pushing the tradition of exposure journalism forward by adding photography as a documentary technique.[18] When American magazines took up muckraking in the early twentieth century, photography played a prominent role in documenting social problems and illustrating exposés.

While Bly and Riis were making headlines in New York, Henry Demarest Lloyd was nurturing the investigative tradition in the Midwest. Spurned by the New York papers, Lloyd joined the *Chicago Tribune* in 1872. A lawyer by training, social reformer by heart, and journalist by instinct, Lloyd burned with indignation at the widespread social ills during America's industrial age. Backed by editor-in-chief Joseph Medill, Lloyd used his position as financial editor and, later, editor of the editorial page to attack big business with the determination of a prosecutor. His targets were men such as oil baron John D.

18. Beaumont Newhall, *The History of Photography*, 138–42.

Rockefeller and railroad magnates William H. Vanderbilt and Jay Gould. Applying his skills as a lawyer, Lloyd exposed the questionable business practices of the railroad trust in a two-page spread in the *Tribune*, including graphs and tables—a visual tool used widely in communicating today's investigative articles. Headlined "Our Land," the lengthy article detailed how the railroad companies had grown rich by selling land given to them by the federal government. He built his case with prosecutorial thoroughness, accuracy, and extensive documentation, including a full-page graphic. As editorial page editor, he wrote editorials attacking the trusts, including Rockefeller and Standard Oil, carefully backing up his arguments with irrefutable facts gleaned from court records, personal interviews, and government and business documents, providing early examples of investigative editorial writing. His attack on the monopolies, and Standard Oil in particular, appeared in the *Atlantic Monthly* as the "Story of a Great Monopoly" and caused a sensation. The magazine went through seven editions to meet reader demand, and Lloyd became a national celebrity. His work set a milestone in the evolution of modern American investigative journalism with the article's comprehensive treatment and exhaustive documentation. The *Atlantic* article became the basis for *Wealth Against Commonwealth*, his book-length attack against the trusts published in 1894. Lloyd became famous as a leader of social reform movements, becoming active in the Populist movement and movements promoting co-operativism, but his celebrity began in connection with his journalism.[19]

Lloyd's work directly influenced the next generation of reform-minded journalists—the early-twentieth-century muckrakers (a pejorative label applied by President Theodore Roosevelt and proudly embraced by the investigative reporters). Some learned from Lloyd by reading his magazine pieces, but Ida Tarbell met him face-to-face for instruction, seeking him out for advice when she was working on her own exposé of the Standard Oil Company. Her in-depth study that appeared as a series in *McClure's Magazine* in 1902 and 1903 mirrored Lloyd's thoroughness and documentary style. Like Lloyd, Tarbell and her contemporaries, influenced by the ideals of the Progressive Party, used their journalism to argue for social and political reforms,

19. Richard Digby-Junger, *The Journalist as Reformer: Henry Demarest Lloyd and* Wealth Against Commonwealth.

reflecting the broader social unrest that challenged the changes wrought by industrialization. Unlike Lloyd, however, the muckrakers were not advocates for particular social movements. Their articles were carefully constructed exposés that provided balanced presentation and left out opinion. This allowed the evidence to speak for itself, and further advanced the credibility of investigative work.

The golden age of muckraking began in January 1903, when *McClure's Magazine* hit the newsstands with three powerful exposés and an editor's note that argued the importance of the magazine's work. Included were Lincoln Steffens's "The Shame of Minneapolis," the second installment of Ida Tarbell's history of the Standard Oil Company, and Ray Stannard Baker's "The Right to Work," which examined working conditions in the nation's coal mines and shortcomings of the union the workers had joined. S. S. McClure, the magazine's owner and editor, provided a short editorial that called attention to the phenomenon of three hard-hitting investigative articles appearing together in one publication, all discussing different subjects, but also discussing the same subject: the threat to democracy from good people doing nothing. It became a constant theme of the muckrakers.

McClure cautioned his writers to provide fully documented articles backed by passionless fact, solidifying and extending the standards of investigative journalism. He counseled that *McClure's* articles should shock readers into demanding social reforms by reporting overwhelming facts, personifying the social conflict by naming names—identifying those in government or corporate America who bore responsibility, and revealing the names and faces of their victims—and writing absorbing narratives using the stylistic techniques of short-story writers. The effect was dramatic and popular. The four hundred thousand copies of the January 1903 *McClure's* quickly sold out, and soon other magazines were copying S. S. McClure's formula. Exposés provided cover stories for *Cosmopolitan, Collier's, Everybody's, Arena, Pearson's, Hampton's, Ladies Home Journal*, and many other general-circulation magazines. Will Irwin wrote on the newspaper trust; David Graham Phillips exposed "The Treason of the Senate"; John O'Hara Cosgrave provided insider information on Wall Street; Samuel Hopkins Adams revealed the fraud of patent medicines; Charles Edward Russell wrote about graft and corruption in state governments; Ray Stannard Baker investigated lynching and the condition of blacks in both the North and South; and Rheta Childe Dorr exposed the plight of women working in factories and sweatshops. In all, more than two thousand investigative articles appeared in American magazines between 1903 and 1912, making the case for widespread social and political reforms and for a short time taking the investigative tradition into mainstream American journalism.[20] Spurred by new technologies—mass-circulation magazines, improvements in printing technology, and photography—and by social upheaval caused by industrialization and efforts to regulate it, muckraking defined journalism during the first two decades of the twentieth century.

Nevertheless, the muckraking era—one of the few times when the tradition of exposure characterized national journalism—succumbed by 1917 to a variety of factors, including America's entry into World War I. The practice also faltered because of libel suits, the purchase of some of the leading magazines by the businessmen they targeted, and growing disinterest from the public, which increasingly viewed the many reforms such as the Pure Food and Drug Act and trust-busting legislation as a resolution to the problems of industrialization. After the general-interest magazines abandoned muckraking, the investigative tradition wavered, but was kept alive by occasional work published in small-circulation opinion magazines, books, and a few newspapers. Investigative work between 1917 and 1950 split into two camps: one continuing the muckraking zeal for reform, pushed by an ideological bent that bordered on socialism; the other evolving into an objective, mainstream version recognizable by today's standards.

Newspapers picked up some of the slack left by the demise of muckraking magazines, and some writers extended the tradition of exposure journalism by adding literary quality to exposure reports. Writing quality had been a concern of the muckrakers. S. S. McClure introduced the use of short-story writing techniques to the exposé, and muckraker Lincoln Steffens counseled journalists on the need for good writing when he was city editor of the New York–based

---

20. Ellen F. Fitzpatrick, *Muckraking: Three Landmark Articles*, 3; for the history of the early-twentieth-century muckrakers, see Walter M. Brasch, *Forerunners of Revolution: Muckrakers and the American Social Conscience*; C. C. Regier, *The Era of the Muckrakers*; and Harold Wilson, *McClure's Magazine and the Muckrakers.*

Commercial Advertiser.[21] Nevertheless, the importance of good writing was underscored by two classic examples of early-twentieth-century newspaper investigations, by legendary newsman Herbert Bayard Swope and his contemporary, Harold A. Littledale.

Swope, at the *New York World*, was widely known for his well-written, fully documented investigations, including the October 27, 1912, article titled "How Police Lieutenant Becker Plotted the Death of Gambler Rosenthal to Stop His Exposé." Swope, an aggressive reporter and brilliant writer, started on the *St. Louis Post-Dispatch*, moved to papers in Chicago, and completed his career at the *World*. He focused on crime and corruption stories, digging deep into the dangerous undergrowth of urban life. His stories sparkled with detail and showed investigative reporters that hard-hitting exposés can sing. Herman Rosenthal was a small-time gambler, gunned down just days before he was scheduled to testify before a grand jury about police payoffs. "'Herman Rosenthal has squealed again,'" Swope began. "Through the pallid underworld the sibilant whisper ran. It was heard in East Side dens; it rang in the opium houses in Chinatown; it crept up to the semipretentious stuss and crap games of the Fourteenth Street region, and it reached into the more select circles of uptown gambling where business is always good and graft is always high." Police Lieutenant Charles Becker, Swope told his readers, was part of the "system, in whose Labyrinthian maze men are killed, others are robbed, and women are made slaves." His narrative takes the reader into the streets and shows them the murder as it happens. Swope's reporting made it impossible for Lieutenant Becker and his accomplices to escape prosecution.[22]

At the *New York Evening Post*, Littledale spent months investigating conditions at the Trenton, New Jersey, state penitentiary that resulted in his January 12, 1917, article, "New Jersey State Prison Breeds Crime." The article employs repetition to hammer at the injustices Littledale had uncovered: "It is a fact that two, three, and even four men are confined together in the same cell in violation of the law. It is a fact that dungeons exist and that men are incarcerated therein and given only bread and water twice a day. It is a fact that men

21. Lincoln Steffens, *The Autobiography of Lincoln Steffens*, vol. 1, 311–26.
22. Herbert Bayard Swope, "How Police Lieutenant Becker Plotted the Death of Gambler Rosenthal," reprinted in Sloan and Wray, eds., *Masterpieces of Reporting*, vol. 1, 319–27.

have been chained to the walls of underground dungeons. It is a fact..." — forty-three paragraphs beginning with "It is a fact..." to list the charges, much like a prosecutor would in an indictment against the state prison system. "That is how the state's wards are kept. That is how they are punished. That is how they are 'reformed.' That is how society is 'protected,'" he concluded. His story won a Pulitzer Prize in 1918.[23]

A few years later, the New York World took on the revived Ku Klux Klan, publishing a scathing exposé on its front pages in 1921, revealing that public relations publicists Edward Y. Clarke and Elizabeth Tyler had helped rebuild the racist organization through a nationwide direct-mail campaign. The effort raised millions for the organization, headed by "Colonel" William Simmons in Atlanta, who used organization funds to enrich himself. Moreover, the newspaper proved that Clarke and Tyler were having an illicit affair contrary to the values championed by the Klan, and documented the group's use of violence and terror. The publicity forced Simmons from the Klan's leadership and drove Clarke and Tyler out of the group, winning the World a Pulitzer Prize. Ironically, the crusade backfired. Klan membership figures went up because of the extensive publicity the World's reports had brought to it. Many early-twentieth-century Americans apparently found the Klan's message of racism and stern morality attractive. Nevertheless, the World's twenty-one-article series inspired other papers to investigate the Klan, ultimately diminishing the organization's political influence.[24]

More socially constructive was the dogged pursuit of the Teapot Dome scandal by the brilliant Paul Y. Anderson of the St. Louis Post-Dispatch. The Post-Dispatch, under the direction of managing editor O. K. Bovard, embarked on numerous local investigative crusades, including an Anderson exposé of the causes of a deadly race riot in East St. Louis that brought him national attention. Anderson went on to be the lone national reporter to reveal how President Warren G. Harding's Interior Department officials took bribes to sell national oil reserves stored at Teapot Dome to major oil companies at discounted prices. The press's general lack of interest in the

23. Harold Littledale, "New Jersey State Prison Breeds Crime," reprinted in Sloan and Wray, eds., Masterpieces of Reporting, vol. 1, 328–32.

24. Silas Bent, Newspaper Crusaders: A Neglected Story, 138–54.

scandal extended from its acceptance of the wider American cultural embrace of the interests, values, and goals of the business class.
Coming out of World War I, the American press, like the rest of
America, wanted a return to normalcy, which President Herbert
Hoover promised. To many, progressivism had won. Government and
business had accepted their responsibilities to society. Reforms were
in place, and the economy was booming. The *Saturday Evening Post*,
which equated American values with those of the business class, was
the most-read publication in the nation. Anderson and his editors
at the *Post-Dispatch*, though, were unwilling to accept their fellow
journalists' contentment. Indeed, exposés, particularly at the national
level, were rare during the 1920s, which only amplifies Anderson's
solitary achievement. His articles generated congressional investigations, during which Anderson testified about what he had discovered, and the investigations led to indictments. Anderson's work
resulted in convictions of Interior Department officials and oil mag-
nate Harry Sinclair, and the return of six million dollars to the federal government, winning the tireless investigator a Pulitzer Prize
in 1928.[25]

The press's complacency toward exposés in the 1920s can be attrib-
uted to more than general satisfaction with the status quo. The sensationalistic crusades of Pulitzer and Hearst and the spectacular muckraking of *McClure's* and other magazines, with which the exposé
had become closely associated, fell on disfavor in the press. An early
salvo came from iconoclastic press critic H. L. Mencken. Though
later he was to fondly remember the crusades he had been involved
in during his newspaper work in the late nineteenth century, in a
1914 *Atlantic Monthly* article Mencken lashed out at the practice. He
accused papers of conducting crusades "for their own profit only,
when their one motive was to make the public read their paper." He
belittled the crusading editors' efforts and declared that their reports
were "gothic, melodramatic." Indeed, he said, even the crusades that
led to better milk handling, creation of parks, the expulsion of corrupt politicians, and other reforms ultimately accomplished little
when the miscreants were replaced by other politicians who reversed

---

25. Edmund Lambeth, "The Lost Career of Paul Y. Anderson"; Arthur M.
Schlesinger, Jr., "Sources of the New Deal," in Schlesinger and White, eds., *Paths
of American Thought*, 373.

the reforms or committed other malfeasances. Moreover, Mencken asserted, the public doesn't care. Ironically, former muckraker Upton Sinclair—writing in *The Brass Check*, his exposé of the nation's newspapers—echoed Mencken's allegation that crusades were undertaken solely as circulation-boosters. The criticism, and journalism's early-twentieth-century complacency with things-as-they-are, pushed the tradition of exposure to the sidelines. Journalist and author Silas Bent, a defender of crusades and exposés, wrote in a 1924 *Atlantic Monthly* article that the crusade was "passé." Moreover, a journalism text published in 1946 denigrated the newspaper crusade and declared "the days of writing crusading stories are far past [though] many newspapers still indulge in this sort of journalism in a more or less limited way." Critics and supporters alike characterized the newspaper crusade as "muckraking" and unfairly associated it with Pulitzer's and Hearst's sensationalism, from which the establishment press tried to distance itself, favoring the professional garment of "social responsibility" instead. Crusade stories were "compounded of bias and special pleading," according to the textbooks, and were to be avoided by responsible newspapers that excised opinion from their news columns. Bent and others offered spirited defenses of crusades, but the exposés that appeared in the establishment press after 1930 rarely embraced the crusade mantel. They instead set "objectivity" as a standard and pushed the tradition of exposure into the era of modern investigative reporting.[26]

The press's suspicion of the newspaper crusade led the industry into an irresponsible quiescence, with some exceptions, during the 1930s and 1940s, when America endured its greatest crises since the Civil War—Prohibition's unrestrained lawlessness that captured many municipal and state governments, the Great Depression, and World War II. As Bent has pointed out, newspapers relinquished their responsibility to support child-labor laws, expose the predatory nature of the Pullman Palace Car Company, campaign against patent medicines, and reveal the abuses of the electric power trust as it attempted to destroy President Franklin Roosevelt's rural electrification program. In addition, the press acquired a shameful record of failing

26. H. L. Mencken, "Newspaper Morals"; for his later comments on crusades, see Mencken, *Newspaper Days*, 37; Upton Sinclair, *The Brass Check*; Silas Bent, "Journalism and Morality"; R. E. Wolseley and Laurence R. Campbell, *Exploring Journalism*, 208–9; Bent, *Newspaper Crusaders*; Miraldi, *Muckraking and Objectivity*.

to expose the causes and effects of the stock market crash of 1929, the human cost of fascism's rise across Europe, and public corruption during these decades of crisis.[27]

Nevertheless, journalism's tradition of exposure appeared sporadically in a few newspapers, and found outlets in small-circulation opinion journals, books, and one nationally syndicated column during the 1930s and 1940s. The *Evanston* (Ill.) *News-Index*, under the editorship of future journalism educator Curtis MacDougall, for example, orchestrated an undercover investigation of voting fraud in 1935, resulting in a dramatic first-person story by Major H. Stephens about how he had taken advantage of Illinois's lax voter registration laws to vote nineteen times in one election. Moreover, the Chicago newspapers ultimately rallied to expose gangster Al Capone's destructive grip on municipal and state government. In St. Louis, Joseph Pulitzer II and his legendary managing editor, Bovard, carried out numerous exposés of local corruption, including an extensive investigation of the corrupt Pendergast political machine's grip on politics in Kansas City. The *St. Louis Post-Dispatch*'s look into Kansas City corruption embarrassed the *Kansas City Star* into doing its own investigation, which produced Paul Fisher's classic "Joe Doakes Knows What It Takes to Stay in Power," but it appeared in June 1939, months after intensive federal investigations into Tom Pendergast's corruption were under way.[28]

Investigative reporting also found an outlet in small-circulation opinion magazines and books during the 1930s and 1940s. Drew Pearson, a reporter for the *Baltimore Sun*, and Robert S. Allen of the *Christian Science Monitor* teamed up in 1931 to write sensationalistic, muckraking books after their newspapers rejected investigative stories they had uncovered. Pearson explained later, "...It is true that the *Baltimore Sun*...declined to publish some of the material... despite the fact that I repeatedly urged its publication.... These and many other instances which I could enumerate have convinced me that...one of the few outlets to free journalism is through the

27. Bent, *Newspaper Crusaders*, 234–53.
28. Major H. Stephens, "I Voted 19 Times in One Election," reprinted in Sloan and Wray, eds., *Masterpieces of Reporting*, 333–36; Lloyd Wendt, *Chicago Tribune: The Rise of a Great American Newspaper*, 509–38; Bent, *Newspaper Crusaders*, 40–41; Paul Fisher, "Joe Doakes Knows What It Takes to Stay in Power," reprinted in Sloan and Wray, eds., *Masterpieces of Reporting*, 337–43.

medium of books." *Washington Merry-Go-Round* appeared in 1931 and was followed by a sequel a year later, both published anonymously in a futile attempt to protect Pearson's and Allen's newspaper jobs. The books were tremendous successes and launched Pearson's and Allen's syndicated column, "Washington Merry-Go-Round," in 1932. Though the column was more akin to biased muckraking than modern investigative reporting, it is credited with goading other Washington journalists into investigative journalism. In addition, the success of *Washington Merry-Go-Round* inspired other book-length investigative looks at Washington and other issues. William P. Helm's *Washington Swindle Sheet* and Matthew Josephson's muckraking *The Robber Barons* and *The Politicos* followed. Cary McWilliams, who would go on to become an editor at the *Nation*, published several muckraking books during the 1930s and 1940s, including an exposé of migrant farm worker conditions, *Ill Fares the Land*, published in 1942. In addition, liberal opinion journals such as the *Nation* and the *New Republic* mixed commentary with exposés, publishing work by Heywood Broun, McAlister Coleman, Lewis Gannett, Louis Adamic, and Fred J. Cook (who sent investigative pieces to the *Nation* that his newspaper, the *New York World-Telegram*, was too conservative to run).[29] Tellingly, iconoclasts I. F. Stone and George Seldes started their own newsletters to publish their investigative articles.

Throughout most of the 1950s, reporting of an investigative nature in newspapers was rare, pushed to journalism's sidelines by the enduring criticism of crusades and a growing complacency in the press. And yet, it was kept breathing by a few visionary newspaper reporters who stoked their professional fires with memories of Lincoln Steffens, Ida Tarbell, and others from the Progressive era, of Paul Y. Anderson of the *St. Louis Post-Dispatch*, and of the long tradition of crusading journalism. Among those working at mainstream newspapers was investigative reporter Clark Mollenhoff of the *Des Moines Register*, who recalled his greatest influence being Lincoln Steffens's autobiography.[30] Mollenhoff reported on police corruption beginning in the late 1940s and early 1950s for the *Register* before moving to

29. Drew Pearson, Letter to the Editor, *Christian Century*, November 30, 1932, 2; Eugene Warner, "The Terrors of Washington," *Collier's*, April 22, 1939, 11; Bruce Locklin, "Digging Without a Shovel."

30. Clark R. Mollenhoff, *Investigative Reporting: From Courthouse to White House*, 14.

Washington for the Cowles newspaper chain, where he focused on labor, agriculture, and other national issues. His contemporaries, Robert Collins at the *Atlanta Journal* and later the *St. Louis Post-Dispatch*, Jack Nelson at the *Atlanta Constitution*, and reporters at the *Utica* (N.Y.) *Observer-Dispatch*, dug up stories during the 1950s about bootleg liquor, prostitution, gambling, race relations, and local corruption.

Mollenhoff, Collins, and Nelson, working in the late 1940s and early 1950s, were the journalistic descendants of Benjamin Harris and James Franklin, who brought the British tradition of journalistic exposure to the American shores, and the scores of exposé writers who followed them. The earliest exposés in seventeenth- and eighteenth-century newspapers used exposure journalism to translate complicated reformist and revolutionary arguments into language easily understood by the general public. In the early Republic, that investigative zeal adapted to the vitriolic partisan attacks carried out by established politicians angling for power in a political world that reduced ideology to personal character. "Over the two centuries since [Benjamin Franklin] Bache," wrote journalism educator and magazine editor Bruce Shapiro, "other inquisitive and relentless American writers—some celebrated, many undeservedly forgotten—have hammered out factual revelations that have evicted from office the highest-level leaders, freed the incarcerated innocent, challenged the logic of wars, exposed predatory corporations.... These writers have defined a distinct tradition of inquiry and exposé: an American tradition of investigative journalism."[31] The penny papers of the 1830s added reportage (interviews and direct observation) and adapted the exposé to crime, developing an exposé narrative that journalists in the latter half of the nineteenth century adapted to expose political corruption and the mounting social problems resulting from industrialization. Sensationalistic crusades making use of detective work, prosecutorial logic, and the new technology of the camera attacked social and political wrongs in the 1880s and 1890s. Early-twentieth-century magazine muckraking crafted a formula of exposure that included use of storytelling techniques and reliable documentation. Its tales of corporate and political greed with clearly identifiable victims and villains were calculated to stir the public's

31. Shapiro, ed., *Shaking the Foundations*, xiv.

demand for reform, and have become models for the writing of modern investigative reporting, which typically establishes clear villains and unmistakably innocent victims.[32] Muckraking carried on the American press tradition begun by Harris and Franklin of challenging the status quo of American institutions and became a bridge from the reformist journalism of the late nineteenth century to the disinterested, modern investigative journalism of the twentieth and twenty-first. The journalistic thread linking Harris and Franklin with Mollenhoff, Collins, and Nelson in the 1950s was the use of exposés to engage the public in local and national dialogues about social and political problems.

32. James S. Ettema and Theodore L. Glasser, "Narrative Form and Moral Force: The Realization of Innocence and Guilt through Investigative Journalism."

The Reemergence of Investigative Journalism, 1960–1975

The United States entered the 1950s confident and self-satisfied. The culture of consumption that had begun in the later years of the nineteenth century had reached maturity. Material abundance appeared to solve all of society's ills. The American media reflected and helped create this idea of progress-through-consumption through its advertising, but also through news and entertainment offerings. Cultural historian Roland Marchand identifies several recurring themes in American advertising that occurred even before World War II. Among them was the theme of the "democracy of goods," which suggested that social equality could be achieved through consumption of goods. "In scores of parables and visual clichés, advertising had served as the society's 'green light,' beckoning consumers to join in a cost-free progress toward modernity," Marchand concludes. Indeed, U.S. media content during the 1950s generally reinforced the image of a just and efficient political and economic system. The mainstream press downplayed news of business leaders and other elites who reaped unfair advantages or benefits. It also paid little attention to class distinctions, religious disagreements, social discontent, political dissidents, or deviations in traditionally respected institutions such as the family, the courts, the community, and schools. "We were confident we had it made," explained *Nation* editor Carey McWilliams in an article critical of the paucity of investigative journalism in the mainstream press during the 1950s. "We had become so infatuated with the great god GNP that we could not see the poor and underprivileged in our midst."[1]

Moreover, nearly every newspaper and magazine publisher shared this myopic view. Publishers accumulated immense wealth, which necessarily situated them within the elite and encouraged them to defend the status quo. Since the Civil War, the newspaper and magazine press had increasingly entered the world of big business, and their owners became comfortably ensconced in the upper crust of society. A U.S. Senate Small Business Committee reported in 1945 that "newspaper publishing has come to be big business in its own right. Even small-newspaper publishing is big business." By the early 1950s, newspaper publishing had become a $4 billion a year business, and two-thirds of the income came from advertising. Moreover, chain ownership dominated the newspaper and magazine industries. By 1946, total newspaper circulation amounted to about fifty-one million a day, and chains controlled more than half of it. "Because the business of newspaper publishing has grown tremendously in the last half century," journalism educator Willard Bleyer wrote in 1934, "newspaper publishers, rather than newspaper editors, are the dominant element in American journalism today. As business men they are likely to take the point of view of other business men."[2]

Profits lulled the press into complacency, but to a considerable extent newspapers and magazines also reflected the attitudes of their audiences. The mainstream news media largely worked within a social and cultural atmosphere that precluded their taking an aggressive stance against institutions and government. Emerging from World War II prosperous and secure, Americans were confident of

1. Roland Marchand, *Advertising the American Dream: Making Way for Modernity, 1920–1940,* 363; McWilliams, "Is Muckraking Coming Back?" 10; on the beginnings of American consumerism, see Stuart Ewen, *Captains of Consciousness: Advertising and the Social Roots of the Consumer Culture,* and T. J. Jackson Lears and R. Fox, eds., *The Culture of Consumption;* on the dominance of consumer culture after World War II, see Allen J. Matusow, *The Unraveling of America: A History of Liberalism in the 1960s.*

2. George Marion, *Stop the Press!;* Willard Grosvenor Bleyer, "Does Press Merit Privileged Place?" *Editor and Publisher,* July 21, 1934, 214–16.

the future and trusted the existing power structure that had led them to victory over Nazism and Japanese imperialism. "The postwar news corporations became overly establishmentarian not just from their own prosperity and stability," press critic Ben Bagdikian remarked in 1968, "but because they also reflected most of us....Most of us, readers and writers, also were too fat and happy." Historian Allen J. Matusow pointed out that America's abundance of wealth eased social and class tensions, encouraged consumption, and "underlay the celebration of American life...and the optimistic conviction... that most American problems could and would be solved." Yet, this barrage of advertising that promoted consumerism would have been wasted on a population unable to afford consumer products. Average family income had risen steadily—up 70 percent between 1929 and 1962, measured in constant 1954 dollars. This growth in personal income established a large middle class in America that, when encouraged by advertising, lusted after material goods that had been luxuries for previous generations. A public opinion poll published by *Look* magazine at the start of 1960 found most Americans were satisfied with their standard of living and most "naturally expect to go on enjoying their peaceable, plentiful existence."[3]

In national and international news reporting as well, the press paid homage to the power structure, particularly to politicians, continuing the press's cooperation with government established during World War II in support of the war effort. Speaking on the "ideals and duties of journalism" during a 1943 symposium, publisher O.J. Ferguson, president of the Missouri Press Association, hoped that self-censorship and restraint shown by the press during the war would continue after the war to convince the community that the media "are not community mendicants." Speaking to the American Chamber of Commerce, newspaper publisher Robert C. Bassett of the *Milwaukee Sentinel* argued in 1955 that the role of the press was to support free enterprise and help fight the spread of communism. Likewise, Henry Luce, publisher of *Time, Life,* and *Fortune,* had counseled his colleagues in the news business two years earlier that one of the press's responsibilities was to help President Eisenhower win the

3. Ben H. Bagdikian, "The Press and Its Crisis of Identity," 10; Matusow, *Unraveling of America,* xiii–xiv, 9; *Historical Statistics of the United States, Colonial Times to 1957,* 165; and *Historical Statistics of the United States, Continuation to 1962 and Revisions,* 23.

Cold War. These pro-government attitudes of publishers filtered into the newsrooms. As late as the 1970s, Leo Rosten, author of *Washington Correspondents*, found that 60 percent of the Washington reporters he interviewed said they were aware of a "fixed" policy on politics at their papers and subjectively slanted stories to fit that policy. Of those surveyed, 55 percent said they had had stories "played down, cut or killed" for policy reasons. Moreover, the American press's embrace of objectivity, which had begun in the early twentieth century, established professional conventions that insulated government and business leaders from routine criticism and challenge. Objectivity, or "straight reporting" — as practiced in the news media — demanded that reporters and editors not only excise personal opinions but also exclude evaluative statements about the institutional pronouncements and policies, unless the reporter was quoting a source of equal status. To do otherwise was considered unprofessional in most newsrooms. Straight-news conventions became "frozen patterns," and were "the absolute commandment of most mass media journalism," journalist Douglass Cater wrote. Its conventions dictated that if a government or business official said something, it was news, and to elaborate on the statement, or to challenge the statement, biased the news. "The trouble," Cater argued in a 1950s issue of *The Reporter* magazine, "is that it precludes investigation..." Indeed, during the 1940s and 1950s, journalists' professional standards in essence protected the status quo. "Objective reporters," writes James Baughman, "by merely announcing a government or business action, in effect publicized rather than analyzed or criticized the behavior of established institutions." Author James Aronson labeled the press's passive performance during the 1950s an "abdication."[4]

Dissident views existed, but they usually came from a radical, leftist fringe and were easily relegated to inconsequence. Allen Ginsberg's *Howl and Other Poems* appeared in 1956 and helped launch the Beat generation of outlaw poets and novelists who protested the conformist, consumer culture. Additionally, there existed a nascent

4. O. J. Ferguson, "Ideals and Duties of Journalism," 193; Robert C. Bassett, *Vital Speeches of the Day*, March 15, 1956, 349–52; Henry R. Luce, "The Functions of Journalism," *Vital Speeches of the Day*, April 1, 1953, 368–72; Leo Rosten, *The Washington Correspondents*, 159, 186–87; Douglass Cater, "The Captive Press," 17; Baughman, *The Republic of Mass Culture*, 13; James Aronson, *The Press and the Cold War*, 10.

civil rights movement as early as the 1940s that challenged Ameri-can society's acceptance of segregation laws and customs that denied blacks equal education and social status. In journalism, the leading rebel of the 1940s was George Seldes, who abandoned mainstream newspapers, which he thought had been co-opted by corporate Amer-ica and conservative politics. Seldes started an independent news-letter, *In Fact*, in 1940 to promote leftist politics and skewer the establishment press. Even among daily newspaper publishers, an occasional dissenter was found. J. W. Gitt, publisher of the *Gazette and Daily* in York, Pennsylvania, stood out as one of the few in the commercial press who championed progressive political ideals.[5] Left-ist social activist Carey McWilliams, a California lawyer, provided a singular voice of protest in books and magazine articles, exposing the unconscionable living and working conditions of migrant work-ers, racism, and other unsavory social problems in American soci-ety, and later became editor of the *Nation* magazine, where he con-tinued to promote muckraking. Another dissident journalist, I. F. Stone, was a leading commentator and muckraker on foreign policy for liberal and leftist publications as early as the 1930s. In 1952 he founded *I. F. Stone's Weekly*, his own newsletter patterned after Seldes's *In Fact*, which had folded in 1950, a casualty of Cold War harass-ment. In politics, the third-party Progressives, a weak derivative of the stronger party from the early twentieth century, offered the most visible opposition to Republican and Democratic policies, though they never garnered a widespread following.

Until the 1960s, the politics of the Cold War effectively eclipsed dissenters such as Seldes, McWilliams, and Stone, regardless of their eloquence and well-documented arguments. Moreover, the mass po-litical hysteria during the McCarthy era, when Americans and their news institutions became obsessed with the fear of communist infil-trators in government and the media, actively suppressed leftist dis-sent and contributed to the general abdication by the press. To Aron-son, "There was a basic reason, however, for the so-called objectivity of the reporters and their editors. This was the acceptance of [Sen. Joseph] McCarthy's stated aim, however much the reporters and edi-

5. Mary Allienne Hamilton, "J. W. Gitt: The Cold War's Voice in the Wilderness."

tors may have deplored his methods (and not all of them did). The aim was to rid the country of the American branch of the 'international Communist conspiracy' which threatened the American way of life." Most journalists regarded themselves as no more than notetakers. Broadcast, radio, and the emerging television news organizations faced additional pressure. Advertisers held sway over broadcasters because they provided 100 percent of the industry's revenues, while the Federal Communications Commission demanded compliance with federal rules regarding obscenity and requirements that licensees serve the public interest as the FCC interpreted it. Consequently, the industry meekly operated under the watchful eye of advertisers and government regulators, both of whom demanded a subservient electronic news medium uncritical of government policy or wanton commercialism.[6]

In addition, media historian James Baughman argues, the press accommodated authority and the elite because reporters felt socially inferior. From the 1930s to the 1960s, pay for journalists was low, and most reporters had little, if any, college education. Russell Baker, the nationally syndicated columnist who entered the journalism profession in the forties, recalled that newspaper reporters "were thought to be a vagabond crowd addicted to booze, vulgar language, bad manners, smelly wardrobes, heavy debt, and low company." While major news outlets paid their Washington reporters comparable to other professions, their counterparts outside of the capital offered much less. In general, reporters outside of Washington made about half the salary of reporters in Washington. Moreover, newspapers paid less than public relations. Legendary *New York Times* reporter James Reston recalled that his pay dropped by a third when he left his publicity job for the Cincinnati Reds to take a newspaper job in New York.[7]

Nevertheless, an inferiority complex cannot explain the lackluster performance of publishers and media owners, who certainly enjoyed a higher social status and wielded considerable social power. As Walter Brasch points out, "in order for journalism to become more

6. Aronson, *The Press and the Cold War*, 71; Boylan, "Declarations of Independence," 31–32; Hodgson, *America in Our Time*, 34–44.
7. Baughman, *Republic of Mass Culture*, 13; Russell Baker, *The Good Times*, 51; James Reston, *Deadline: A Memoir*, 40, 45.

than a superficial recording of current events, it's necessary that publishers go beyond the superficial." And yet, most media managers did not encourage aggressive, in-depth reporting during the 1940s and 1950s because they accepted the government's and the power elite's point of view. In his speech to the American Chamber of Commerce, publisher Bassett of the *Milwaukee Sentinel* declared there was "no room for a newspaper which cutely and snidely foists the Marxian class struggle upon its readers while it masquerades under the guise of enlightened idealism," a stance that devalues the practice of exposing social problems. Moreover, and probably more important, publishers did not see a financial profit in investigative reporting, an expensive, risky enterprise that, given their self-satisfied audience, usually failed to sell more newspapers.[8]

But during the 1960s and continuing into the 1970s, journalism attracted better-educated, less-roguish practitioners, and pay improved. In addition, influenced by rebellious social and cultural changes, many younger journalists viewed the press as an institution for social change. According to research by John Johnstone and his colleagues, reporters saw the press's responsibilities to include being an investigator, a watchdog on government, an interpreter of the news, and an educator. By 1978, according to Stephen Hess, most Washington-based correspondents had college degrees and one-third had advanced professional or graduate degrees. Throughout the 1960s, enrollments in college journalism programs increased, which Michael Schudson attributes to increased salaries in the field, new journalistic opportunities for women, and "most of all the continuing influence of national events of the 1960s." When asked why he became an investigative reporter, Bret Hume, an associate of columnist Jack Anderson and later a Washington-based television reporter, passionately asserted that he entered journalism to fight corruption and protect democracy. During the 1950s, reporters who strongly held a belief that the press was the watchdog of government and its role was to protect the public felt stymied by institutional and managerial restraints and rarely conducted aggressive and investigative reporting. During the 1960s, though, institutional barriers began to break down as a new generation of publishers took over newspapers and magazines, and reporters in the field argued that their professional-

8. Brasch, *Forerunners of Revolution*, 155; Bassett, *Vital Speeches*, 351.

ism, with its strong insistence on social responsibility and objectivity, gave them the authority to control the content of their stories.[9]

Several specific events, in addition to more general cultural and social developments, chipped away at the facade of consensus cultivated during the Eisenhower era and awakened, particularly in the press, a questioning, often cynical response to the prevailing wisdom of those in power. David Broder observed that clashes between the press and the government had been part of the American journalistic tradition, but "...events in the 1960s and 1970s [including the civil rights movement, the Vietnam War, Watergate, and a series of U.S. presidents willing to lie to the American people] increased the clashes between journalists and government officials.... This period established the investigative role for reporters." To Boylan, "the great surprise, in retrospect, is the speed with which the bedraggled, victimized press of the 1950s came to see itself as an apparently potent, apparently adversary press in the 1960s." Researchers also have documented this shift in perspective. Leon Sigal found, for example, that between 1949 and 1969 the reliance by reporters on routine, official sources declined significantly and their pursuit of enterprise stories showed a corresponding increase. William Rivers, in a series of studies of the Washington press corps, found a growth in the adversarial relationship between government and the press. "Watergate was less coup d'etat than it was climax," Rivers concluded. "It was the end of a long evolution..." Additionally, the government's public relations apparatus expanded to feed politicians' growing desire to manage the news, increasing the adversarial relationship with reporters who fought to retain control of their stories.[10]

9. J. W. C. Johnstone, E. J. Slawski, and W. W. Bowman, *The News People*; Stephen Hess, *The Washington Reporters*; Schudson, *Watergate in American Memory*, 111; David H. Weaver and G. Cleveland Wilhoit, *American Journalist: A Portrait of U.S. News People and Their Work*, 2d ed.; Hume is quoted in William L. Rivers, *The Other Government: Power and the Washington Media*, 122; Walter Gieber, "News Is What Newspapermen Make It," 173–80; Edwin Diamond, "Reporter Power Takes Root," 241–49.

10. David S. Broder, *Behind the Front Page: A Candid Look at How the News Is Made*, 139–40; Boylan, "Declaration of Independence," 31; Leon Sigal, *Reporters and Officials: The Organization and Politics of Newsmaking* (New York: D.C. Heath and Co., 1973), 129; Rivers, *Other Government*, 10. Others have argued less convincingly from critical studies positions that this strain in the relationship was superficial; see, for example, Daniel C. Hallin, "The Media, the War in Vietnam, and Political Support: A Critique of the Thesis of an Oppositional Media."

In many ways, the evolution in the press began with its experience in covering the controversial Senator Joseph McCarthy, the Wisconsin Republican who manipulated the press's commitment to objectivity in order to generate publicity for his demagogic ends. The media's deference to government officials during the early 1950s, for the most part, allowed McCarthy to spread lies and exaggerations about supposed communistic influences in American society. McCarthy made good copy for print as well as broadcast reporters, and because he was a U.S. senator, the media published and broadcast his accusations without question. Rarely were the senator's charges challenged in the same news columns that carried his accusations. His statements were often published without evidence to support his ever-expanding conspiracy theory because of the press's commitment to objectively cover what officials were saying, and also because of preconceived Cold War notions among reporters, editors, and publishers that even if McCarthy was exaggerating the issue, the issue was legitimate. Many who favored Republican politics also failed to challenge the senator because they appreciated his attacks on Democrats.[11]

"McCarthy exploited the news convention that what a public man says is news, and that the reporter doesn't go back of the quotation to test its truth," Louis Lyons pointed out in 1965. To Boylan, "McCarthy was a news diet of choice," although others have shown that this assessment must be tempered by the qualification that some in the media worked to expose the senator's flaws even though they gave his accusations space on the front page. Indeed, a few reporters began their opposition to McCarthy soon after his now-famous 1950 Wheeling, West Virginia, "I have a list" speech. Murrey Marder of the *Washington Post*, CBS's Edward R. Murrow, and columnist Drew Pearson were three of several reporters who worked admirably to expose McCarthy's lies. In his study of how the press covered McCarthy, Edwin Bayley concludes that the press's investigation of McCarthy's affairs "was no less thorough [than the press's work during Watergate], and no minor wrongdoing was left undisclosed. But no one cared." Two highlights of coverage were Edward R. Murrow's scathing indictment of McCarthy's tactics on his popular *See It Now* program and television's live coverage of McCarthy's attack during a Senate

11. Edwin R. Bayley, *Joe McCarthy and the Press*, 215.

hearing on the U.S. Army. Murrow's report allowed news film clips of McCarthy to reveal his tactics and his lies. Two networks, ABC and DuPont, carried every day of the hearings live and drew as big an audience as the popular *Arthur Godfrey Show*. McCarthy came off like a bully during the hearings, and the public was repulsed. Journalist James Reston of the *New York Times* reveals, though, that much of the press's criticism of McCarthy was not necessarily adversarial to government. He points out that the *Times*'s attacks on the senator were often coordinated with and helped by the Eisenhower administration. Most observers agree that journalism ultimately did little to deflate McCarthy's power. Republicans in the Senate, backed by President Eisenhower, finally censured out-of-control McCarthy after he foolishly accused U.S. Army leaders of being traitors. The press and television news media, in fact, came out of the McCarthy era embarrassed by their overall lackluster performances. Journalists felt not only frustrated by their inability to adequately counter McCarthy's unsubstantiated charges in a meaningful way, but also chagrined that the senator had intimidated them. The once-trusting relationship between government and the press suffered severe damage. By the mid- to late 1950s, there was a general understanding in the press that the press-government relationship and journalistic conventions needed adjustment. Journalists began to move toward more in-depth coverage to better explore and explain the meaning of events.[12]

The next major test for the press was the civil rights movement. While the 1950s perception of social harmony was criticized throughout the decade by leftist intellectuals and the counterculture Beats, it was the civil rights movement more than any other single factor that forcefully challenged the notion that America was trouble-free. The movement not only raised questions about the integrity of American institutions and the ability of government to maintain social order but also changed the definition of news by turning social justice issues into daily stories for both the print and the broadcast media. Recounting his experiences with United Press International in its Mississippi bureau, John Herbers wrote that racial strife during

12. Louis M. Lyons, "Introduction: *Nieman Reports* and Nieman Fellowships," 30; Boylan, "Declarations of Independence," 31; Bayley, *Joe McCarthy*, 204, 216; Reston, *Deadline*, 216.

the late 1950s and early 1960s consumed the energy of the news staff and on some days news of racial events accounted for half of the state wire's contents.[13]

David Broder considers the coverage of the civil rights movement as the first of a series of major clashes between the press and the government that ultimately led to a more adversarial relationship. Almost immediately, in fact, there came from within the media a call for more in-depth, comprehensive reporting. Declared *Arkansas Gazette* Editor Harry S. Ashmore in 1958: "It remains, then, journalism's unfulfilled responsibility... to add the why to the what [and]... to recognize that news is not merely a record of ascertainable facts and attributable opinions, but a chronicle of the world we live in cast in the terms of moral values." Additionally, George P. Hunt, managing editor of *Life* magazine, argued in 1965 that the success of civil rights reform depended largely on the media's willingness to engage in in-depth coverage of the race issue. Like the early-twentieth-century muckrakers who had come before them, journalists in the 1960s saw in-depth reporting as a responsibility to society in the face of great injustice and social upheaval. It was a defining moment for the news industry in the postwar era. Harrison Salisbury points out that coverage of the civil rights movement in the South resulted in the formation of a *New York Times* team of reporters, "skilled, physically courageous, battle-trained," that went on to cover the racially charged riots in Northern cities, the student movement, the Vietnam War and its opposition, and "the widening and bitter action which marked the rising tensions and new politics of the sixties and seventies."[14]

Trust in government and other social institutions by the American people and the press weakened during the late 1950s. During the early 1960s, it collapsed. By 1968 a number of disillusionments had created a "credibility gap" of immense proportion. Of lasting relevance to the news media were the 1960 U-2 spy plane incident, in which Eisenhower lied to the press and the American people; the 1961 Bay of Pigs fiasco, after which President John F. Kennedy regret-

13. John Herbers, "The Reporter in the Deep South." On the left and counterculture Beat movements, see Todd Gitlin, *The Sixties: Years of Hope, Days of Rage*, 1–77, and Milton Viorst, *Fire in the Streets: America in the 1960's*, 55–88.

14. Broder, *Behind the Front Page*, 140; Harry S. Ashmore, "The Story Behind Little Rock"; Harrison Salisbury, *Without Fear or Favor: An Uncompromising Look at the* New York Times, 362.

ted convincing the press not to report the planned invasion of Cuba, and a senior administration official argued the government had the right to lie; and the 1966 exposure by muckrakers Drew Pearson and Jack Anderson of corruption by the respected Senator Thomas J. Dodd of Connecticut, leading to the senator's censure by his colleagues.

The U-2 spy plane incident cooled relations between the United States and the Soviet Union on the eve of a major international summit to discuss arms control. The Soviets shot the plane down on May 1, 1960, as it flew into Soviet air space. President Eisenhower attempted to cover up the incident by first denying the plane had been shot down, and later told the press that it was a research plane—a flying laboratory used to make weather observations—assigned to the National Aeronautics and Space Administration. An Associated Press story filed from Moscow on May 5, 1960, reported Soviet Premier Nikita Khrushchev, in a speech to the Soviet parliament, described the plane as a "U.S. military craft." The article repeated the Eisenhower administration's assertion that the plane accidentally flew into Soviet air space while conducting scientific tests after taking off from a base in Turkey. Obviously wanting to protect their position with the Soviets, President Eisenhower and his staff maintained the charade until the Soviets paraded Francis Gary Powers, the captured pilot of the U-2, in Moscow. Once Powers was put on display and confessed to his Soviet captors, the U.S. government could no longer deny the plane's spy mission. Editors, reporters, and columnists, who had trusted the White House to tell them the truth, were astounded that they had accepted the administration's words at face value.[15]

About a year later it was the new U.S. president, John Kennedy, who lied to the American people and the world. Kennedy and his administration inherited from the Eisenhower administration a Central Intelligence Agency plot to help anti-Castro exiles invade Cuba from a secret base in Guatemala. The Kennedy administration's lie that distressed the nation's press was not its denial of U.S. aid to the anti-Castro rebels, though it transparently denied the help. Unlike the mission of Francis Gary Power's U-2 spy plane, the truth about plans for the U.S.-aided invasion of Cuba was well known by the press. In fact, most of the press purposely ignored or downplayed the invasion plans during the weeks leading up to the attack. They did

15. Boylan, "Declarations of Independence," 31.

so because of an even bigger and more damaging lie by the Kennedy administration. While mounting an attack against Cuba with the intention of overthrowing Fidel Castro, the country's communist dictator, the Kennedy administration falsely warned that Cuba was preparing to invade South and Central American countries to build a base from which it would eventually attack the United States. Our nation's security was at risk, the Kennedy administration warned. American publishers accepted President Kennedy's interpretation of events. The news media withheld reports about the planned invasion to protect the lives of Americans who would participate in the raid, and because they accepted the Kennedy administration's view that Castro was an imminent threat to America's security. Later, Kennedy was embarrassed by the disastrous failure of the Bay of Pigs invasion, during which Castro's forces killed or captured the entire CIA-trained force of Cuban exiles. Kennedy told editor Turner Catledge of the *New York Times* during a meeting at the White House: "If you had printed more about the operation you would have saved us from a colossal mistake." In this context, many in the press chafed at Pentagon spokesman Arthur Sylvester's argument that the government has the right to lie to the press and the American people when "national security" is at stake. The *New York Times* ran an editorial to rebut Sylvester's argument, headlined "The Right Not To Be Lied To," a few days following the Bay of Pigs fiasco. "Neither prudence nor ethics can justify any administration in telling the public things that are not so," the *Times* argued. "A democracy — our democracy — cannot be lied to... The basic principle involved is that of confidence [in our leaders]."[16]

Correspondent David J. Kraslow of the *Los Angeles Times* summed up his colleagues' reaction to being deceived by Presidents Eisenhower and Kennedy: "We ought to be raising hell about an official mentality which seems too ready to tamper with the credibility of the United States government for the sake of alleged short-term gain," he told a symposium on Washington reporting. "The U-2 business of 1960, the Bay of Pigs in 1961, the Cuban [missile crisis] mess of 1962... Three times in less than three years the American people were misled by their own government on matters of major import."[17]

16. Aronson, *The Press and the Cold War*, 163–66.
17. David J. Kraslow, "National Security Fibs."

Many in the press and much of the public were indeed worried, evidenced by public opinion polls that showed a growing lack of respect for government and other social institutions. Until about 1958, Americans' confidence in their government and institutions slowly grew, but by the early 1960s, this confidence had seriously eroded, evolving by the mid-1960s into a credibility gap between what government and institutions said and what the public perceived.[18]

The press's growing adversity toward government was exhibited in the exposure of Democratic Senator Thomas J. Dodd of Connecticut, which resulted in a scandal that focused journalists' growing lack of confidence in government on Congress. Dodd was a highly respected senator, well ensconced in the Washington establishment. He was best known for being the executive trial counsel for the Nuremberg trials after World War II, but he also had a solid background as a special assistant in the U.S. attorney general's office, where he prosecuted sabotage and industrial fraud cases during the war. After serving two terms in the House, he was elected in 1959 to the U.S. Senate, where he gained recognition as a champion of gun control, civil rights, and the protection of children. Hidden behind Dodd's solid public reputation, however, lay a sullied trail of corruption. Aided by two of Dodd's staff members, James Boyd and Marjorie Carpenter, muckrakers Drew Pearson and Jack Anderson exposed in their "Washington Merry-Go-Round" column that Dodd had systematically mined his public office for personal gain. He exchanged favors with industries he was supposed to be investigating as a committee chairman; he diverted campaign funds for personal use and cheated on his income taxes; he got jobs for people who paid him money or gave him no-interest loans; and he intervened with government agencies on behalf of his law clients. The journalists' revelations shocked Washington and led the Senate to censure the wayward senator. Criminal charges were never brought, but voters refused to give him a third term. The scandal emphasized to the press that the government could not be trusted to govern its own.[19]

18. Arthur Miller, "Political Issues and Trust in Government," *American Political Science Review* 68 (September 1974): 951–72.

19. Robert Yoakum, "The Dodd Case: Those Who Blinked," *Columbia Journalism Review*, Spring 1967, 13–20; James Boyd, "The Indispensable Informer," *Nation*, May 5, 1979, 495–97.

A watershed for the nation and for journalism was the Vietnam War and the "years of discord," as historian John Morton Blum calls the 1960s and early 1970s. The war disillusioned Americans about the role of the United States in international affairs and whether politicians in Washington could be trusted to tell Americans the truth about foreign *and* domestic policies. It also spawned a counter-culture and radicalized a generation. In journalism, it fractured the relationship between the press and government and caused a split among many journalists over the extent to which management should dictate the content of news stories. The journalistic result was a new appreciation for on-site, behind-the-media-event, direct-observation reporting.[20]

The impact of the Vietnam War on American society and culture, and on its journalism, has been well documented. Historian Jim Heath summarizes the conclusions of many historians who have written about the war's effects on American society: "[A]fter eight years of Democratic leadership under Kennedy and Johnson, the United States was being rocked by more dissension, tumult, and violence than at any time since the Civil War. Many of the accepted dogmas of American life were seriously questioned: the social and economic system, cultural values, the merit of technological expertise, New Deal–style liberalism, big government, and the whole concept of presidential power." Godfrey Hodgson points out that between 1960 and 1972, "the legitimacy of virtually every institution had been challenged, and the validity of virtually every assumption disputed." While the Vietnam War was not the only catalyst for the disruptions of the 1960s, it became the focal point of discontent. The counterculture of radical politics, drug use, promiscuous sex, and rock 'n' roll music evolved from the antiwar movement, according to Hodgson. Moreover, it spawned other movements, including the New Left and other revolutionary political movements, the free-speech movement, Black Power, and other distinct social movements

20. John Morton Blum, *Years of Discord: American Politics and Society, 1961–1974,* 287–318; Boylan, "Declarations of Independence," 33–34; Salisbury, *Without Fear or Favor,* 37–46; Stanley Karnow, "The Newsmen's War in Vietnam"; Kathleen J. Turner, *Lyndon Johnson's Dual War: Vietnam and the Press,* 170–211; Robert J. Donovan and Ray Scherer, *Unsilent Revolution: Television News and American Public Life 1948–1991,* 87–93, 98–102.

seeking student rights, feminist rights, poor people's rights, gay and lesbian rights, consumer rights, and environmental protection.[21]

A direct connection between the reemergence of investigative journalism in the United States and the discontent of the 1960s came through the founding of numerous underground and alternative newspapers, radio stations, and other alternative media by various social and cultural movements, which adopted muckraking as a means of separating themselves from the mainstream media as well as for political and cultural criticism, identity creation, and political and cultural organizing. New offset printing technology and typewriter improvements that became available in the 1960s provided a relatively inexpensive means of publishing small-circulation papers (about one hundred dollars for four thousand copies of an eight-page paper), while the oppositional culture provided the material to fill them and the audiences to read them. At least five hundred underground papers appeared in American cities, in addition to hundreds of alternative high school papers, nonprofit cooperative FM radio stations, muckraking magazines, independent documentaries, and two alternative news services, Liberation News Service and Pacific International News Service. A "golden age" of alternative and underground media occurred as leaders of antiwar, alternative-lifestyle, and cultural radical movements sought communication outlets beyond the mainstream media, which refused to provide them a forum for their radical perspectives.[22]

In their zeal to condemn established culture and policies, many alternative and underground publications in the late 1960s and early 1970s turned to a radical brand of muckraking, which used exposure journalism to promote their fiery reform and revolutionary politics. *Ramparts*, a magazine published in California, carried in its May 1971 issue an exposé revealing the involvement of South Vietnam's Marshal Nguyen Cao Ky in heroin trafficking. The investigative story outlined the Southeast Asia connection in the illegal

21. Jim F. Heath, *Decade of Disillusionment: The Kennedy-Johnson Years*, 12; Hodgson, *America in Our Time*, 12.

22. David Armstrong, *A Trumpet to Arms: Alternative Media in America*, 32; Robert Glessing, *The Underground Press in America*; Laurence Leamer, *The Paper Revolutionaries: The Rise of the Underground Press*; Abe Peck, *Uncovering the Sixties: The Life and Times of the Underground Press*.

drug trade, but also aided the radicals' opposition to the Vietnam War, the CIA (Ky was on the spy agency's payroll), and the Nixon administration, which had taken a hard line against illegal drug use. Mainstream newspapers and broadcast news outlets generally ignored the story until Senator Albert Gruening of Alaska opened congressional hearings on the allegations. After coverage of the hearings, though, the mainstream press dropped the story. "The 'underground' press is, to some extent, trying to exploit what it regards as the general press' reluctance to engage in investigative journalism," Carey McWilliams, editor of *Nation* magazine, pointed out in 1970.[23]

Ramparts, transformed from a Catholic journal for liberals into a brash muckraking publication by Warren Hinkle in 1964, "was at the forefront of the revival of investigative journalism," according to Godfrey Hodgson. It specialized in investigative stories about the Vietnam War and the civil rights and student movements. One of its biggest exposés was the revelation in March 1967 that the National Student Association, a group organized to promote liberalism and thereby counter the leftist Students for a Democratic Society, was funded by the CIA. Scrappy publications such as *Los Angeles Free Press, Berkeley Barb, The Black Panther, The Great Speckled Bird, The Village Voice, Rat, Rolling Stone*, and *The Rag* challenged status quo American values, promoted cultural experimentation, and organized opposition to racism, sexism, the Vietnam War, and the excesses of capitalism. They challenged objective reporting techniques found in the mainstream media, but embraced the tradition of exposure. Usually less disciplined than the muckrakers of the early twentieth century, they instead drew inspiration from the reform and radical alternative papers of the late nineteenth century. Alternative media muckraking, however, would sometimes rise above subjective ideological rant to offer hard-hitting analysis and exposure. The alternative press also provided an outlet for professional journalists who could not get controversial stories into the mainstream media, further supporting the resurgence of investigative journalism.[24]

When former Associated Press reporter Seymour Hersh could not interest traditional news sources in his carefully documented reports about the My Lai massacre, a story about how American soldiers

23. McWilliams, "Is Muckraking Coming Back?" 13.
24. Hodgson, *America in Our Time*, 344; Armstrong, *Trumpet to Arms*, 99–100.

killed about three hundred unarmed civilians in a Vietnamese ham-
let, he turned to the alternative press. In late 1969, the alternative
press's Liberation News Service wire was the only outlet willing to
disseminate the reports, which established Hersh as one of America's
foremost investigative journalists and eventually landed him a job
with the *New York Times*. LNS also scored hits with stories exposing
Operation Phoenix, the Pentagon's assassination squad operating in
South Vietnam, and the first reports of the dangers of Agent Orange,
the cancer-causing chemical sprayed by the United States on the jun-
gles of Vietnam.[25]

Eventually, the Vietnam War transformed mainstream journalism
as well. Reporters covering the war from Saigon and the antiwar
movement in the United States grew disillusioned with American
politicians and generals. In Vietnam, what the military's information
officers told reporters and what reporters learned in the field did
not mesh. Faced with the alternative perspectives of the war that
developed from the events and personnel in the field, some reporters
refused to report the perspective of American successes and the
prospects for the Diem government that the U.S. military and government wanted published—and that their editors and news directors wanted to see. Reporters such as Homer Bigart and David
Halberstam of the *New York Times*, Malcolm Browne and Peter Ar-
nett of the Associated Press, Neil Sheehan of UPI, Peter Kalischer and
Morley Safer of CBS, and Charles Mohr of *Time* told Americans that
American military strategy was failing, conclusions they drew only
because they went beyond the official U.S. military press briefings
to find sources among soldiers in the field. The Pentagon and the
White House harshly criticized their reports, and editors questioned their conclusions. Nevertheless, after the Tet offensive in 1968,
when North Vietnamese troops and the Viet Cong briefly overran
American and South Vietnamese troops, the reporters who investigated and, hence, challenged official reports from military spokesmen
were vindicated, to some extent, and many American news media
outlets grew more skeptical and critical of official American policy
in Vietnam.[26]

25. Seymour Hersh, *My Lai 4: A Report on the Massacre and Its Aftermath*,
128–203; Armstrong, *Trumpet to Arms*, 105–7.
26. Boylan, "Declarations of Independence," 33–36; Reston, *Deadline*, 313–21.

This is not to say that media coverage of the war and the antiwar protesters at home turned overwhelmingly antagonistic toward government. Several researchers have documented this did not happen. In separate studies, Daniel Hallin and Clarence R. Wyatt argue that the press coverage of the Vietnam War complemented the government's purposes more than it conflicted with them, to use Wyatt's phrasing. Hallin, in particular, argues that opposition to the federal government's policy for the Vietnam War came from within the government, not from the media. In this view, the media simply mirrored the opposition that congressional and other government officials presented and, hence, remained a captive of the power elite in American society, albeit an opposing faction of the power elite. Yet, an alternative reading of Hallin's data suggests that the "oppositional media" he was looking for exists within the framework of the social structure in which the American media must operate. As Hallin points out, the media broadened its vision of the "sphere of legitimate controversy," allowing the critics in and giving their arguments legitimacy. Because of the media's power to expose or exclude violators of consensus values, the act of allowing the power elite critics of American Vietnam policy into the sphere of legitimacy can be seen as an oppositional act. Some reporters gave more coverage to those within the military and government who disagreed with the official U.S. policies concerning the war and other social issues, and through that provided legitimacy to critical arguments and furthered the ability of the critics to challenge official policies. After Vietnam, the reporters who covered the war and those who covered the antiwar activities at home were more cynical about institutions and governments, their newsrooms were more willing to accept their cynicism, and their audiences were more willing to listen.[27]

Evidence of how the audience had changed and how that change affected the media can be found in the interviews with 1960s student antiwar and civil rights activists. Rennie Davis, founder of the Progressive Student League at Oberlin College, recalls being inspired by reports of the 1958 civil rights sit-ins in Greensboro, North Caro-

27. Daniel C. Hallin, The "Uncensored War": The Media and Vietnam, 22; Clarence R. Wyatt, Paper Soldiers: The American Press and the Vietnam War, 217; Donovan and Scherer, Unsilent Revolutions, 87–93, 98–102; Hodgson, America in Our Time, 263–73.

lina: "Here were four students from Greensboro who were suddenly all over *Life* magazine. There was a feeling that they were us and we were them.... Communications made a tremendous difference.... [It] was a subtle reinforcing of the belief that, if we took action, we could get results." When the media covered the civil rights protest events, Davis, a member of an audience very different from the mainstream, interpreted the message of the events in Greensboro in a way meaningful to him. He and others like him then orchestrated events that would gain further media attention. Another leader in the antiwar movement, Jerry Rubin, recalls that media manipulation came from "an intuitive understanding": "...Stopping troop trains, a little violence, students and police clashing on the railroad tracks. The media loved it. They exaggerated the event on television, and then the papers exaggerated it some more. The people who read it or saw it exaggerated it even more when they talked about it to others...and from that the movement grew." During a civil rights sit-in in Nashville, student leader John Lewis and others were arrested. But, according to Lewis, they resolved to stay in jail because "the press was giving us a lot of attention then, and the television, and we wanted to use the jail to involve our parents, the university, the people of Nashville, and the entire country."[28]

In this way, the media provided what media researcher James Ettema has called the "many small stories of various kinds" that made their way through the news to inspire politics that were alternative to those of the power elite. These new politics, in turn, inspired calls for adversarial news reporting. "If reason is not to fail men in our time, we of the press must give men the information, the knowledge, to sustain reason," Carl Rowan lectured in 1968. He argued that much of the social dissent of the 1960s resulted from the press's failure to dig out news about social conditions. Facts about malnutrition and hunger in America were made public, not by the press, but by "church groups, foundations, and private citizens." Why was it, he pointedly asked, "That some team of dedicated reporters did not put these facts before the people?" Bill Moyers, publisher of *Newsday* in 1968, reviewed government-press relations and stressed that social upheavals show the need for an independent

28. Viorst, *Fire in the Streets*, 176, 428.

press: "For the press and the government are not allies. They are adversaries....For it is the nature of a democracy to thrive upon conflict between press and government..."[29]

In 1977, Howard Simons, managing editor of the *Washington Post*, reviewed the press's experiences since his entry into journalism. Journalists in the mid-1970s "practice a kind of in-depth reporting that was rare when I became a reporter twenty-two years ago," Simons reported. "There is more skepticism now. Reporters and reporting have taken on a tougher edge..." When researcher William Rivers surveyed Washington reporters for a 1982 book, he found that 90 percent of those who responded indicated government lying during the Vietnam War was one of the causes of their becoming more skeptical of and adversarial toward officials.[30]

This break between official government sources and the news media had occurred before in American history. Adam Gopnik, writing in the *New Yorker*, found that the media became adversarial toward government during the Civil War, when conflicts between the generals and the press broke what had been a close relationship between government and reporters. In a sense, journalists lost their access to the power elite and, hence, sought out alternative sources and turned "mean" toward those in power. Press historians support him. Mark Wahlgren Summers, in his study of press and politics between 1865 and 1878, reaches a similar conclusion. When the press embraced an adversarial stance in the nineteenth century, the age of reform journalism dawned and the golden age of muckraking was right around the corner. When twentieth-century reporters cooled their cozy relationship with political and business leaders that had flourished following World War II, they embraced a questioning, skeptical attitude that nurtured modern investigative journalism.[31]

Significantly, the press's adoption of a newfound antagonism to-

29. James Ettema, "Discourse That Is Closer to Silence than to Talk: The Politics and Possibilities of Reporting on Victims of War," 4; Carl T. Rowan, "The Mass Media in an Era of Explosive Social Change"; Bill D. Moyers, "The Press and the Government: Who's Telling the Truth?"
30. Howard Simons, "The Realism of What Actually Appears in Print," speech to graduates at Northeastern Illinois University commencement exercises, May 12, 1977; Rivers, *Other Government*, 231.
31. Adam Gopnik, "Read All About It," 84–102; Summers, *The Press Gang*.

ward government and business paralleled theoretical writings about the press and the meaning of the First Amendment that, if their practical implications are recognized, made further demands for a more aggressive, questioning, and active press.

During the United States' turbulent first one hundred years, press liberty competed directly with an equally compelling concern for public safety and national security, and rarely won. The press operated within an atmosphere in which the public generally agreed that unfettered discussion furthered democracy, but restrictions on press freedom garnered little protection from the courts. Protection from libel prosecutions and censorship, as well as access to government information — the tools of a free press — received scant consideration from the courts. Faced with repeated attempts by state and federal governments to repress public speech, libertarian legal scholars concentrated on articulating a coherent theory of freedom under the First Amendment.

The federal government imprisoned and fined Republican editors who criticized Federalist government officials between 1798 and 1800 under the Alien and Sedition Acts; abolitionist and women's rights newspapers were attacked and destroyed by unruly mobs prior to the Civil War; and during the war, generals suppressed Northern newspapers sympathetic to Southern secession while Southern publications operated under strict censorship guidelines enforced by the Confederate military. In the immediate decades following the Civil War, repression of labor, birth-control, sexual-freedom, and anarchist publications focused the attention of legal scholars on natural-rights arguments for individual autonomy. Until World War I, much legal scholarship on the First Amendment centered on opposition to government attempts to restrict free speech with such laws as the Comstock Act, enacted in 1873. Anti-vice activist Anthony Comstock agitated for a federal law restricting obscene publications after New York officials failed to successfully prosecute the free-love newspaper *Woodhull and Claflin's Weekly* in 1872 for revealing the details of an adulterous relationship between the Reverend Henry Ward Beecher, a leading moralist, and his best friend's wife. The result was "An Act for the Suppression of Trade in, and Circulation of, obscene Literature and Articles of immoral Use," universally referred to as the Comstock Act. As special agent for the U.S. Post Office, Comstock unleashed an attack on publications that advocated a wide range of social and cultural reforms.[32]

World War I ushered in its own pernicious attacks on press freedom. Faced with dangers from without, the U.S. government reacted by restricting speech and press within the country. Determined to prevent dissent over the war effort, Congress passed the Espionage Act of 1917 and the Trading with the Enemy Act of 1918, which together allowed repression of newspapers that published comments critical of the U.S. government. Nearly two thousand prosecutions resulted and more than a hundred publications were suppressed, effectively redirecting free-press theorists away from issues of individual autonomy and toward arguments that defended a free press within the context of its benefit to society. Beginning with Zechariah Chafee, Jr.'s 1919 *Harvard Law Review* article, "Freedom of Speech in War Time," free speech and press scholars focused their arguments on the relationship between free political speech and society, grounding the defense of free speech and press in its usefulness to the survival of democracy. The shift represented a watershed in the history of free speech and press theory, forever linking freedom with responsibility. Whereas prior to World War I, scholars perceived liberty of speech and press as a necessary condition for individual fulfillment, after the war they viewed it as a necessary condition for society's betterment. This was a change that would impose obligations on the press that gained currency in modern free-press theory as framed in 1947 by the Commission on Freedom of the Press, headed by University of Chicago President Robert M. Hutchins and heavily influenced by none other than Zechariah Chafee, Jr., its resident free-press theorist.[33]

Time founder and editor Henry Luce bankrolled the Hutchins Commission's exploration into the relationship between press freedom and democracy. Its members included Hutchins, Chafee, theologian Reinhold Niebuhr, political scientists Harold D. Lasswell and Charles Merriam, philosopher William E. Hocking, historian Arthur M. Schlesinger, poet Archibald MacLeish, and five other prominent scholars. No journalists served on the commission. The primary con-

32. David M. Rabban, *Free Speech in Its Forgotten Years*, 27–30.
33. Ibid., 3–5; Fred Blevens, "The Hutchins Commission Turns 50: Recurring Themes in Today's Public and Civil Journalism" (paper presented to the third annual Conference on Intellectual Freedom, Montana State University–Northern, April 1997).

cern of the men who served on the commission was whether the news media and other American institutions were providing citizens with the information and knowledge required to make decisions on important public matters.

After conducting interviews and collecting data on the press, the commission issued its conclusions in one primary document, *A Free and Responsible Press*, and several individual reports, including one on press liberty penned by Chafee. The commission raised concerns that the concentration of media ownership was robbing American democracy of free and vigorous public debate, and called on the news media to be more responsible. "Clearly a qualitatively new era of public responsibility for the press has arrived," the commission declared. A set of broad guidelines for the press offered by the commission suggests a demand for a type of reporting that goes beyond the stenographic report of press conferences and media events: Put the facts of events in a meaningful context, provide a forum for public discussion, provide information about constituent groups of society, present and clarify the values and goals of American society as a whole, and offer "full access" to the intelligence of the day.[34]

The connection between ideas and practice is usually difficult, if not impossible, to establish with scientific certainty, but seen at a different magnitude the importance of ideas is that they set boundaries for what is possible at any historical moment. Intellectual historian Gordon S. Wood stresses that it is irrelevant to ask whether an idea causes an action, such as whether the idea of social responsibility causes investigative journalism. "Close up we see individuals acting freely, randomly, and purposefully," he points out. "But at a distance, at a different order of magnitude, the accumulated multitudes of ideas and thoughts transcend the particular intentions and wills of the historical participants and form a collective cultural system that sets limits on what individuals can say and think and hence do at any particular moment." Indeed, there are indications that the Hutchins Commission proposals were not isolated, idle theorizing by academics barricaded in ivory towers. To be sure, the

---

34. Commission on Freedom of the Press, *A Free and Responsible Press* (Chicago: University of Chicago Press, 1947), 20–29, 125; Zechariah Chafee, Jr., *Government and Mass Communications*, vol. 2.

press was generally hostile to the commission's report when it was released. Charlene Brown and her colleagues point out, though, that the commission's recommendations and ideas about the role and responsibility of journalism did not substantially conflict with the opinions of working reporters, editors, and publishers. The theme of the press's "social responsibility" dominated this public dialogue, and specific issues addressed by the commission, such as concentration of media ownership and fairness of press coverage, also concerned these commentators and critics. That suggests that the press's criticism of the commission's report was a rejection of the commission, not the ideals and goals identified by the commission.[35]

Throughout the 1950s, 1960s, and early 1970s, the idea that the mass media had a *duty* to report beyond the superficial handouts from those with social and political power gradually gained acceptance among press law theorists—and among journalists—even if for no other reason than that it made economic sense. The more prominent press law theorists of the postwar era, including Chafee, Alexander Meiklejohn, Thomas Emerson, and Vincent Blasi, argued for an unfettered, protected press so that it could fulfill its responsibility to fully inform the public. Meiklejohn argued for absolute protection of political speech and insisted the role of public communication was to help citizens govern themselves. Emerson theorized a "system of free expression" can be found in the words of the First Amendment that provided for a free press as well as collateral rights to obtain information and protect the identity of sources. The strongest argument for an aggressive press, though, came from Blasi, whose "checking value" theory of the First Amendment directly assigns a role for the press as watchdog of government. While the concept was not new—Blasi himself traced the checking-value theory in U.S. press theory to James Madison and other framers of the U.S. Constitution—its explication in a systematic way by Blasi gave it contemporary prevalence. The role of the press in a democratic society, Blasi counseled, is to be a critic of government, to be a "fourth estate" capable of challenging the ideas and policies of those in political power. To Blasi, the press in a modern democracy is a surrogate

35. Gordon S. Wood, "Intellectual History and the Social Sciences," 27–41. Charlene J. Brown, Trevor R. Brown, and William L. Rivers, *The Media and the People*, 178–208; Margaret Blanchard, "The Hutchins Commission: The Press and Responsibility Concept."

for the public and therefore must go beyond reporting what those in power want disseminated. Like theorist Thomas Emerson, Blasi argues for shield laws and open records laws. Emerson supported such laws to facilitate self-government. Blasi demands them so that the "professional critics" of government, including journalists, can have access to information needed to expose corruption by public officials. Blasi's interpretation of the First Amendment is reflected in the justification investigative reporter Jack Anderson gave in the mid-1970s for doing reporting that concentrates on the wrongdoing of public officials. "We must have an independent watchdog," Anderson explained, "... who will keep an eye on government."[36]

Admittedly, the ideas of the Hutchins Commission and Blasi and other legal theorists had at best indirect influence on the working press. References to these theorists rarely appear in the memoirs and reporting of journalists. But the Supreme Court's decisions during this time, many of which quote these legal theorists to justify rulings, did directly influence the working lives of reporters and editors. And none had more direct impact on investigative journalism than the 1964 Supreme Court decision in *New York Times v. Sullivan*. The court's decision revolutionized libel law in America.[37]

Ironically, *Times v. Sullivan* did not result from investigative reporting, though the U.S. Supreme Court's decision removed libel as a serious challenge to exposé reporting. In 1960, Montgomery City Commissioner L. B. Sullivan and four other Alabama public officials, including Governor John Patterson, sued the *New York Times* and four Alabama clergymen. The suit, filed in an Alabama circuit court, claimed the newspaper had libeled the officials by publishing an advertisement placed by a group seeking donations to support civil rights activist Dr. Martin Luther King, Jr. Alabama had charged King with felony perjury in connection with his state income tax filings, a charge many within the civil rights movement saw as the

36. Alexander Meiklejohn, *Free Speech and Its Relation to Self-Government*; Thomas I. Emerson, *The System of Free Expression*; Vincent Blasi, "The Checking Value in First Amendment Theory"; Elizabeth Blanks Hindman, "First Amendment Theories and Press Responsibility: The Work of Zechariah Chafee, Thomas Emerson, Vincent Blasi and Edwin Baker"; John C. Behrens, *The Typewriter Guerrillas: Closeups of 20 Top Investigative Reporters*, xx.

37. 376 U.S. 254 (1964); Lewis, *Make No Law*; Harry Klaven, Jr., "The New York Times Case: A Note on 'The Central Meaning of the First Amendment.'"

Alabama officials' attempt to imprison and silence Dr. King because of his civil rights activities. To bolster its claims, the advertisement recounted abusive incidents against civil rights demonstrators in Alabama. While the theme of the ad was accurate, several of the facts were not. For example, the advertisement claimed black student demonstrators were expelled from Alabama State College after singing "My Country 'Tis of Thee" on the State Capitol steps. In fact, the college expelled the students for leading a sit-down strike at the Montgomery County Courthouse grill, and the students had sung "The Star Spangled Banner," not the song the ad mentioned. The ad also wrongly stated that college authorities had padlocked the college's dining hall in an attempt to starve student demonstrators into submission and that heavily armed law enforcement officers had "ringed" the campus.

Commissioner Sullivan's suit was the first to be tried. The advertisement didn't attribute the incidents to any specific Alabama official, but Sullivan claimed the ad indirectly identified him because he was in charge of police operations in Montgomery, the state capital, county seat, and home of Alabama State College. The Alabama courts agreed, ruling that the newspaper had libeled Sullivan and awarding him five hundred thousand dollars in damages, an astronomical amount for a libel judgment in 1960.

Attorneys for the *New York Times* appealed to the U.S. Supreme Court, arguing that the Alabama court decision violated the press's First Amendment freedom to publish information about public matters. The newspaper argued that the errors, for which it had apologized, were not intentionally made, and that the Alabama courts were wrong to say that Sullivan was identified in the ad. The stakes were sky high. The *Times* faced libel suits by the four other Alabama officials, as well as libel suits filed by other Alabama officials over *Times* reporter Harrison Salisbury's reporting of civil rights incidents that occurred in Birmingham, Alabama. Together, the remaining suits were seeking more than six million dollars in damages, enough to bankrupt the financially struggling *New York Times*. Moreover, other public officials in Alabama and throughout the South had adopted L. B. Sullivan's strategy of using libel suits to silence other Northern journalists who were reporting on civil rights in the South. By the time the U.S. Supreme Court agreed to hear *Times v. Sullivan* in 1964, Southern officials had brought libel suits totaling three hundred million dollars against newspapers and television networks that dared to reveal to Northern and national audiences the South's ugly race story.

In previous libel cases, the Supreme Court had explicitly ruled that journalists were not constitutionally protected when they published false information. Had the Court strictly followed its earlier decisions, the mistakes contained in the *Times* advertisement would have been enough to sink the newspaper's case. Instead, in a unanimous opinion written by Justice William Brennan, it used *Times v. Sullivan* to revise the nation's libel laws to better protect the press's right to publish news and commentary on political and other public issues. After *Times v. Sullivan*, public officials would have to prove that false statements were published with "actual malice"—that the newspaper or TV news operation knew or should have known the information was false. The Court believed it was important for the survival of democracy in the United States that the press be allowed to aggressively report on public matters without an excessive fear of being sued for libel. Accepting innocent factual mistakes, the Court reasoned, was the price of ensuring vigorous public debate. Justice Brennan's opinion reflected the free-press theories of Alexander Meiklejohn and Zechariah Chafee, and presaged those of Thomas Emerson and Vincent Blasi. Harry Kalven, Jr., commenting on the case shortly after the Court's decision was rendered, argued that it had used *Times v. Sullivan* to explicate what it believed to be the central meaning of the First Amendment, that democracy cannot function without the people's right and freedom to criticize government. After *Times v. Sullivan*, Kalven wrote, "it is not now only the citizen's privilege to criticize his government, it is his duty."[38]

Commentary by Kalven and others provided academic justification for aggressive, investigative reporting, and the practical result of the *Times v. Sullivan* decision was to actively encourage investigative reporting by substantially lessening the threat from libel suits. While libel remained a concern for publishers and editors, the press gained an obvious advantage. Justice Brennan had specifically written that discussion of public issues was to be protected, even if the discussion includes mistakes, as long as the false information was not intentionally or recklessly included. Legal affairs reporter and commentator

38. Lewis, *Make No Law,* 158; Behrens, *Typewriter Guerrillas,* xiii.

Anthony Lewis has argued that without the *Times v. Sullivan* ruling, "the rise of... investigative journalism would not have been possible if the old law of libel had still shielded officials from criticism." John Behrens, in his book about investigative reporters, said the *Times v. Sullivan* decision "served to give an additional sense of assurance to newspapers. It began to be respectable and responsible, once again, to muckrake."[39]

In addition to the *Times v. Sullivan* decision, the Supreme Court provided other decisions in the 1960s and 1970s that effectively made aggressive reporting more acceptable, more protected, and more possible. Eugene Methvin, senior editor of *Reader's Digest*, recalled during a 1979 speech that *Times v. Sullivan* was the first of a series of Supreme Court decisions that "vastly enlarged our power and privilege." In 1972, former reporter/editor Frederic Coonradt declared in a journalism trade publication that "the law of libel which the American communications media long lived with, and were inhibited by, has been all but repealed." While there are no opinion surveys of journalists for the 1960–1975 time period regarding the connection between libel law decisions and their activities or sense of freedom, the attitudes of reporters and editors working during the 1980s are instructive when contrasted with Coonradt's optimism. A 1983 survey of investigative journalists found that almost two-thirds agreed that there were stories of importance not being covered because of fears of being sued, indicating that libel judgments during the latter half of the 1970s and the early years of the 1980s had a chilling effect on their work, in contrast to the more confident years of the late 1960s and early 1970s. Likewise, Douglas A. Anderson and Marianne Murdock found that by 1980 editors perceived an erosion of press protection based on recent Supreme Court decisions, indicating that there was more perceived protection from the courts in the early years of the 1970s.[40]

---

39. Eugene H. Methvin, "Supreme Court Decisions," speech delivered to the Annenberg School of Communications, University of Pennsylvania, Philadelphia, October 19, 1979.

40. Frederic C. Coonradt, "The Law of Libel Has Been All but Repealed"; Richard E. Labunski and John V. Pavlik, "The Legal Environment of Investigative Reporters: A Pilot Study"; Douglas A. Anderson and Marianne Murdock, "Effects of Communication Law Decisions on Daily Newspaper Editors"; *Gertz v. Robert Welch, Inc.*, 418 U.S. 323, 94 S.Ct. 2997, 41 L.Ed.2d 789 (1974).

In fact, a series of decisions during the 1960s and 1970s expanded the *Times v. Sullivan* doctrine's protection of the press. In *Curtis Publishing Co. v. Butts* and *Associated Press v. Walker*, the court extended the actual-malice standard to public figures. And the court applied the public-figure test to a variety of people, some of whom were public employees and some of whom had acquired public status through their jobs or through their actions. In 1971 the court went so far as to apply the actual-malice test to private citizens in *Rosenbloom v. Metromedia*. Although the *Rosenbloom* standard was eventually reversed in *Gertz v. Robert Welch, Inc.* three years later, for a time it signaled to the press that libel would be of little worry.[41]

The growing aggressiveness of the press during the 1960s and early 1970s and its use of anonymous sources to report on antiwar protesters, counterculture figures, and revolutionaries spawned a series of cases that challenged whether journalists had the right to withhold the identities of their secret sources, as well as to withhold notes, tapes, and other materials collected during the reporting process. While the Supreme Court has generally rejected absolute privilege, its decisions encouraged news reporters that their activities would be protected to a considerable degree. In the controlling case, *Branzburg v. Hayes*, three cases were combined for a ruling. The Court ruled that forcing journalists to testify before grand juries about criminal activities is not unconstitutional, but it explicitly affirmed that "news gathering is not without its First Amendment protections." Indeed, Justice Stewart, in a dissenting opinion, argued "a corollary of the right to publish must be the right to gather news." He also laid out a three-part test that went far to protect journalists and which, by the early 1980s, had become accepted law. Stewart insisted that before a journalist can be forced to testify, the government must first show that the journalist's information is "clearly relevant" to a criminal case, that the information sought from the journalist cannot be obtained from any other source, and that there is a demonstrated compelling and overriding interest in the information. The Court's actions, while not overwhelmingly in favor of protections for the press, were sufficient to give journalists confidence.

41. *Curtis Publishing Co. v. Butts*, 388 U.S. 130, 87 S.Ct. (1975); *Associated Press v. Walker*, 18 L.Ed. 2d 1094 (1967); *Rosenbloom v. Metromedia*, 403 U.S. 29, 91 S. Ct. 1811, 29 L.Ed. 2d 296 (1971); *Gertz v. Robert Welch Inc.*, 418 U.S. 323, 94 S. Ct. 2997, 41 L.Ed. 2d 789.

In 1972 the *Georgetown Law Journal*, in a survey of First Amendment law, optimistically declared that confidentiality of news sources was an "emerging constitutional protection." By the late 1960s, as Vincent Blasi found, only 8 percent of the journalists who were surveyed indicated that their reporting was affected during the previous eighteen months because of the possibility of a subpoena.[42]

While privacy law would become a greater concern to the media in the 1990s, the Supreme Court's approach to false-light privacy suits during the 1960s was beneficial to the press as well. The leading case was *Time Inc. v. Hill*, decided in 1967.[43] Escaped convicts held the Hill family hostage in 1952 in their suburban Philadelphia home. Though treated well by their captors, a novel and a Broadway play based on the incident fictionalized some abuse and depicted the family as being heroic. *Life* magazine ran an article about the theatrical production, implying heroics by the family, and the Hills sued for false-light invasion of privacy. After losing in the lower courts of New York, Time Inc. appealed to the Supreme Court, arguing that the *New York Times v. Sullivan* actual-malice decision should be applied to the invasion of privacy suit. The court agreed, extending the actual-malice test to private matters as long as the case meets a newsworthiness test, which *Time v. Hill* did. In essence, the court established the standard that people's privacy can be invaded for newsworthy purposes, a standard that still carries considerable weight.

A final area of the law that bolstered the press's position in the 1970s emerged from *New York Times v. United States*, or the Pentagon Papers case, when President Nixon's administration attempted to halt the publication of classified documents about the government's policy-making during the Vietnam War. A former consultant for the Pentagon, Daniel Ellsberg, leaked the documents to *New York Times* reporter Neil Sheehan in June 1971. Under the cloak of secrecy, Sheehan and a team of reporters and editors sifted through seven thousand pages of classified documents and crafted a multipart series that began on the front page of the *Times* on June 13, 1971, under the headline "Vietnam Archive: Pentagon Study Traces Three Decades of Growing US Involvement"—hardly an inflammatory title. Neverthe-

42. *Branzburg v. Hayes*, 1 Med.L.Rptr. 2617, 408 U.S. 665 (1972); Vincent Blasi, "The Newsman's Privilege: An Empirical Study."
43. *Time Inc. v. Hill*, 1 Med. L. Rptr. 1791, 385 U.S. 374, 87 S. Ct. 534, 17 L. Ed. 2d 456 (1967).

less, President Nixon's national security adviser, Henry Kissinger, was outraged. Nixon showed little concern because the papers revealed the workings of his predecessors, Presidents John Kennedy and Lyndon B. Johnson, and he was not mentioned. But Kissinger, who had worked in Johnson's administration, was, and he convinced Nixon that the publication threatened national security. Consequently, Nixon commanded Attorney General John Mitchell to seek an injunction, and launched the most notable prior restraint test in modern U.S. history. The newspaper published three segments before the Justice Department secured a temporary injunction from a New York federal district court. Angered that the *Times* had been censored, even briefly, Daniel Ellsberg gave a portion of the papers to the *Washington Post*, which published them as well. Government lawyers opened a second front of attack against the *Post* in a Washington, D.C., district court and were turned down. When the *Boston Globe* and the *St. Louis Post-Dispatch* each published an article based on the classified papers, the government sought and received restraining orders against them as well.[44]

In record time, the Pentagon Papers case landed at the Supreme Court. In line with earlier cases, the Supreme Court unanimously ruled that prior restraint, under certain limited circumstances, is constitutional, but said the Justice Department had not proved that the nation's security was at risk. The injunctions were lifted. It was a remarkable decision, given that the government had alleged publication would endanger troops fighting in Vietnam and hinder peace talks under way with the North Vietnamese government. Nonetheless, in rendering the Court's 6–3 decision on June 30, 1971, Justice Hugo Black, with Justice William O. Douglas concurring, forcefully defended the rights of the press in no uncertain terms: "I believe that every moment's continuance of the injunctions against these newspapers amounts to a flagrant, indefensible, and continuing violation of the First Amendment.... In my view it is unfortunate that some of my Brethren are apparently willing to hold that the publication of news may sometimes be enjoined. Such a holding would make a shambles of the First Amendment." Justice Douglas, in his

---

44. *U.S. v. New York Times*, 403 U.S. 713, 91 S. Ct. 2140, 29 L. Ed. 2d 822 (1971); Sanford J. Ungar, *The Papers and the Papers: An Account of the Legal and Political Battle over the Pentagon Papers.*

concurring opinion, made reference to the works of legal theorists Emerson and Chafee. While the Pentagon Papers articles were not classic investigative reporting (they were not the result of independent investigation by the press), they were a remarkable example of the press's willingness to expose the government's secrets.[45]

Later reflection by legal scholars and journalists found little in the Pentagon Papers decision to be enthusiastic about, mainly because the Court did not rule out the possibility of prior restraint in the future and also because Black's and Douglas's comments were not supported by other members of the Court. Yet, at the time, it was a heady experience for the press. The newspapers had stood up to the government at great risk, and the courts had made the Nixon administration back down.

Although the victory gave the media confidence in confronting the government, journalists were embarrassed by what the Pentagon Papers showed, and they resolved to become more aggressive toward government officials. The classified documents revealed that the Kennedy and Johnson administrations had lied to the public about policies concerning Vietnam, lies that the press had not uncovered. As journalist Sanford Ungar explained, "the press had also learned that, if anything, it should be more bold and outspoken in digging behind official policy, both domestic and foreign; the Pentagon Papers showed how little the public really knew about the origins of the war in Vietnam. Newspapers were painfully aware, after the crisis was over, that they had been too cautious about printing government secrets..."[46]

The media did not win all their battles in the courts from the 1950s to the early 1970s, though. While winning major concessions in the areas of libel, protection of confidential sources, privacy, and prior restraint, the press also lost many specific cases within each area. Actual malice was ultimately not extended to cases involving private individuals, and the costs of libel suits, even when winnable, would soon become prohibitive; privilege was not made absolute; privacy law remained unsettled so that in later years it would loom as a major threat to press freedom; the possibility of prior restraint was not eliminated; and considerable restrictions were placed on

45. *U.S. v. New York Times.*
46. Ungar, *Papers and the The Papers*, 95.

broadcasters. But in many ways it was an expansive time for the First Amendment. The Warren Court during the 1960s, in particular, extended press freedoms and protections. These advances in mass media law and First Amendment theory gave the press confidence and encouraged it to be more aggressive and investigative. Overall, the legal developments created an atmosphere in which investigative journalism could flourish. As Harrison Salisbury of the *New York Times* explained, "Placing the Pentagon Papers ruling and *Sullivan* back to back a careful analyst could see that there were few matters, indeed, which were likely to resist the probing powers of the press if the will to probe was present." Embarrassed that they had allowed government officials to lie to them and manipulate them, and emboldened by favorable court rulings, journalists breathed new life into the press's tradition of exposure journalism.[47]

Significantly, technological developments, including television, also pushed journalists toward investigative reporting. By the mid-1960s, television dominated mass communication. From 1948 to 1956, the percentage of homes with television sets increased from 4 percent to nearly 65 percent. While primarily an entertainment medium, TV proved to be an effective news communicator as well, capable of covering some types of breaking news better than the print media. Its live coverage of the Army-McCarthy hearings in 1954, CBS's Edward R. Murrow documentaries and *See It Now* programs, television's vivid portrayals of battles from Vietnam during the 1960s, and its dramatic capture of the 1963 assassination of President Kennedy, among other programming, made the medium a first-rate contender in the news business. "Magazines and newspapers no longer drew the eyes of so many readers. TV was no fad," Baughman points out. "The light from the sets kept burning as competitors plotted ways to douse it."[48]

Some in the print media saw investigative reporting as a means of exploiting its primary advantage over television—the ability to provide in-depth, detailed coverage that could be clipped, saved, and pondered. Writing in 1970, *Nation* editor Carey McWilliams reported that "in general, both newspapers and magazines have begun to feel that muckraking or investigative journalism is a useful means of

47. Salisbury, *Without Fear or Favor*, 390.
48. Baughman, *Mass Culture*, 30–47.

countering network news." Magazines and newspapers increasingly turned to investigative journalism. Magazines such as the *Saturday Evening Post, Cosmopolitan, True,* and, later, *Life* and *Look,* led the mass periodicals in such reporting. Newspapers, encouraged by the likes of Otis Chandler, the publisher of the *Los Angeles Times,* could "escape the tyranny of news as nothing more than a string of events and analyze information in a more sustained fashion than any TV newscaster could achieve," as Baughman explained.[49]

Meanwhile, parallel technological and legal developments provided the tools for doing such work. One of the more critical was the emergence of the freedom of information movement in the late 1940s, which led to new laws that guaranteed open meetings and open records. The American Society of Newspaper Editors formed a Committee on World Freedom of Information late in 1948. Despite its name, the committee's concentration was primarily on opening meetings and records in the "court houses, the state houses, city councils, school boards" and the U.S. federal government. When the committee started its work, there was no federal open records law and fewer than half the states had such laws, most of which were weak and ambiguous.[50]

The work of ASNE in this regard and the efforts of Congressman John Moss from 1955 to 1964 as head of a special House committee (later dubbed the Moss Committee) to push for less secrecy in government led ultimately to passage of the Freedom of Information (FOI) Act in 1967. The act codified the ideal that federal records should by definition be open to public inspection, unless officials could give specific reasons for their closure. Nine exemptions to disclosure were allowed. However, the original act failed to prevent all government secrecy. Bureaucrats found ample loopholes and delaying tactics to thwart inspection of their documents. Consequently, the debate over open records continued into the early 1970s, eventually resulting in 1974 in important amendments to the 1967 law. However, the deficiencies and criticisms of the law notwithstanding, for the first time probing reporters had specific tools for prying open government records. In 1977, Congress further endorsed open gov-

49. McWilliams, "Is Muckraking Coming Back?" 12; James Phelan, *Scandals, Scamps, and Scoundrels: The Casebook of an Investigative Reporter.*
50. George Kennedy, "Advocates of Openness: The Freedom of Information Movement" (Ph.D. diss., University of Missouri, August 1978), 24.

ernment when it passed the Government-In-Sunshine Act, which required fifty federal agencies, commissions, boards, and councils to open their meetings to the public and the press. Though slower to come and somewhat less sweeping, similar open records and open meetings laws were passed at state and local levels.[51]

Reporters' memoirs are replete with evidence that open records laws provided valuable aid for their investigations. For James Phelan, state lobbyist and corporation records on file in California provided key information needed to reveal the backers of a lobbying effort trying to halt an agreement between the state and the city of Long Beach over distribution of revenues from Pacific Ocean oil leases near the city. On a national level, the work of investigative reporter Clark Mollenhoff, who testified before the Moss Committee on behalf of open records legislation, used the FOI act as Washington bureau chief for Cowles Publications during the late 1960s to investigate grain trading and practices of the U.S. food industry. The probes revealed malfeasance, conflicts of interest, and unethical practices, and set off several congressional investigations.[52]

Two little-studied and usually overlooked technological developments from the 1950s, 1960s, and early 1970s that made investigative reporting more accessible were photocopiers and portable tape recorders. The FOI act, for example, provides for copying of documents, so it became possible for reporters outside of Washington to have copies of documents mailed to them. Photocopies of federal, state, and local documents, in addition to business documents, were added documentation for an investigation. Making use of documents became an important skill developed by investigative reporters by the 1960s, and photocopying became an important means of managing the documentation. The sensational exposés of Senator Thomas J. Dodd in 1967 by Drew Pearson and Jack Anderson would have fizzled

51. 5 U.S.C.A. at 552. The exemptions are national security, if agency rules require nondisclosure, if a statute requires nondisclosure, trade secrets, inter-agency and intra-agency memos that would not ordinarily be available by law, personal medical and personnel records and other private files, investigatory files for a current case, financial information about banks and other financial institutions, and locations of private oil and gas wells. Donald Gillmor et al., *Mass Communication Law* (St. Paul, Minn.: West Publishing, 1990), 465–76.

52. Phelan, *Scandals, Scamps, and Scoundrels,* 77–78. For other examples, see Leonard Downie, Jr., *The New Muckrakers*; Behrens, *Typewriter Guerrillas*; and Brit Hume, *Inside Story*; Dygert, *Investigative Journalist,* 46.

had the journalists not obtained photocopies of incriminating documents. Disillusioned employees and former employees of the senator
photocopied approximately six thousand pages of documents from
the senator's files and passed the copies to Pearson and Anderson.
Without the photocopied documents to back up the details of their
charges, the reporters and their sources would have had their credibility destroyed by the aggressive counterattack mounted by Dodd
and his supporters.[53]

The portable tape recorder, which appeared in economically available models during the mid- to late 1960s, allowed reporters to tape
interviews without the awkward use of reel-to-reel, desktop players.
The recordings improved accuracy and provided a verifiable record
of an interview. They also made possible the taping of telephone
calls and even surreptitious surveillance of conversations. While
few discussions of journalism make mention of specific instances
when a portable tape recorder was used and how that may have
helped the reporter, their usefulness was touted in journalism texts
and books on interviewing. David Anderson and Peter Benjaminson, the authors of one of the earliest texts on investigative journalism, included a chapter titled "Gadgets." They describe various electronic devices available to investigative journalists by the mid-1970s,
including wiretaps, bugs, pocket calculators, and cassette tape
recorders. Anderson and Benjaminson enthusiastically described the
advantages of recordings: "Obviously tape recorders can go places
where a reporter can't, such as to secret meetings." The authors go
on to describe a tape recorder secreted in a briefcase and another hidden in a belt.[54] Some reporters saw recorders as a way to be certain
of accuracy, and to provide proof of an interview. Bob Greene, head
of an investigative team for *Newsday*, insisted on tape recording key
interviews, using the tapes during the writing process to clarify
handwritten notes and to transcribe exact quotes.[55]

Related technological developments, still cameras and television
cameras in small sizes, also contributed to investigative reporting.
Perhaps the best-known investigation that used surveillance cameras
and recorders was the 1978 Mirage Bar investigation. The *Chicago*

53. Yoakum, "Dodd Case," 13; Donald R. Shanor, "Can a Congressman Sue a
Columnist?" *Columbia Journalism Review*, Spring 1967, 20–23.
54. Peter Benjaminson and David Anderson, *Investigative Reporting*, 140–47.
55. Paul Williams, *Investigative Reporting and Editing*, 91.

Sun-Times opened a tavern in downtown Chicago, staffed it with re-porters, and collected evidence of corruption by city inspectors while photographers from the paper and crews from CBS's 60 *Minutes*, which often used hidden cameras and recorders, captured the officials soliciting bribes on film, tape, and video. While the ethics of such surreptitious surveillance remained to be worked out — the *Chicago Sun-Times* was denied the Pulitzer Prize because some judges objected to the surreptitious investigation — the possibilities of secret record-ings and videotaping inspired some reporters toward investigations.[56]

The most dramatic technological development in the 1960s, though, was the computer. While general use of computers in inves-tigations would wait until development of the personal computer in the late 1980s, there was groundbreaking computer-assisted report-ing as early as the late 1960s. Philip Meyer, a member of the *Detroit Free Press*'s Washington bureau in 1967, was a pioneer in the use of social science methodology and computer analysis in news report-ing. Applying the social science methodology he learned during a Harvard University Nieman fellowship, Meyer led a team of reporters in uncovering the story behind the story of a 1967 racial riot in De-troit. In a sidebar to his main story, Meyer described the methodol-ogy used: "Interviews were taken from a random probability of 437 Negroes living in the main riot areas...An IBM 360 computer was used to cross-tabulate the responses and test their relationships for statistical significance." The story's reporting techniques enabled the *Free Press* to explode the myth that the rioters were Southern immigrants who could not adjust to big-city life and to report that participants in the riots cut across all education and income levels. The key to the cause of the rioting, the story was able to say, was alienation. He detailed his methodology in a textbook, *Precision Jour-nalism*, which inspired the next generation of reporters. To ethics pro-fessor Edmund Lambeth, Meyer's reporting systematically advanced the practice of journalism.[57]

Another pioneering use of computers in investigative journalism occurred in 1972, when reporters Don Barlett and James Steele of the *Philadelphia Inquirer* published their results of a computer

56. Zay N. Smith and Pamela Zekman, *The Mirage Bar.*
57. Philip Meyer, "The 'How' Behind This Special Survey," *Detroit Free Press,* August 20, 1967; Philip Meyer, *Precision Journalism: A Reporter's Introduction to Social Science Methods*; Lambeth, "Waiting for a New St. Benedict," 100.

analysis of Philadelphia criminal court records. The reporters spent four months in dusty storerooms carefully combing through nineteen thousand file folders holding the documentation of twenty-five years of Philadelphia criminal cases. They selected more than one thousand violent crime cases to examine more thoroughly, tabulating forty-two items for each case. Using punch cards, they fed the data into a mainframe IBM computer, cross-referencing the items and obtaining statistically valid comparisons. What they discovered stunned the legal community, as well as the public. The analysis documented that politics, racial bias, and other factors routinely affected justice in one of the Northeast's largest cities.[58]

Computers, tape recorders, and other technological developments, changes in libel law and other interpretations of the press's First Amendment freedoms, open meetings and open records statutes, and the shifting attitudes of the press toward government all contributed to the reemergence of modern investigative journalism from the late 1950s to the early 1970s. But it would be inaccurate to present these developments as though they contributed equally to the reemergence of investigative journalism in the United States. Because of the nature of social and cultural interaction, some had more impact than others.

When investigative journalism reemerged during the 1960s and early 1970s, it was not a new form of reporting. Veteran investigative reporter Clark Mollenhoff pointed out that serious interest in investigative journalism had started in the early 1950s and had risen steadily in intensity. But even then, it was an old form of reporting with a long tradition in American journalism that was resurrected and reestablished as a dominant news form. The experiences of investigative reporting throughout the history of American journalism, then, can be helpful in determining which of the examined sociocultural aspects were of primary importance for its reemergence in the mid–twentieth century. While technological developments usually promote change, the new technologies and the new open records/open meetings laws were no more than encouragement and help; they were not decisive. None of the technological changes appear sufficient to cause a rebirth of the practice on their own.

58. Steve Weinberg, *Telling the Untold Story: How Investigative Reporters Are Changing the Craft of Biography*, 111–12.

Good investigative journalism was being done prior to television and the availability of tape recorders, cameras, computers, and the other devices. At most, one can say that these devices made new subjects or different analyses available to investigators and made the chores of investigation easier, more efficient, and perhaps more accurate (computers, in particular, provided all of these advantages). In the case of television, the new technologically driven competition for audiences prodded newspaper and magazine publishers and editors to make more use of investigative journalism. The rotary press provided similar stimulation, though in a different manner, during the golden age of muckraking. Nevertheless, competition alone does not adequately explain the reemergence, because publishers could have chosen other journalistic traditions, including literary journalism.[59]

Likewise, it seems logical that the developments in First Amendment theory and case law also were contributory, but not sufficient, factors in the reemergence of investigative journalism. The early-twentieth-century muckrakers flourished without the benefit of Blasi's First Amendment theory (although the concept of the watchdog role of the press was alive and well at the time) and without the help of *Times v. Sullivan*. There is evidence, however, that the threat of libel prosecutions which would not have been possible under *Times v. Sullivan* may have contributed to the demise of the early muckraking age, although other theories for its faltering provide more compelling arguments.[60]

The third category of sociocultural developments, then, appears in several ways to be the determining factor in investigative journalism's

59. Dygert, *Investigative Journalist*, 53; David Mark Chalmers, *The Muckrake Years*, 10.

60. The impact of *Times v. Sullivan* remains in dispute, although I think the evidence and logic suggests a positive effect on the press's perception of its freedom just as surely as it had a positive effect on its actual experience with libel suits. But for an opposing view, see D. A. Anderson, "Libel and Press Self-Censorship." One possible effect on the reemergence of investigative journalism not considered here is the fact that newspapers, at least by the late 1960s, were wealthy, which brought power and inspired expensive investigative projects. Protess et al., *Journalism of Outrage*, 47–54, makes this argument, although with little documentation. It appears true that there is a positive relationship between the wealth of publishers and television station owners and their willingness to do investigative journalism. But a good case has not been made that wealth inspires an adversary stance to government and the institutions of society, while the opposite argument has been strongly argued.

reemergence. These developments provide incentives from within and from without journalism. To an extent, they give clues to motivation. The sociocultural conflicts caused journalists and media owners to be more accepting of adversarial, investigative reporting and editing. And they account for an audience that appears to have become receptive to this kind of journalism. From a cultural studies perspective, this issue of audience becomes particularly relevant. If mass communication is primarily and most meaningfully seen as ritual, as scholar James Carey argues, then its primary purpose is to provide confirmation, not information. Communication is conversation, not soliloquy, and reality is created through a shared understanding arrived at through dialogue. There is evidence that the American public's relationship to government and traditional institutions changed during this period just as surely as the relationship between government and the press changed.[61]

While the violence of the civil rights marches and the horrors of the Vietnam War were brought in graphic detail to the American people through television, radio, and print media, they did not need the mass media to conceive of the injustices, for these injustices were part of their lives. And it was with their own eyes and ears (albeit, often via the mass media) that they captured the lies and inadequacies of their elected political representatives. So ultimately it was not decisive that the news coming out of Birmingham or Saigon upheld the official government perspectives, as some researchers have asserted it did. Many in the audience had formed their own, alternative understandings, derived in part from news reports that either confirmed their perceptions or were interpreted through an oppositional reading, and the news media were required to alter their messages if they wanted to remain relevant to the audience. Likewise, when reporters sought unofficial or dissenting official views because they were either shut out of or quit believing in the official views, their reports changed in character.[62]

The press was called upon to reassert itself as the watchdog of government, a role originally proposed by the framers of the U.S. Constitution in the eighteenth century, but that had succumbed

---

61. Carey, *Communication as Culture*, 18–19.
62. Hallin, "Media, War in Vietnam, Political Support"; Todd Gitlin, *The Whole World Is Watching: Mass Media in the Making and Unmaking of the New Left.*

to partisanship and commercialism during the nineteenth and early twentieth centuries. From the mid-1950s, society expected a more aggressive message from the media, and the tools became available to support it. In response, investigative journalism reemerged as an accepted form of news reporting. Nevertheless, investigative journalism was not the only alternative form of news reporting vying for acceptance during this time period. Interpretive (or explanatory) reporting, which achieved legitimacy in reaction to the press's objective reporting stance during the coverage of McCarthy in the mid-1950s, and literary journalism (or New Journalism) and advocacy journalism, which were also championed as acceptable forms during the turbulent 1960s and early 1970s, all competed with investigative journalism for institutionalization in the mainstream media. All had healthy traditions within the history of American journalism. But investigative reporting succeeded in gaining a stronger role in modern journalism than the others, and that factor is significant to gaining an understanding of the practice and for an understanding of society. Moreover, investigative journalism, not the other alternative forms of news production, evolved into an important standard for the judgment of journalistic institutions.

3

Defining the Practice, 1960–1975

By the mid-1970s, investigative journalism had matured into a well-defined, viable practice, with clearly established methodologies, goals, values, standards, and rewards that embraced and extended journalism's long tradition of exposure and crusading for reform. It was largely an individual pursuit, with little interaction among other investigative journalists outside one's own news organization. From the late 1950s to about 1975, as reporters, editors, and TV producers pursued coverage of graft and corruption, injustice and ineptitude, they learned by doing. Values and standards were defined mostly by trial and error, and techniques and goals were sharpened through mentoring and discussions with other practitioners in trade publication articles and occasional workshops. Eventually, those engaged in investigative journalism came to an understanding of what the practice was, how it should be done, and what standards and values should guide their work.

One of the practitioners' greatest challenges was defining what they were doing. Indeed, journalists disagreed about whether it was a specialty at all. Many argued that investigative reporting was not unique within journalism. When prominent journalist Carl Bernstein accepted an honorary degree from Boston University in 1975 in recognition of his work in helping to reveal the Watergate scandal, he insisted that the reporting he and Bob Woodward had done for the *Washington Post* was no different from conventional police reporting. "I don't particularly buy... the idea of so-called investigative reporting as some kind of separate pseudo-science.... All good reporting really is based on the same thing, the same kind of work..." Bernstein's colleague at the *Post*, Robert Maynard, an editorial writer and former associate editor, agreed: "I'd be surprised if anyone... can tell me how it differs consistently from all other kinds of reporting," he told the same Boston University audience. Former investigative reporter Stephen Hartgen, however, argued in a 1975 article that investigative journalism was indeed different from other reporting. His point was that investigative reporting "involves two talents not found to the same extent in any other kind of reporting. One is the ability to use public records.... The other is the ability to see and understand relationships between people and institutions." Jack Nelson, investigative reporter for the *Los Angeles Times*, told an interviewer in the mid-1970s that investigative journalism is a "specialty" that requires special skills for digging up information, more-than-normal stamina, and tough-mindedness. To some, modern investigative journalism was a separate, coherent social activity, differing from conventional journalism in its intensified use of traditional reporting methods and in the manner in which it conceptualizes a reporting project. Investigative editor and educator Paul Williams called it an "intellectual process" as much as a collection of skills.[1]

As early as 1962, John Hohenberg, curator of the Pulitzer Prizes, wrote about the previous year's entries for the Pulitzer Prize public service category and drew distinctions between exposure journalism and routine reporting. Hohenberg labeled this reporting "investigatory." Other than the late-nineteenth-century label of "detective reporting" assigned to the work of Nellie Bly and others, Hohenberg's term was perhaps the first published attempt to name the practice.

1. Walter Lubars and John Wicklein, eds., *Investigative Reporting: The Lessons of Watergate*, 11; Stephen Hartgen, "Investigative Reporting: There's More Here Than Meets a Dragon's Eye," 13; Dygert, *Investigative Journalist*, 58–59; Williams, *Investigative Reporting and Editing*, 12.

The reporting was different from routine journalism, Hohenberg said, because reporters who produced it dug beneath the surface of events; they were what Hohenberg called "digging" specialists. Hohenberg singled out Clark Mollenhoff of the *Des Moines Register and Tribune*, who gained national recognition for his exposés of Teamster Union corruption published in the late 1950s, and Jack Nelson, then of the *Atlanta Constitution*, who was noted for his exposure of gambling payoffs in Biloxi, Mississippi, in 1948 and his coverage of civil rights violence during the late 1950s and early 1960s. Hohenberg's examples of investigatory journalism shared the element of exposure and revealed graft, corruption, or criminal behavior.[2]

In 1964 the element of exposure continued to define investigative journalism when Hohenberg again described examples of the reporting including *Newsday* and Robert Caro's exposés of land-sale frauds by Florida and Arizona promoters; the *Cleveland Plain Dealer*'s exposure of corruption by the Cuyahoga County, Ohio, recorder of deeds; and the *Philadelphia Bulletin*'s undercover photographs of city policemen at a south Philadelphia gambling concern that resulted in a department shake-up and four arrests.[3]

During the mid-1970s, journalists consistently defined investigative journalism as the exposure of corruption, graft, and abuse of power. When journalist John Behrens published a book about investigative journalists in 1973, for example, he interviewed Bill Anderson of the *Indianapolis Star* about a series Anderson and fellow reporters Richard Cady, Myrta Pulliam, and Harley Bierce had published that exposed corruption within the ranks of the Indianapolis police. Likewise, investigative reporter Gene Cunningham of the *Milwaukee Sentinel* told Behrens her most satisfying story was the exposure of a corrupt county board chairman who was indicted after her exposé was printed. Jim Polk, an investigative reporter at the *Washington Star*, the Associated Press, and *NBC News*, spoke about his investigative journalism with educator Paul Williams, describing a story he aired on NBC about two U.S. senators who accepted a free trip to a ski resort and in turn tried to influence the U.S. Housing and Urban Development Department to speed up approval of a federal sewage

2. John Hohenberg, "New Patterns in Public Service"; Dygert, *Investigative Journalist*, 50–52.
3. John Hohenberg, "Public Service: A 1964 Honor Roll," 11.

treatment grant. In 1971, Mike Baxter and Jim Savage formed an investigative team for the *Miami Herald*. Their first major story, according to Leonard Downie, Jr., was an exposé of a U.S. senator's shakedown of construction company executives hoping to get low-interest loans and other advantages from the Federal Housing Administration. In interview after interview, when journalists described investigative reporting, they made the connection between it and exposure of public official misfeasance and malfeasance.[4]

Another characteristic of investigative journalism during the 1970s that was frequently mentioned by journalists concerned the unveiling of secrets about important public matters. One of the earliest attempts at defining investigative journalism was offered in a 1972 *Quill* article by K. Scott Christianson. An investigative reporter for the *Knickerbocker News-Union Star* in Albany, New York, Christianson defined the practice as the gathering of "important secret information that somebody is determined to keep secret." This definition adds two elements: The subject matter has to be of public importance, and the information revealed has to have been previously kept secret from the public. The examples of investigative reporting offered by Hohenberg in his 1962 and 1964 articles included these elements as well. Gambling payoffs in Biloxi, civil rights repression in Georgia and Mississippi, public-official corruption in Ohio, consumer rip-offs in New York, and dishonest policemen in Philadelphia were serious questions of public concern, their full comprehension hidden from public view until the newspapers published the stories.[5]

The Christianson definition, however, was broad enough to include investigative reporting other than that which reveals corruption, malfeasance, or criminal behavior. While investigative journalism primarily is aimed at revealing wrongdoing, it also documents inefficiencies or inequities in public policies. That is what Tom Miller of the Huntington, West Virginia, *Herald-Dispatch* did in 1974. Miller won a Gerald Loeb Award and a John Hancock Award for his series, "Who Owns West Virginia?" — an analysis of land ownership patterns in the West Virginia coal country. While there were no revelations

4. Behrens, *Typewriter Guerrillas*, 15–23, 83–84; James Polk interview with Paul Williams, 1975, Investigative Reporters and Editors Resource Center, University of Missouri School of Journalism (hereafter referred to as "IRE files"); Downie, *The New Muckrakers*, 121–44.

5. K. Scott Christianson, "The New Muckraking," 10–15.

of criminal behavior or corruption, the series spurred legislators to revamp the state's tax laws to correct inequities and to discourage land speculation by absentee owners. In a 1974 speech, *Washington Post* publisher Katherine Graham distinguished the two kinds of investigative reporting. The first, she said, is the more widely understood definition of exposing hidden illegalities and public official malfeasance. The second, she said, "zeroes in on systems and institutions, in the public or private realm, to find out how they really work, who exercises power, who benefits and who gets hurt."[6]

In addition to Miller's work, there are other published examples of this second kind of investigative reporting. In 1974, Graham's own *Washington Post* published a detailed study of the U.S. Postal Service that revealed inefficiencies and poor management, not corruption. Likewise, the *Philadelphia Inquirer's* investigative team of Donald Barlett and James Steele carried out extensive analyses of social institutions and business enterprises, including the Philadelphia court system and the oil industry. Steele explained: "We don't see ourselves as righting wrongs, but merely looking at complicated public issues for patterns that haven't been seen before."[7]

In his 1962 and 1964 articles, Hohenberg identified another key element of investigative journalism—digging. This element has two dimensions. First, it implies that the reporting process involves lengthy and persistent efforts to uncover information not generally available to the public. Second, it requires that reporters themselves do the investigation, rather than simply reporting the results of a law-enforcement investigation or the proceedings of congressional investigators. Veteran investigative reporter Clark Mollenhoff said investigative reporting is primarily "hours and days—and sometimes weeks—of tedious work in combing records; countless interviews with people who do not really want to talk to you; the running out of endless leads...and the impenetrable stonewalling of responsible officialdom." Miller, of the Huntington, West Virginia, *Herald-Dispatch*, spent one full year compiling information for his series on land ownership. And Barlett and Steele at the *Philadelphia Inquirer* spent six months investigating the Internal Revenue Service for a 1974

6. Behrens, *Typewriter Guerrillas*, 148–49; "More Investigative Expertise Urged," *Publishers Auxiliary*, 1.
7. Dygert, *Investigative Journalist*, 69.

Pulitzer Prize winning series on tax law enforcement. Their work underscores the investigation's being the work product of the reporters themselves. "The two spent most of their time pulling together facts and statistics from several different sources, sometimes computing or estimating new statistics," James Dygert writes. They examined twenty thousand tax liens in four cities, pored over published IRS reports, traveled to eight states to access thirty thousand pages of court records and transcripts, and examined "five thousand pages of real estate records, probate reports, congressional committee files, medical licensing records, and government agency hearing transcripts." Seeing his contemporary investigative journalists as folk heroes, Dygert said the practice "blossomed in the late 1960s and early 1970s into a widely scattered force for informing the public about misconduct in government and prodding authorities to act against crime and corruption." He described investigative journalists as "dispassionate professionals" probing beneath the surface "to uncover the whole truth." Robert Greene of *Newsday* suggested a definition similar to the one proposed by Christianson in his 1972 article; namely, that investigative journalism is the exposure of information important to the public that someone wants to keep secret. "Pulling out something that somebody or some organization is trying to keep secret is one of the elements of investigative reporting," Greene told Paul Williams, who was researching his text on investigative journalism. Greene, a pioneer investigative journalist who at *Newsday* had founded the nation's first permanent investigative team of reporters, added a further requirement—that the reporting must be the journalist's own work product, not the reporting of an investigation by police or other government or private agency. As he told Williams, some reporters with good sources can report on investigations by the police or the Justice Department or the Rand Institute. "That is fine reporting," Greene said, "but it isn't investigative reporting. It is not their own work product."[8]

In addition to the elements of exposure, time, persistence, revealing important public issues, and independent "digging," investigative journalism also contains a desire to bring about reform, or what

8. Clark Mollenhoff, "Investigative Reporting: The Precarious Profession," 37; Dygert, *Investigative Journalist*, vii-viii, 118; Robert W. Greene interview with Paul Williams, 1975, IRE files.

David Protess and his fellow researchers have referred to as "implicit or explicit normative appeals." As Jack Anderson associate Les Whitten has remarked, investigative journalists have a desire to expose the villains and get them removed from positions of power. Investigative journalists, Whitten said, must maintain "a sense of outrage."[9]

This reformist element is most pronounced in those who seek a specific connection to the early-twentieth-century muckraking tradition. Carey McWilliams, editor of the *Nation*, assumed in 1970 that investigative journalism and reform journalism, or muckraking, were the same type of journalism. In an article for the *Columbia Journalism Review*, McWilliams used the terms "muckraking," "reform journalism," and "investigative journalism" interchangeably to describe the press's renewed interest in stories that aggressively exposed the secrets of the powerful and unjust. After reviewing several developments in investigative journalism from 1960 to 1970, McWilliams concludes: "From all this, it should be apparent that the muckraking or reform tradition is very much alive in American journalism." Others agreed with him. Jessica Mitford, who as a freelancer exposed the unethical practices of morticians in *The American Way of Death* in 1963 and problems in the penal system in *Kind and Unusual Punishment* in the early 1970s, published a how-to book on investigative journalism in 1979 and subtitled it *The Gentle Art of Muckraking*. She first thought of herself as a muckraker, she said, after *Time* magazine labeled her "Queen of the Muckrakers" following publication of her 1969 article exposing the Famous Writers School as a fraud. Likewise, syndicated columnist Jack Anderson readily referred to himself as a "muckraker." Clark Mollenhoff of the Cowles papers saw his reporting as only a prelude to pushing for reforms, often appearing before congressional committees with suggestions for reformist legislation.[10]

The degree to which this reformist desire becomes overt, however, depends upon the individual investigative journalist. Ronald Kessler of the *Washington Post*, for example, argued, "it's dangerous for a re-

9. Protess et al., *Journalism of Outrage*, 215; Theodore L. Glasser and James S. Ettema, "Investigative Journalism and the Moral Order"; Dygert, *Investigative Journalist*, 107.
10. McWilliams, "Is Muckraking Coming Back?" 8–15; Jessica Mitford, *Poison Penmanship: The Gentle Art of Muckraking*; Jack Anderson with James Boyd, *Confessions of a Muckraker*; Jack Anderson, *The Anderson Papers*; Behrens, *Typewriter Guerrillas*, 155–66.

porter to think of it as a personal campaign or crusade." He explained: "It's not my business what happens afterwards. What I enjoy is bringing out the truth. In the long run that will bring reform, though it might not happen right off." But even for those investigative reporters who agree with Kessler, the hope that one's reporting will in and of itself instigate reform of a bad situation—if the public deems reform necessary—is a strong motivator. "The satisfaction is in lifting the corner of the curtain on various activities which a government or an official may at times conceal from the public it serves and to whose judgment it must be held responsible," said investigative reporter Jim Polk. Researchers James Ettema and Theodore Glasser go even further to explicate the role of the investigative journalist as a reformer, arguing that an investigative report is a "call for public moral indignation," summoning the public to correct the problems revealed by his journalism.[11]

In summary, the definition of investigative journalism that emerges from comments by investigative reporters and from examples of investigative stories has five distinct elements: 1) exposure of information 2) about an important public issue 3) that someone or some organization does not want reported 4) that is revealed through the original, time-consuming "digging'" of the reporter 5) for the purpose of inspiring reform.

The first element usually has been interpreted to mean the exposure of illegal or immoral behavior that affects the public, but it also could include the revelations of inefficiencies or inequities through systemic analysis. In addition, the skills employed by investigative journalists are similar to traditional skills of all journalists, but are used more intensely, more aggressively, and more systematically.

Nevertheless, this definition of the investigative practice formed slowly over the years between 1960 and 1975 as practitioners of investigative journalism sought a niche for themselves within the general regimen of journalism. Consequently, it was a time of experimentation in the use of various methods and skills. Methods were tried and evaluated, accepted, or rejected. Skills, including interviewing and document searches, were identified and nurtured, allowing the practice to mature and remain viable. Many of the methods used, such

11. Dygert, *Investigative Journalist*, 69; Behrens, *Typewriter Guerrillas*, 204–5; Ettema and Glasser, *Custodians of Conscience*, 10–13.

as team-reporting and undercover work, were adaptations or refine-
ments of methods used in earlier exposé reporting. Some, including
persistent digging for covered-up facts and organization of an investigation, were methods used by the earlier muckrakers and reform
journalists, but they were improved on by practitioners of modern
exposé reporting. A few of the methods, including computer use and
polygraph tests, were introduced because new technologies became
available.[12]

Investigative reporter Bruce Locklin has argued that modern investigative reporting differs from the muckraking tradition because the
modern version of investigative journalism involves "systematic investigative reporting," whereas much of the early-twentieth-century
muckraking involved distillation and interpretation of already known
information. And, indeed, there was an attempt during the late
1960s to develop a systematic investigative reporting methodology.
In the late 1960s four men working at the American Press Institute
in Reston, Virginia—J. Montgomery Curtis, Ben Reese, former editor
of *The St. Louis Post-Dispatch*, John Seigenthaler of the *Nashville Tennessean*, and Clark Mollenhoff of the Cowles papers—developed
checklists for investigative reporters and blueprints for investigative
reporting that could be applied to studies of government or private
institutions, offices, or agencies. Mollenhoff described the system in
a 1976 article: "It involves an analysis of the history of the agency, its
purposes, and a study of how those purposes are being advanced from
a standpoint of possible conflicts of interest and the administration
of its laws and regulations. It comes complete with a check list for the
investigative reporter, so he doesn't forget any areas of potential mismanagement or corruption." The system became the basis for a series
of investigative reporting seminars sponsored by API beginning in
1968 and was expanded upon by journalism educator Paul
Williams in his 1978 textbook, *Investigative Reporting and Editing*.[13]

12. Warren T. Francke discusses team investigations during the muckraking
era and earlier in "Team Investigation in the 19th Century: Sunday Sacrifices
by the Reporting Corps" (paper presented to the History Division, Association
for Education in Journalism and Mass Communiction annual convention, 1988,
Portland, Oregon). The history of undercover reporting is included in Tom
Goldstein, *The News At Any Cost: How Journalists Compromise Their Ethics to Shape
the News*, 133.

13. Mollenhoff, "Precarious Profession," 39; Locklin, "Digging Without a
Shovel," 51.

After interviewing ninety-nine investigative reporters and editors in the mid-1970s, Williams provided one of the earlier models of investigative journalism methodology. He observed that investigative projects proceeded, consciously or unconsciously, through several stages from conception to publication. At several points along the way, evaluations were made. The general outline, according to Williams, was: Conception; Feasibility study; Go/no-go decision; Planning and base-building; Original research; Reevaluation; Go/no-go decision; Key interviews; Final evaluation; Final go/no-go decision; Writing and publication.[14]

This model illustrates what Protess et al. would conclude more than ten years later, namely that investigative reporting involves "highly distinctive processes" that take considerable time, include implicit or explicit normative appeals, and involve inductive generalizations from specific facts to larger social issues. Throughout the process, investigative reporters and editors constantly reevaluate their conception of the story. Much of this process is also regularly done during routine daily news reporting, of course, but the emphasis on original research, the framing of the story as being a comprehensive look at a public problem, and the delay of key "target" interviews until most of the research is completed separate investigative journalism from routine news reporting.[15]

Four projects from the period reveal modern investigation journalism's methodology, as perceived in the early 1970s:

1. The heroin trail project published by *Newsday* in 1973. It won the Pulitzer Prize for meritorious public service in 1974.

2. The investigation of police brutality in Chicago by the *Chicago Tribune* in 1973.

3. The study of the Philadelphia criminal justice system by the *Philadelphia Inquirer* in 1972.

4. The 1972 investigation by the *Chicago Tribune* of voter fraud in Chicago, which won a Pulitzer Prize for local reporting.

Each of these investigations pushed the methodology of investigative journalism beyond the practice's previous limits.[16]

14. Williams, *Investigative Reporting and Editing*, 14.
15. Protess et al., *Journalism of Outrage*, 215.
16. The projects spotlighted here were chosen because they represent the range of methodologies used from 1960 to 1975. *The Heroin Trail* (New York: New American Library, 1974); *Chicago Tribune* reprint, "Police Brutality," November

Bob Greene founded *Newsday*'s investigative team in 1967, and it became the model for teams at other newspapers and broadcast news operations. The *Boston Globe*, for example, studied the *Newsday* team organization before setting up its Spotlight Team in 1970. The *Newsday* team had its own office and secretary, and members of the team answered only to Greene, who closely coordinated the reporting and editing.

To report the flow of heroin into Long Island, *Newsday* sent Greene and two associates, Knut Royce and Les Payne, to the poppy fields of Turkey in June 1972. They interviewed villagers and opium processors and observed the initial phase of heroin production. From Turkey, team members went to France to investigate how opium gum was processed into heroin and smuggled out of Europe. Other *Newsday* reporters reported the story from the United States, interviewing law enforcement officials, drug dealers, and drug users.

Before embarking on the fact-gathering portion of the investigation, Greene and other team members spent two months reading extensively about the heroin problem, interviewing selected sources about drug smuggling, and developing contacts for their international visits. They took a crash course to learn the fundamentals of the Turkish language. And they mapped out a detailed plan for the investigation, including devising a cover for themselves as travel writers for *Newsday*.

Newsday spent more than one hundred thousand dollars on the heroin trail investigation. Its reporters did original research by interviewing hundreds of sources in thirteen countries in person and examining hundreds of pages of official documents. They presented a complete picture of the heroin problem from the poppy fields of Turkey to the arm of a Long Island addict. The project took six months to complete. The methods employed included team reporting, personal interviews, document searches, deception (Greene posed as a lawyer while in France), collection of evidentiary photographs (Greene took Polaroid photos of poppy seeds, among other things), identification of drug dealers by name, use of insider informants (in the qualitative research sense of finding someone knowledgeable

---

1973; the *Philadelphia Inquirer* series is detailed in Meyer, *Precision Journalism*, 366–89, and in Weinberg, *Telling the Untold Story*, 111–12; "How Voting Frauds Were Uncovered by Chi Tribune," *Editor and Publisher*, May 26, 1973, 55.

who can help set up interviews and provide guidance for the researcher), and presentation of massive amounts of evidence to prove their accusations (the final version of the report consisted of thirty-two parts and was so long it had to be shortened when it was published as a book).

To investigate police brutality in Chicago, the *Chicago Tribune* team of George Bliss, Emmet George, Pamela Zekman, and William Mullen sifted through evidence of more than five hundred cases of reported police abuse, eventually selecting thirty-seven to present to the public in their eight-part series. Spending five months, the team questioned at length hundreds of alleged victims of police violence and hundreds more who claimed to be witnesses of abuse. Thousands of police, court, and medical documents relating to charges of brutality were examined. In addition to talking to the people who accused the police of abuse, the reporters also talked to the police officers accused of the violence. The *Tribune* paid for polygraph tests to be administered to both victims and accused police officers as an additional verification of the veracity of the sources. The result was a series that gave numerous examples of police brutality, often telling the victims' tales as narratives, backed up by stories written in the more conventional expository form. The examination of each case amounted to a mini-investigation, each thoroughly researched and documented. Each had its own, delayed "key interview" when the offending police officer was confronted with the evidence. At every step, the decision to use the case had to be reexamined. The articles concluded that the police department's internal investigative division was ineffective and that "police brutality can happen to anyone, that it is not reserved for blacks, the poor, or the so-called radicals."

In Philadelphia, reporters Donald Barlett and James Steele used a computer to analyze data from more than thirteen hundred individual criminal cases to tell the story about the administration of justice in Philadelphia courts. The reporters mastered the skill of document use. They scrutinized indictments, bail applications, court hearing summaries, police complaints, prior arrest records, psychiatric evaluations, probation reports, hospital records, trial transcripts, sentencing records, defendant's backgrounds, prison records, and other public records. They painstakingly collected more than one hundred thousand pieces of information about the cases and the defendants, had the data transferred onto more than ninety-six hundred IBM computer cards, and fed the cards into a computer. After analyzing the data, the reporters interviewed crime victims, judges, prosecutors, defendants, and defense lawyers. They discovered that in Philadelphia courts, justice was not blind. Building on the innovation of Philip Meyer's computer analysis of survey data for the *Detroit Free-Press*'s study of the 1967 Detroit inner-city riots, the success of the *Inquirer* series and its use of computer analysis of public documents set a new standard for other investigative reporters embarking on investigations of local criminal justice systems.

When the *Chicago Tribune*'s team of investigative reporters decided to investigate voter fraud in Chicago in 1972 by going undercover, the paper had already experimented with clandestine investigations. Two years previously, team member William Jones had posed as an ambulance driver for two months to investigate the private ambulance companies in Chicago. Later, team members Pamela Zekman, Jones, and two other reporters got jobs working undercover inside nursing homes to see firsthand how patients were treated. In 1971, the team used surveillance techniques to investigate waste and mismanagement in Cook County government. Building on the experience of these earlier investigations, the *Tribune* task force placed seventeen *Tribune* staff members and eight outside investigators as Republican election judges and poll watchers in order to study voter fraud in 1972. In addition, team leader George Bliss carried out surveillance on one polling place from the outside. The resulting series revealed multiple voting, voting machine tampering, and cash payments to voters, in addition to other abuses, all to the benefit of the city's Democratic politicians. Prior to beginning their undercover work, the reporters mailed registered letters to a sampling of 5,495 voters in precincts where voter fraud was suspected and thereby were able to prove that about 13 percent of the registered voters were dead or never existed.

Undercover investigations were not new to investigative journalism. In 1971, Clarence Jones of WHAS-TV in Louisville, Kentucky, used a camera hidden in a lunch box to investigate walk-in bookie parlors and after-hour liquor sales for eight months. But because the *Tribune*'s voter fraud series won a Pulitzer Prize, it became an example for other investigative reporters and temporarily legitimized the controversial use of undercover work. The controversy came to a head by 1978, however, when the *Chicago Sun-Times* was denied a Pulitzer

Prize for its Mirage Bar series detailing corruption among city employees, precisely because undercover techniques and hidden cameras were used.

Newsday's heroin trail investigation, the exposé of police brutality in Chicago, the study of the Philadelphia court system, and the revelation of voter fraud in Chicago all serve to show the breadth of methodology applied by investigative journalists by the mid-1970s. These case studies reveal that investigative reporters developed the skills necessary for:

— Conceptualizing stories at a systemic level, concentrating on patterns of abuse, illegalities, and corruption rather than on a few wrongdoers;

— Organizing, correlating, and evaluating massive amounts of information and sifting through thousands of documents;

— Interviewing hundreds of sources for an individual story or series;

— Analyzing with computers otherwise unmanageable amounts of data;

— Persisting in an investigation over months of inquiry, even when faced with what appear insurmountable odds, such as following up hundreds of leads to find information and develop evidence;

— Collecting evidence that people and institutions want to keep hidden, even if collecting it means surveillance or undercover work by the reporters;

— Conducting tough interviews with targets of their investigations;

— Verifying the truth of evidence, such as through the use of polygraph tests in the police brutality series;

— Cooperating in teams to accommodate investigations that go beyond the scale that individuals could handle alone.

Modern investigative journalists learned during the 1970s that skill alone would not sustain a specialized practice, however. The type of reporting these journalists were pursuing was controversial, challenging, daunting, and sometimes dangerous. They were carrying out reporting projects of considerable sophistication, and they were going up against people and institutions that held positions of power within society. The journalists found that to do serious investigations they would have to embrace intangible qualities of character that would infuse their work with legitimacy. Moral philosophers and media ethicists call these qualities "virtues." Philosopher

Alasdair MacIntyre argues that a social practice such as investigative journalism cannot be elevated and extended over time without its practitioners displaying virtues such as courage, justice, honesty, and a sense of tradition. Media ethicist Edmund Lambeth suggests three additional time-tested principles for journalists: freedom, humaneness, and stewardship. Through the application of the virtues and the pursuit of excellence, social practices thrive. They produce "goods"—internal and external—that either sustain the practice and cause it to grow, or detract from it and cause it to decay. Internal goods, MacIntyre asserts, are those goods that relate to the virtues and that partially define the practice. Their achievement is a good for all who participate in the practice. For investigative journalists, such internal goods would include comprehensiveness, vividness, reporting on matters of public importance, truth-telling, originality, and impact. They contrast with external goods, which are those goods derived from outside the practice as a personal benefit to those doing the practice or as a benefit to the institutions that support the practice. For journalists, these external goods include money, fame, social power, and prestige.[17]

Standards of excellence change, however, and internal goods are sometimes redefined. It is in this way, in fact, that a practice either progresses or decays. The conceptions of the standards and the internal goods are "systematically extended"; in other words the practice progresses, in what Lambeth calls a "MacIntyrean moment." This is when, by applying the virtues and by pursuing goods internal to a practice, the practitioner reaches beyond the accepted standards to establish new standards and through this process causes the practice to reconceptualize the standards of excellence and, perhaps, the internal goods themselves.[18]

Lambeth, for example, argues that when reporters Barlett and Steele of the *Philadelphia Inquirer* used computer analysis in 1972 to study the administration of justice in Philadelphia courts, they pushed the practice of investigative journalism forward by establishing new standards. After Barlett's and Steele's investigation, other reporters wanting to study the administration of justice within a particular

17. MacIntyre, *After Virtue*, 175–79; Edmund Lambeth, *Committed Journalism: An Ethic for the Profession*, 23–34; Lambeth, "Waiting for a New St. Benedict," 103–4.
18. Lambeth, "Waiting for a New St. Benedict."

court system would have to match the now reconceived standards of computerization, thoroughness, and documentation. In addition, Barlett and Steele caused the practice to reconceptualize what the internal good of "telling the whole story" means.

In contrast, the *Chicago Tribune*'s 1974 investigation of voter fraud in Chicago and the *Chicago Sun-Times*/CBS 1977 investigation of city-official corruption through operation of the Mirage Bar did not advance the practice of investigative journalism because in reaching for the internal good of "truth-telling," and in attempting to set new standards of documentation, they did not apply all the virtues. While they were courageous, justice-seeking, and somewhat conscious of tradition, they were not honest. In both cases, undercover reporting and deception were used to collect information for the stories. As a result, controversy and embarrassment resulted rather than an extension of the practice.

The statements of investigative journalists and commentators from 1960 to the mid-1970s reveal the virtues, standards of excellence, and internal goods for the practice of investigative journalism as perceived by those involved in the practice during that time. By the mid-1970s there was a level of maturity in the practice of investigative journalism, a recognition of the virtues and principles, an understanding of the standards of excellence, and a perception of the internal goods. A study of the *Chicago Tribune*'s 1973 series on police brutality in Chicago, which won the 1974 Pulitzer Prize for local reporting, shows how virtues, standards of excellence, and internal goods were present within the practice of investigative journalism by the mid-1970s.

The *Tribune*'s report on police brutality toward citizens of Chicago ran in a six-part series in November 1973. It involved the paper's Task Force investigations team, headed by veteran investigative reporter George Bliss. Other members of the team were Pam Zekman, William Mullen, and Emmet George. Discussing the series after it ran, *Time* magazine described it as "probably the most thorough examination of police brutality ever published in a U.S. newspaper."[19]

The *Tribune*'s investigation was prompted by a concern that the Chicago Police Department's Internal Affairs Division (IAD) was not adequately responding to complaints of physical and verbal brutality

19. "Police Brutality," 45.

leveled by citizens against individual police officers. In 1972, IAD had sustained twenty-nine cases of abuse out of 827 it had received. As of November 1973, it had sustained 8 percent of the complaints. At the same time, the newspaper and numerous community organizations and civic leaders were receiving thousands of complaints that the police department allegedly was not investigating. A statement published later by *Tribune* publisher Stanton R. Cook pointed out that what the paper was after were the "few policemen [who] have abused their powers and the rights of citizens they are sworn to protect." The paper's position was consistent with James Dygert's requirement that investigative journalism "promote reform, expose injustice, enlighten the public" as well as discover "why an institution doesn't do its job." It also met the test proposed by investigative journalist Gene Cunningham of the *Milwaukee Sentinel* that investigative reporting concentrate on "telling the public something it should know—it must know—and otherwise wouldn't." The purpose of the *Tribune* investigation, in other words, was to achieve the journalistic internal good of reporting on a matter of public importance.[20]

By choosing the subject it did, the *Tribune* team met the standard of confronting the powerful (the police department) and consequently had to display the virtue of courage. The series points out that some alleged victims refused to talk to the reporters for fear of retaliation by the police, and Pam Zekman related in a later interview that police officers were often aggressively defensive about the questions the reporters asked. In addition, getting interviews with alleged victims or with witnesses to brutality also demanded courage, Zekman pointed out. The reporters often had to seek out people who lived in crime-infested sections of Chicago, and Zekman said she and others did not know whether "people would quietly submit to questioning or shoot us." As Dygert observed in his book about investigative journalists in the mid-1970s, "treading on the toes of a community's power structure...takes real courage."[21]

The *Tribune* reporters also sought the other investigative journalism internal goods of telling the whole story, truth-telling, originality, and impact. Telling the whole story meant looking at the range

20. Ibid., 1; Dygert, *Investigative Journalist,* 147; Behrens, *Typewriter Guerrillas,* 84.
21. Dygert, *Investigative Journalist,* 273.

of accusations of police abuse — not just one or two cases, but thirty-seven out of five hundred cases selected for investigation to show that abuse was happening to all kinds of people, "that it is not reserved for blacks, the poor, or the so-called radicals." It also meant including the stories of those who were accusing the police department, as well as the stories of the police officers who were accused. It meant investigating more than just that abuse was going on, but also what the police department was doing about the allegations of abuse and what was not being done, but what could be done to stem the brutality. It meant not writing one article, but a series that included thirty-eight articles and sidebars. As investigative reporter Jack White of the Providence, Rhode Island, *Journal-Bulletin* told an interviewer in the mid-1970s, "Perhaps the most satisfying thing is that when you're done...you are able to say to people: 'This is the whole thing.' When you can give people the whole story in one package or a series, they really understand it."[22]

By telling the whole story and looking at all angles of perspective, the *Tribune* reporters also exhibited the virtue of justice. They were concerned about the injustice of the brutality; they also were concerned about being just to those on whom they reported. Also, they carried out their investigation employing the virtue of humaneness, wanting to prevent harm to innocent civilians and wanting to prevent harm to those they reported on. And they diligently sought fairness. As publisher Cook explained, a newspaper must be both tough and fair, "and at the *Tribune*, we take great pains to be both."[23]

Truth-telling also was a primary objective for the *Tribune* reporters. "We knew that each complaint we used in our series had to be perfect," Pam Zekman recalled later. "If the police department found one hole in any single account they would drive a truck through the whole series." The reporters acknowledged that some of the people who had complained about police brutality "were lying, trying to mask their own wrongdoing by making false charges against the police." But they found others who were telling the truth, and "what emerged was a pattern of brutality by some policemen that could not be ignored." By exposing that some complaints were bogus, the reporters exhibited the virtue of honesty. "It takes a real gut desire

22. "Police Brutality," 2; Behrens, *Typewriter Guerrillas*, 212.
23. "Police Brutality," 1.

to get at the truth," as investigative reporter Ronald Kessler of the *Washington Post* explained to an interviewer. "It goes beyond a professional interest in getting good stories. It takes a drive to find out what's really going on."[24]

By striving for the standards of thoroughness and documentation, the *Chicago Tribune* reporters sought to guarantee truth-telling. They met the standard set forth by magazine editor Lewis H. Lapham, who in 1973 wrote that "the gathering of information can be a tedious process, but the relevant facts can be found if a man will search diligently enough among the available records, if he will talk to a sufficient number of people, and if he will work out the implications of his evidence." As Ted Driscoll of the Hartford, Connecticut, *Courant* explained to an interviewer in the mid-1970s, accusations by investigative journalists must be backed up by solid research. A reporter must talk to sources on both sides of the issue to verify complaints and must pull together documentation. "When you write that the [paper] 'has evidence of widespread instances...,' it must mean just that."[25]

Like other investigative journalists who helped set the standard that a journalistic investigation must involve the search of numerous public records and interviews with dozens, if not hundreds, of people, the *Tribune* reporters examined thousands of documents— starting with five hundred written complaints to the IAD provided to Bliss by an inside source—and interviewed hundreds of people who complained of brutality or were witnesses to brutality. In a later interview, Pam Zekman related her experience of trying to document one woman's accusation that a police beating led the woman to have a miscarriage. Zekman said she spent considerable effort to get an interview with the woman's doctor, who agreed the beating could have resulted in a miscarriage—had the woman been pregnant. The doctor explained that the woman had come to him for a pregnancy test, but had not returned for the test results, which were negative. In addition, the *Tribune* team extended the standard of documentation by requiring, at the paper's expense, that alleged victims

24. Behrens, *Typewriter Guerrillas*, 226; "Police Brutality," 2; Dygert, *Investigative Journalist*, 72.
25. Lewis H. Lapham, "The Temptation of a Sacred Cow," 44; Behrens, *Typewriter Guerrillas*, 99.

and some police officers pass polygraph tests administered by an independent polygraph firm with a national reputation.[26]

The internal good of originality also was sought by the *Tribune*. Original work was not clearly established by 1973 as a good associated with investigative journalism, but it quickly became so. *Life* magazine had built a reputation for investigative reporting during the late 1960s and early 1970s, including the exposure of Supreme Court Justice Abe Fortas's acceptance of a twenty-thousand-dollar annual fee from a foundation associated with a convicted criminal whose case would come before the Supreme Court. William Lambert, the magazine's chief investigative reporter, also had exposed Maryland's U.S. Senator Joseph Tydings's failure to provide full disclosure of his financial assets. But the investigations by *Life* were criticized by some investigative reporters. Robert Walters, a freelance investigative journalist, argued that the stories *Life* was publishing were not investigative reporting because the exposés did not result from original work by the reporters, but came instead from leaks by prosecutors who were unable to complete their investigations sufficiently for prosecutions.[27]

The standard of originality, however, eventually developed through criticism and self-examination by practitioners such as Walters. By the mid-1970s, Bob Greene of *Newsday* could confidently assert that the "essence" of investigative journalism is that it is the reporter's own work. And it is apparent that the reporters and editors at the *Chicago Tribune* clearly accepted the standard of originality when they set out to investigate police brutality. They did not accept the findings of the IAD that most accusations of abuse were unfounded. And they were not content to simply repeat the accusations of "bar associations, federal study groups, and respected police organizations" who had offered "scathing criticism of half-hearted brutality investigations." Instead, showing independence from the police department and other institutions, the reporters carried out their own investigation, interviewing victims, witnesses, police administrators, police department critics, and police officers, as well as searching public records for evidence. The reality of police brutality became "clear to the reporters" because the reporters had conducted their own investigation. Moreover, in carrying out an independent investigation,

26. Behrens, *Typewriter Guerrillas*, 226; "Police Brutality," 2.
27. Dygert, *Investigative Journalist*, 172, 177.

the *Tribune* editors and reporters were continuing a tradition of the paper and of journalism in general, according to publisher Cook. The brutality investigation "typifies the kind of tough, thoroughly-researched investigative reporting which . . . has won the *Tribune* two Pulitzer prizes in the past three years," Cook asserted. And, he said, it "illustrates the kind of commitment that a responsible metropolitan newspaper should make to its city and people."[28]

Investigative journalists by the mid-1970s did not agree on the importance of an investigation's having impact on a community, however. The *Washington Post*'s Ronald Kessler, for example, argued that it was dangerous for a reporter to push for reforms beyond laying out the facts of a problem. Kessler conducted investigations and presented his findings. "It's not my business what happens afterwards," he argued. But others clearly saw the need for impact and argued that following up an investigation with questions about whether reforms were being made must be a standard of excellence for the practice. Clark Mollenhoff of the Cowles papers, for instance, always followed his investigations with demands that changes be made. "If you want to be effective in this business, you've got to follow through," he argued. *Boston Globe* investigative reporter Gerard O'Neil told an interviewer that his most rewarding story was an investigation of fraudulent vocational schools because "it did the most good. It brought the biggest response . . . which can be the investigative reporter's best measurement [of success]." Moreover, Downie began his book about investigative reporting by admiringly listing the numerous changes that investigative journalism had wrought. Pointing out that Bob Woodward and Carl Bernstein helped topple President Nixon's corrupt administration, that Seymour Hersh helped turn around public opinion about the Vietnam War by reporting on the My Lai massacre, and that William Lambert's reporting on Supreme Court Justice Abe Fortas led Fortas to resign from the court, Downie concludes that "journalists have not had such a telling impact on the country's affairs since the brief golden age of the original 'muckrakers' just after the turn of the century."[29]

28. "Police Brutality," 1.
29. Dygert, *Investigative Journalist*, 69; Behrens, *Typewriter Guerrillas*, 186–87; Downie, *New Muckrakers*, 7–8.

At the *Chicago Tribune*, there is no evidence that the investigative team began its study of police brutality with a goal of effecting change, but it can be inferred that impact was a good being sought. For example, the series included interviews with law enforcement experts about how police brutality can be curbed, providing suggestions for change. The series also provided perspective on the brutality, first by exposing it as a problem, then by suggesting how the police department had failed to control it, including the revelation that a nationally recognized psychological screening program for new officers had been systematically eliminated by the department. Further, the paper followed up the series with reports of reactions to the investigation's findings. An afterword included in the paper's reprint of the series listed the various responses from the city, the police department, the state legislature, and other institutions.

The standard of vividness in reporting the findings of the investigation also contributed to the *Tribune*'s wanting to make an impact. It was recognized among investigative journalists by the 1970s that the way in which one told the story was an important factor in producing an exposé that catches people's attention. "Major projects are massive and intricate, but they are of little use if the reader can't understand and digest them," investigative reporter K. Scott Christianson advised. "The writer must know how to build and keep the reader's interest, structuring it in a manner which allows it to intensify until the last tumultuous day [of the series]." The cases of brutality detailed in the *Tribune*'s series sought to achieve vividness. They were reported in narrative form, telling short stories of police violence against individual citizens. The stories used a mixture of dialogue, graphic detail, chronological structure, irony, and other literary devices to help tell the individual stories. One of the stories began with ironic detail and observation:

> Harold Williams couldn't believe he had violated any traffic regulations when two policemen in a squad car pulled him over at 19th Street and Kostner Avenue.
>
> He was right. They had stopped him because they couldn't see the city vehicle tax sticker on his windshield.
>
> It was 10 p.m. Oct. 16, 1971, and Williams, 44, of 237 N. Long Av., was alone in his car, driving home.
>
> He never got home that night....

Another story added dialogue to its chronological description of events:

> Bennye [Moon] screamed at Winfield, "That's my son. Oh, my God, don't hit my son."
>
> [Officer] Winfield swung his revolver and hit Bennye across the face, shattering her lower left jaw. She started to sag to the street and grabbed his lapels to keep from falling....
>
> "Get out of here, bitch," Winfield told Diane [Bennye Moon's daughter].
>
> "That's my momma," she protested, but Winfield pulled her up by her maternity shirt and hit her in the mouth....
>
> "I'm hurt," she moaned. "I'm bleeding."

In addition, the series was complemented with photographs of the victims, some of which showed the effects of the abuse.[30]

Shortly after the series appeared, according to City Editor Bill Jones, phone calls and letters poured into the newsroom and did not stop for several weeks. "The series obviously had struck a delicate chord in the public," he said. In addition, several police officers were indicted on criminal charges, new programs and policies were introduced in the police department, and an independent citizens council was created to investigate police brutality complaints.[31]

The *Tribune* reporters and their editors had carried out the investigation of police brutality responsibly, according to publisher Cook, whose comments after the series ran suggested that the principles of freedom and stewardship had guided the paper's work. Lambeth points out that freedom includes the concept of autonomy, or independence, and stewardship involves acting in such a way that the freedom of the press and America's free society are maintained. "Today, more than ever before," Cook said, "a newspaper must be a spotlight on our system because only the press has the resources, energy and staff to examine such wide-ranging and complex stories as this [investigation of police brutality].... It must practice professional investigative journalism, but it must do so in a responsible manner.... Fairness breeds trust. And trust, the public's belief that a newspaper makes every effort to be fair, is the life's blood of a free

---

30. Christianson, "New Muckraking," 15; "Police Brutality," 12.
31. "Chicago's Rogue Cops," *Newsweek*, April 23, 1973, 48.

press." Clearly, the *Tribune*'s publisher saw the need for journalists to operate in such a way that social and individual freedoms were protected. In addition to their publisher's observations after the fact, the individual reporters and editors who carried out the investigation and put its findings in the paper applied the virtues of freedom and stewardship during the investigation. They did this by working to achieve the recognized internal goods of investigative journalism (reporting on matters of public importance, telling the whole story, truth-telling, originality, and impact); by striving for the standards of excellence established by investigative journalists (confronting the powerful, showing independence, documentation, thoroughness, vividness, perspective, and follow-up); and by applying the other recognized virtues and principles (courage, justice, honesty, humaneness, and sense of tradition).[32]

By the mid-1970s, modern investigative journalism had matured to the point where it was well defined, its skills and methodology were developed, and its internal goods and standards were, for the most part, in place. That maturity was accomplished largely through informal mentoring and recruitment among journalists who shared the skills and values that sustained the practice.

Alasdair MacIntyre explains that a social practice evolves and gains sustenance through the practitioners themselves and the work they do, as well as from the social institutions that host the practice. "Every practice requires a certain kind of relationship between those who participate in it," MacIntyre asserts. There must be a sharing of purposes and standards "which inform the practices." That is to say, members of a practice must have a means to train new practitioners, recognize and develop standards of excellence, and define internal goods. In addition, institutions play a role because "no practices can survive for any length of time unsustained by institutions." The institutions provide the external goods — in the case of investigative journalism, the salaries, the means of publication, the social power to gain information, and the awards and rewards that encourage and allow investigative journalists to carry out investigations. Jim Savage of the *Miami Herald* pointed out, for example, that "having the power of the *Miami Herald* behind me usually meant that some action would be taken on what I helped uncover." And from 1960

32. Lambeth, *Committed Journalism*, 29, 32; "Police Brutality," 1.

to the mid-1970s, the evidence shows, the media and other social institutions also provided the means of recruitment of new practitioners and to a large extent the training and development of investigative journalists.[33]

From the early 1960s to the mid-1970s, journalists got involved in investigative reporting through self-motivation to expose wrongdoing and corruption or through recruitment by editors who sought out reporters with relevant characteristics to carry out specific exposés. Training was carried out primarily through self-education and one-on-one mentoring. In a few cases, including those of two prominent investigative reporters from this era, Clark Mollenhoff of the Cowles papers and Robert Greene of *Newsday*, training came through education in law and/or employment with congressional committees involved in specific investigations.

Rarely did reporters perceive themselves as becoming the type of reporter that could be called "investigative journalist." Some reporters regularly doing investigative stories, such as Richard Dudman of the *St. Louis Post-Dispatch* and Jonathan Kwitny of the *Wall Street Journal*, rejected the investigative reporter label when interviewed in the mid-1970s. Dudman said he did not consider himself an investigative specialist, in spite of the fact he regularly used investigative methods. And Kwitny denied there was a specialty of investigative reporting and argued that "every story is an investigation." Many entered investigative reporting in the same way as Carl Bernstein of the *Washington Post*. Because he had a reputation for being an aggressive reporter, Bernstein was given the nod to help Bob Woodward in the investigation of the Watergate scandal in 1972. Neither Bernstein nor Woodward had the title of "investigative reporter." Bernstein explained in an interview in the mid-1970s: "I've always approached especially long pieces by digging into things. It's what I like to do. Most of the work I've done hasn't been about Watergate-type stories or people who have broken the law or anything of that kind. But it's been about how people live . . . but again I don't think you do such stories any differently." Ironically, it was Bernstein's and Woodward's book about how they reported the Watergate scandal, *All the President's Men*, that provided one of the few how-to books in the mid-1970s for would-be investigative journalists who tried to train

33. MacIntyre, *After Virtue*, 178–81; Downie, *New Muckrakers*, 134.

themselves in investigative journalism techniques. Another available source for self-study was Philip Meyer's *Precision Journalism*, first published in 1973. As a text on reporting and the use of social science methods in journalism, *Precision Journalism* offered step-by-step advice on how to carry out in-depth reporting through the use of public surveys, public records, and public polls. It also, significantly, offered aspiring investigative reporters three case studies of reporting that made use of social science methods. Other examples were available through reprints of investigations offered by the newspapers that carried them out.[34]

Another means of training was through mentoring. Investigative reporter Steve Weinberg, for example, recalls being mentored by Tom Duffy, city editor of the *Columbia Missourian*, where he worked as a student at the University of Missouri School of Journalism. Duffy, a former editor of an East St. Louis, Illinois, paper, guided Weinberg in doing investigative projects that were published in the *Missourian*. Likewise, reporter Jim Savage learned investigative skills in 1965 when he joined the Fort Lauderdale bureau of the *Miami Herald* and met Hank Messick, a veteran investigative reporter. Messick allowed Savage to watch and later help Messick's investigation of wrongdoing in local sheriffs' offices. That exposure to techniques and standards allowed Savage to develop into an investigative reporter and to go on in the mid-1970s to reveal bribery in the office of U.S. Senator Edward J. Gurney, Republican from Florida.[35]

Additionally, some communication of standards and methods was offered through articles published in journalism reviews and other magazines. The *Columbia Journalism Review* carried articles that assessed reporting on congressional aide Bobby Baker's influence-peddling scandal (1964), praised reporting by *Fleet Owner* magazine on drug use by over-the-road truck drivers (1965), analyzed undercover reporting by the *Philadelphia Bulletin* (1966), criticized the less-than-aggressive reporting about corruption in the office of Congressman Thomas J. Dodd (1967), and reported on the general comeback of muckraking (1970). *The Quill*, a publication of the Society

34. Dygert, *Investigative Journalist*, 30, 138; Behrens, *Typewriter Guerrillas*, 29; Bernstein and Woodward, *All the President's Men*; Downie, *New Muckrakers*, 1–53.

35. Steve Weinberg, interview with author, April 16, 1992, Columbia, Missouri; Downie, *New Muckrakers*, 134.

of Professional Journalists, carried articles such as investigative journalist K. Scott Christianson's assessment of the "new muckraking" (1972) and former investigative journalist Stephen Hartgen's analysis of investigative journalism (1975). [MORE], a journalism review published during the early and mid-1970s, also published assessments of investigative journalism and case studies of investigative projects. By publishing such articles, the trade press, particularly the journalism reviews, provided a critically informed forum for discussions of investigative journalism techniques, standards, and goals.

From 1960 to 1975, however, the dominant influence on the recruitment, training, and sustenance of investigative journalists was the news organizations and other social institutions interested in investigative reporting. Some newspapers, magazines, and broadcast news organizations saw investigative reporting as a duty of journalism and as a means of generating readership and viewers. Davis Taylor, publisher of the *Boston Globe*, encouraged investigative journalism during a speech to fellow publishers attending the American Newspaper Publishers Association 1974 annual meeting: "It's a trend—so far as newspapers are concerned—that is way overdue. It is something that newspapers can do better than any other medium.... I must cast my vote for more aggressive investigative reporting." Katherine Graham, publisher of the *Washington Post*, also encouraged more investigative journalism.[36]

By the mid-1970s, there were investigative teams and investigative reporters at *Newsday* on Long Island, the *Globe* in Boston, the *Philadelphia Inquirer*, the *Chicago Tribune*, the *Chicago Sun-Times*, the *Miami Herald*, the *Minneapolis Tribune*, the *Indianapolis Star*, the *St. Louis Post-Dispatch*, the *Atlanta Journal*, the *Cincinnati Enquirer*, the *Daily Oklahoman*, the *Wall Street Journal*, the *New York Times*, the *Nashville Tennessean*, and many other newspapers. On many teams, including *Newsday*'s and the *Chicago Tribune*'s, staff reporters were recruited from daily assignments to special assignment on an investigative team or to do individual investigations.

Nation editor Carey McWilliams encouraged muckraking and sought out reporters who could do stories for the magazine. *Life* and *Look* magazines saw investigative journalism as a means of expanding readership and perhaps saving the magazines from folding.

36. Behrens, *Typewriter Guerrillas*, 121; "More Investigative Expertise Urged," 1.

Other magazines, such as *Ramparts* and *New Times*, were oriented toward investigative reporting, albeit with a muckraking, reformist agenda.

Broadcast news operations also saw investigative journalism as a means of attracting larger audiences. CBS, which had broadcast Edward R. Murrow's documentary investigations on *See It Now* and as individual specials during the 1950s and early 1960s, founded 60 *Minutes* in 1968 with a decidedly investigative reporting agenda. NBC-TV had an investigative reporting team headed by Stanhope Gould and including James Polk, a veteran of the Associated Press investigative team founded in 1967 and the *Washington Star.* ABC-TV did investigations through its ABC News *Close-Up* show, which featured a former Jack Anderson associate, reporter Brit Hume. Some local television stations also pursued investigative reporting, including WHAS-TV in Louisville, WCCO-TV in Minneapolis, WMAQ in Chicago, and WPLG-TV and WCKT-TV in Miami.

Without the demand for investigative journalism from the mainstream media organizations, it would have been impossible to sustain the practice of investigative journalism. They provided the outlets for the products of the investigative journalism practice, hired investigative reporters, recruited journalists to do investigative reporting, and encouraged development of the skills of investigative journalism. The mainstream media's interest in investigations, for example, led the American Press Institute to organize its series of investigative journalism seminars that trained journalists from more than one hundred newspapers. In addition, a private foundation, the Urban Policy Research Institute of Beverly Hills, California, sponsored workshops on investigative journalism in Orange County, California, in September 1975 and in San Diego in 1976.[37]

But there was a danger in allowing media institutions to lead the development of the practice of investigative journalism. As MacIntyre warns, "practices must not be confused with institutions." Institutions are "characteristically and necessarily" concerned with acquiring external goods — making money and gaining power and

37. Christianson, "New Muckraking," 12; Urban Policy Research Institute, "Orange County Workshop," transcript of seminar held in Newport Beach, California, September 13, 1975; Urban Policy Research Institute, "The Public Record and Investigative Reporting," transcript of seminar held at San Diego, January 10, 1976.

status, and distributing money, power, and status as rewards. But the care for what MacIntyre calls the "common goods of the practice" or internal goods often come into conflict with the acquisitiveness of the institution sustaining the practice. The result can be a corruption of the practice. Such a conflict developed at the *Boston Herald-Traveler*, which established an investigative team in 1967 headed by Nicholas Gage. But only months after its formation, the team was disbanded after its investigations began revealing unflattering information about some of the businessmen on the paper's board of directors. The conflicts also were present in the magazine industry. When Jessica Mitford attempted to market her article about the Famous Writers School, she had initial rejections from *Atlantic, McCall's*, and *Life* because the magazines did not want to lose hundreds of thousands of dollars in advertising from the school, even though her article proved it was defrauding people. *Atlantic* eventually agreed to publish the piece after *Harper's* indicated an interest in it.[38]

Hank Messick, a member of the ill-fated *Boston Herald-Traveler* investigative team, argued that an investigative journalist "must understand that while his paper wants to look like it is aggressive and crusading, it doesn't want anyone rocking the boat." But the hesitancy of editors and publishers to invest in investigative journalism may have been more complicated. There were also other concerns for publishers. In addition to the possibility of offending board members or advertisers, there were concerns over libel suits as well as perceptions that the public was tiring of investigative journalism and that, perhaps, investigative journalism was having a negative effect on American democracy by undercutting the credibility of government institutions.[39]

Libel was a growing concern, in fact. The *Saturday Evening Post*, for example, faced a libel suit in the late 1960s that damaged its pride and its financial standing. While the decision in the case by the Supreme Court extended the *New York Times v. Sullivan* constitutional test for libel to public figures and thereby continued to

38. MacIntyre, *After Virtue*, 181; Downie, *New Muckrakers*, 135; Mitford, *Poison Penmanship*, 172.

39. Dygert, *Investigative Journalist*, 245; Robert M. Smith, "Why So Little Investigative Reporting?" 7–9.

expand the freedom of the press, the case still harmed the reputation of investigative journalism because of the sloppiness of the investigation by the magazine's writer and editors. University of Georgia football coach Wally Butts sued the *Post* when the magazine accused him of conspiring to fix a game against the University of Alabama. The story was based primarily on information inadvertently obtained by an insurance salesman who overheard a telephone conversation between Butts and Alabama coach Paul Bryant. The Supreme Court ruled against the *Post*, saying the magazine should have shown more care in verifying the accusation. According to the court's majority opinion: "The evidence is ample to support a finding of highly unreasonable conduct constituting an extreme departure from the standards of investigation." The high court let stand the $3,060,000 damage award against the *Post*. The ruling served as a warning to publishers that investigative stories could be second-guessed in the courtroom and could be expensive.[40]

In addition, while *Times v. Sullivan* and other Supreme Court decisions provided constitutional protections to the press in regards to libel law, the costs of defending one's self against a libel suit was becoming exceedingly expensive. In the mid-1970s, for example, *Harper's Magazine* spent nearly one hundred thousand dollars defending itself against a libel suit filed by a public official, tax assessor George Crile of Gary, Indiana. Arthur B. Hanson, general counsel for the American Newspapers Publishers Association in 1975, estimated that from 1964 to 1975, eleven hundred libel suits were filed against newspapers alone.[41]

Some editors and publishers also perceived that the public might be tiring of investigative journalism. After the first two years of Watergate scandal stories, *Time* magazine reported in 1974, some newspapers were backing off on their coverage out of concern that readers had had enough news of corruption. Indeed, a 1979 poll taken just five years after President Nixon's resignation indicated that more than

40. Lewis, *Make No Law*, 183–218; "Slander Suit Imperils Investigative Reporting," *Editor and Publisher*, February 2, 1974, 14; David M. Rubin, "The Perils of Muckraking," 5–9, 21; *Curtis Publishing Co. v. Butts*, 388 U.S. 130, 87 S.Ct. 1975, 18 L.Ed.2d 1094 (1967).

41. Lois G. Forer, *A Chilling Effect: The Mounting Threat of Libel and Invasion of Privacy Actions to the First Amendment*, 65; Rubin, "Perils of Muckraking," 5–9, 21.

70 percent of the respondents thought newspapers carried too much bad news and 64 percent thought television carried too much bad news.[42]

Some news executives also saw the trend of investigative journalism as being a danger to the stability of the United States. Howard Simons, managing editor of the *Washington Post*, warned in 1974 that the media may be overreacting in their search for corruption, "that is, looking and seemingly finding scandals everywhere." He continued: "What I mean by this is that I regard Watergate and related stories now as a kind of bloody body in the water and, therefore, an invitation to a shark frenzy during which reporters will take bites of the body and rather than carefully chew over them, swallow the bites whole. Some of this already has happened, resulting in some loss of credibility as the press has had to correct, retract, refine and recoup." Similarly, Martin S. Hayden, editor and vice president of the *Detroit News*, argued during a 1976 speech that since 1966 "the American regime has been crippled by a series of tragic events heavily-propelled by *strident, over-simplified, one-sided* American journalism, much of it described by its practitioners as 'investigative journalism'" (italics in original).[43]

Those were the concerns of news executives responsible for the financial health of their publications. So it is clear that the pursuit of external goods sometimes collided with the pursuit of the internal goods of investigative journalism. MacIntyre points out that practices are always vulnerable to the acquisitiveness of institutions, and it is very difficult for practices to "resist the corrupting power of institutions." And, indeed, there were signs in the mid-1970s that investigative journalism was not healthy.[44]

Writing in the *Quill* in April 1975, Stephen Hartgen argued that the practice of investigative journalism suffered from "serious weaknesses": "More systematic issues, such as land-use patterns and reform

42. "Covering Watergate: Success and Backlash," *Time*, July 8, 1974, 68–73; D. Charles Whitney, "The Media and the People: Americans' Experience with the News Media: A Fifty-Year Review," 14.
43. Howard Simons, "Watergate As a Catalyst," *Montana Journalism Review* 18 (1975): 14; Martin S. Hayden, "Investigative Reporting: An Assault on the Basic Regime," *Vital Speeches of the Day* (July 1, 1976): 575.
44. MacIntyre, *After Virtue*, 181.

in the criminal justice system, are generally ignored because patterns are difficult to document, and the subjects are too broad to be handled by instant analyses.... The real problem is that much investigative reporting focuses on a one-shot effort to sketch an abuse. It is rarely followed by other reports, and almost never results in substantive change." Hartgen was not alone in his criticisms. K. Scott Christianson argued that investigative journalism needed to refocus itself on topics of broader social importance and be more selective about who is allowed to engage in the practice. Investigative reporter Robert M. Smith, who worked in the Washington bureau for the *New York Times*, reflected Christianson's concern about who was being allowed to do investigative journalism. In an article for *[MORE]*, he argued that it must be recognized that it takes sophistication to be an investigative reporter. He also argued that investigative journalism takes time to do. "It is not getting the story one day ahead," he warned. Robert Greene of *Newsday* told an interviewer about his investigative team's attempt in 1971 to document accusations that President Nixon's close friend and business associate "Bebe" Rebozo had ties to organized crime. After spending several months, sifting through forty thousand documents, and conducting four hundred interviews, the organized-crime tie failed to materialize. Consequently, it was not included in the series *Newsday* ran about Nixon and Rebozo. However, Greene complained, others "with no more evidence than we had" wrote about the organized crime connection. "But if you can't prove it, it's just innuendo, and publishing it is a disservice to our profession." But, as Greene's comment shows, some investigative reporting was being published that did not meet the accepted standards of the practice. "There are always too many well-meaning but reckless adventurers in this business and too many scoop-happy opportunists," Clark Mollenhoff pointed out in 1975.[45]

These criticisms of investigative journalism made by practicing investigative journalists showed concern about the direction of the practice. Commentators were worried that the practice tended to concentrate on narrow corruption issues because they were easier to

45. Hartgen, "Investigative Reporting," 13; Behrens, *Typewriter Guerrillas,* 75; Smith, "Why So Little?" 9; Dygert, *Investigative Journalist,* 114; Mollenhoff, "Precarious Profession," 40.

prove than more important systemic issues, that there was a trend to require investigative work in addition to regular daily responsibilities, that there appeared to be practitioners who rushed into print with accusations not fully documented, and that some practitioners were not well trained. These types of criticism—going after easy targets, lack of training, rushing into print, insufficient resources to carry out investigations—are the types of criticism one would expect of a practice that is dominated by the institution supporting it. There was an underlying and largely unarticulated criticism that the news organizations, in attempts to cut costs (and, hence, acquire larger profits), and some practitioners, who were more interested in fame and fortune than in maintaining high standards, were leading the practice into troubled waters. Investigative journalism had matured by the mid-1970s, but there was wide concern about the direction it was taking.

4

The Founding of IRE

On the morning of February 22, 1975, approximately six months after President Richard M. Nixon had resigned because of the Watergate scandal, eleven journalists noted for publishing exposés met in Reston, Virginia, to create a national group dedicated to the type of journalism that had helped force Nixon's resignation.[1] The journalists were worried that the glamour associated with investigative journalism after Watergate would undermine the integrity of the practice. They had good reason to be.

The Watergate scandal and President Nixon's resignation had made celebrities of *Washington Post* reporters Bob Woodward and Carl Bernstein, who followed up their Pulitzer Prize with a best-selling book detailing how they had peeled back the facade of respectability around the Nixon White House. *All the President's Men*

---

1. Myrta Pulliam et al., "Report to Charles Williams, vice president, Lilly Endowment, Inc.," March 12, 1975, IRE files. President Nixon resigned from office on August 18, 1974.

dramatized the reporters' exploits with "Deep Throat," Woodward's mysterious informant; secret meetings and coded signals; and other adventures. Thousands of young reporters — the ethical and unethical, the competent and incompetent, the skilled and unskilled — wanted their own Watergate to bring them fame and fortune. Evaluating the investigative journalism published and broadcast after Watergate, two researchers declared in 1986 that "some of what has passed for investigative reporting since then has been pretty shoddy. Hyped headlines and glittery graphics have too often substituted for careful research and meticulous documentation."[2]

While enrollment in college journalism programs had begun to swell by the end of the 1960s — and consequently *not* as a direct reaction to *All the President's Men* — the book and film had created an alluring myth that changed the way young people perceived journalism. Earlier enrollment increases were propelled by the excitement of television news and interest in advertising, but enrollments after Watergate were driven by a fascination with investigative journalism. Flush with a rare enthusiasm for investigative reporting among editors, publishers, and broadcast managers, newspaper, TV, and magazine reporters cranked out exposés at a scale unmatched since the heyday of muckraking seventy years earlier, and many of them were more flash than flame. Some leaders in journalism were aghast. The Associated Press had started its own investigative team in 1967, but a month after *All the President's Men* premiered in 1976, Wes Gallagher, the Associated Press's general manager, saw journalism's zest for adversary digging as "an investigative reporting binge of monumental proportions."[3]

Nevertheless, 1974 was a heady time for investigative reporting. Four Pulitzers were awarded for newspaper investigations: *Newsday* on Long Island, New York, won the Public Service award for its *Heroin Trail* series that tracked the illicit narcotic traffic from Turkey to the arm of an addict on Long Island; reporters Arthur Petacque and Hugh Hough of the *Chicago Sun-Times* won the Local General or Spot News Reporting award for their investigation into the 1966 murder of Valerie Percy that led authorities to reopen the case; William Sher-

---

2. Bernstein and Woodward, *All the President's Men;* Margaret Jones Patterson and Robert H. Russell, *Behind the Lines: Case Studies in Investigative Reporting,* 1.
3. Michael Schudson, *The Power of News,* 149; *New York Times,* May 4, 1976.

man of the *New York Daily News* won in the Local Investigative Specialized Reporting category for digging into abuses of the New York Medicaid program; and Jack White of the *Providence Journal and Evening Bulletin* and James Polk, then of the *Washington Star-News*, shared the National Reporting award for exposing irregularities in President Nixon's income tax payments for 1970 and 1971 and questionable practices in the financing of the president's 1972 election campaign, respectively. *Time* magazine declared it "The Year of the Muckrake," and *Newsweek* cautioned that "scarcely a reporter in the country is now immune to fantasies of heroic achievement and epic remuneration. Woodstein envy is rampant." Harley Bierce of the *Indianapolis Star*, one of the Reston meeting's organizers, wrote to J. Montgomery Curtis of Knight-Ridder that self-regulation by journalists through a national organization was critical. "As you know," he earnestly wrote, "investigative reporting has become an important tool on many papers but there is a danger it could turn into a fad, attracting reporters seeking notoriety. A few lousy jobs and the whole field could get a bad name."[4]

And that, indeed, is what happened during the late 1970s and early 1980s as reporters dug into one national story after another, none of which amounted to much. This was particularly evident during President Jimmy Carter's administration. Carter had emphasized the moral degeneracy of the Nixon White House during his campaign, and reporters, still excited from the role the press had played during the Watergate scandal, saw new "gates" everywhere. Among others, there was "Billygate," when reporters dogged the president's brother, who had unwisely used his family connection to finagle business dealings with Muammar al Qaddafi's Libya without registering with the State Department as a foreign agent, which was required by law. A feeding frenzy occurred, as reporters dug around trying to prove related accusations, seeing scandal behind every rumor. Newspapers published exposés that suggested, wrongly, numerous extensions of the story, including a supposed presidential cover-up. But nothing of substance came of it. Billy Carter was a minor political figure whose actions were ill-advised but relatively harmless.

4. Hough, "Truth Be Told"; Harley R. Bierce to J. Montgomery Curtis, February 6, 1975, IRE files.

The irresponsibility of some scandalmongers peaked in 1978, however, when reporters pursued a false story about Carter aide Hamilton Jordan. Steve Rubell, an owner of Studio 54, the trendy New York nightclub where Jordan had partied one night, tried to deflect his own troubles over tax evasion by alleging he had seen Jordan sniff cocaine in the club's basement. A drug dealer facing criminal charges of his own supposedly offered details of the crime. The drug-dealer, called "Johnny C," was presented as quite a catch by ABC's 20/20, where he repeated his allegations for the show's cameras. After an exhaustive four-month investigation, though, a court-appointed prosecutor, Arthur Christy, who had made his reputation bringing Mafia kingpins to justice, concluded that the charges were baseless.

Such high-profile excesses by "investigative" reporters drove the public to question the reliability of the press, and of investigative journalists in particular. Conservative columnist Suzanne Garment stressed that new government ethics rules during the post-Watergate period contributed to the misguided scandals of the Carter administration, but the Washington press corps was obviously an enthusiastic participant.[5]

Overzealous, poorly reasoned investigations such as those that occurred after Watergate are what Harley Bierce and his colleague at the *Indianapolis Star*, Myrta Pulliam, hoped to counter with a national organization that could prod practicing investigative journalists to seek out the best practices for the craft. It would take several years before the organization could hope to have much impact, but eventually, they believed, it could set higher standards for the craft and educate reporters in the techniques of proper investigations. They worked with journalism educator and former newspaper editor Paul Williams of Ohio State University, and Robert Friedly, director of communications for Christian Church, Disciples of Christ, Indianapolis, to organize the meeting at Reston, Virginia, where Investigative Reporters and Editors, Inc., was founded. A thirty-one-hundred-dollar grant from the Lilly Endowment of Indianapolis paid the expenses for the meeting. The American Newspaper Publishers Association Foundation, by request of Gene Pulliam, publisher of the *Indianapolis Star*, made the arrangements.

5. Suzanne Garment, *Scandal: The Culture of Mistrust in American Politics*, 47–56.

Bierce and Myrta Pulliam were members of the *Indianapolis Star* investigative team that had revealed police corruption in Indianapolis two years earlier. After a six-month investigation, the team had uncovered bribery, extortion, and thievery by Indianapolis police. Their reports won a Pulitzer and other journalism prizes. In subsequent reporting, they attempted to expand their investigation into a nationwide study of police corruption. While struggling with the national story, Bierce and Pulliam grew frustrated by their limited skills and knowledge for a nationwide investigation. Moreover, the lack of reliable contacts among reporters across the United States hindered their reporting, and they believed a national network of reporters could help one another. During discussions with Williams and Ron Koziol, a reporter at the *Chicago Tribune*, the idea of a national service organization took hold.[6]

Among those in attendance at the meeting were columnist Jack Anderson and his associate, Les Whitten. Anderson, perhaps the best-known investigative reporter in the room, produced "Washington Merry-Go-Round," a popular investigative column he took over from the venerable Drew Pearson in 1969, when the column appeared in four hundred newspapers. Anderson had won a Pulitzer Prize for national reporting three years earlier for exposing President Nixon's secret support of Pakistan during the 1971 Indo-Pakistani war when the United States was claiming neutrality. Anderson also had contributed exclusive columns on aspects of the Watergate conspiracy that led to Nixon's resignation, particularly a stunning revelation that Attorney General John Mitchell had secretly settled the Nixon administration's anti-trust case against International Telephone and Telegraph Company, on terms generous to ITT, in exchange for a four-hundred-thousand-dollar campaign donation. Anderson's scoops had so enraged the Nixon White House that dirty operations figure G. Gordon Liddy had offered to assassinate him.[7]

David Burnham of the *New York Times* also attended. Burnham's investigation of the New York Police Department had led to formation of the Knapp Commission that probed police corruption and suggested governmental reforms. His work on the Frank Serpico

---

6. "Organizational letter," undated, IRE files.
7. Fred Emery, *Watergate: The Corruption of American Politics and the Fall of Richard Nixon* (New York: Random House, 1994), 98.

police corruption case had earned him a George Polk Award for community service. Expanding his reach beyond law enforcement, Burnham developed a specialty for investigating regulatory agencies, including nuclear energy agencies. One month before the Reston meeting, in fact, Burnham was in Oklahoma waiting for nuclear industry whistleblower Karen Silkwood to arrive with evidence she said showed that the Kerr-McGee Corporation was manufacturing faulty fuel rods at the plant where she worked and exposing workers to plutonium. On her way to meet Burnham after attending a union meeting, Silkwood was killed in a one-car crash on a lonely stretch of highway. No documents were found in her wrecked car.

Paul Williams brought equally impressive credentials to the meeting. He was then a journalism professor at Ohio State University, but before that he had been an investigative reporter and editor for *Sun* Newspapers of Omaha and led his paper to a Pulitzer Prize for reporting in 1973, the first time a reporting Pulitzer had gone to a weekly. The paper's target had been a sacred cow to most in the media—Boys Town of Nebraska, the Catholic home for troubled boys made famous in a 1938 movie starring Mickey Rooney and Spencer Tracy, who played the venerable Father Edward Flanagan. Through extensive and careful investigation, *Sun* Newspapers showed that Boys Town administrators inflated their need for money when they sent out fund-raising materials, making the organization appear poor when in fact it was flush with millions of dollars in the bank.

Other journalists who attended the Reston meeting included the *Washington Post's* metropolitan editor, Len Downie, Jr., who was working on *The New Muckrakers,* a book about investigative reporters that would be published the following year; and Jack Landau, a legal affairs correspondent and columnist for the Newhouse News Service's Washington Bureau. Journalists also respected Landau for his work with the Reporters Committee for Freedom of the Press, which had started in 1970 to fight government attempts to force investigative reporters to reveal unnamed sources. He had gained national recognition while a reporter at the *Washington Post* in the early 1960s by covering congressional corruption linked to Vice President Lyndon Johnson through the business dealings of Senate secretary Bobby Baker. Frank Anderson, associate editor of the *Long Beach* (California) *Independent*; Robert Peirce of the *St. Louis Globe-Democrat*; and John

Colburn, executive vice president of the media corporation Land-mark Communications, in Norfolk, Virginia, completed the group of journalists.[8]

Still other prominent journalists were expected at the meeting but did not attend for various reasons, including Katherine Graham, publisher of the *Washington Post*; Otis Chandler, publisher of the *Los Angeles Times*; Norman Isaacs, dean of the Columbia University Graduate School of Journalism and who would later publish *Untended Gates*, a book of press criticism; William Hornby, executive editor of the *Denver Post*; Dick Pyle, a reporter on the Associated Press's investigative team; Pamela Zekman, head of the *Chicago Tribune*'s investigative team; Andrew Greeley with the National Opinion Research Center; and Fred Graham of *CBS News*. While these luminaries did not attend, their interest in the group shows the appeal an organization dedicated to investigative journalism had for leaders in the profession.

At the meeting, it was quickly agreed that a service organization for investigative journalists would be worthwhile. During debate over what to call the organization, Les Whitten pointed out that a defining characteristic of investigative journalists was their sense of outrage. So someone grabbed a dictionary to find synonyms of "outrage" and came up with "ire," which would work as an acronym for "Investigative Reporters and Editors Group." So IRE became the organization's acronym.

One of the more important decisions the group had to make concerned who should be allowed into the organization, and it proved to be one of the more debatable issues. How they decided the question would define the organization and determine the fate of the group, as well as the impact on journalism it would eventually have. The question was whether to limit the organization to experienced investigative reporters, or to open the group to all reporters.

Some participants, particularly those who had already gained notoriety as investigative reporters, wanted the organization to be an elite association of journalists who had proved themselves. "I suggest

8. Attending as observers were Donald McVay, acting executive director, American Newspaper Publishers Association; Stewart Macdonald, executive director, ANPA Foundation; Steve Palmedo, ANPA Foundation staff member; and Malcolm Mallette, managing director, American Press Institute.

we accept only the experienced reporters," said Jack Anderson. "There are very few of the type of reporters I'm talking about."[9] The purpose of such a select group, according to David Burnham, would be to publicize investigative journalism in an attempt to change the definition of news from just reporting what public officials said to reporting what is going on behind the public announcements. There was precedent for an organization with restricted membership. The American Society of Journalists and Authors, founded in 1948, served freelance journalists and nonfiction book authors and limited membership to writers with impressive résumés showing publications in leading magazines or publication of at least two books by leading publishers.

In contrast, John Colburn of Landmark Communications argued for a broad-based organization, seconding Robert Peirce's position that "the real need is a general upgrade" of investigative reporting skills among regular reporters. Malcolm Mallette of the American Press Institute acknowledged his sympathy for Colburn's desire to reach out to all reporters but also saw the benefits of an elite group as proposed by Jack Anderson: "If you want to go Jack's way for a prestige thing, then you are aspiring to something. There is a ripple effect in this industry."

"I wonder about being too selective," cautioned Robert Friedly, who argued that the organization should be open to all reporters and editors, not just to those who have proved themselves. "It's the guy in 'Kokomo' who needs this to rub off," he explained, "but if it's too exclusive, you won't get the ones who need the help."

"How about writing 'Kokomo' and asking the city editor to nominate someone?" Les Whitten suggested. "That's still selective, but you avoid some yo-yos."

Whitten and others wanted to establish authority over the craft by excluding reporters who had not yet gained reputations as investigators. This attitude resurfaced at a later meeting when it was discussed who would be listed in a directory of investigative journalists. But at Reston, the consensus shifted to openness. David Burnham acknowledged, for example, that to limit the organization would

9. Notes taken by Myrta Pulliam during the Reston meeting, IRE files. The following dialogue is recreated from Pulliam's notes.

exclude reporters who are not assigned to investigative beats but who nonetheless produce tough, investigative reporting. Later in March 1975, writing in a trade magazine to publicize the new organization, Harley Bierce of the *Indianapolis Star* emphasized that the organization would provide services to any reporter needing assistance on an investigative story. "We want to stress that this won't be an exclusive organization," he wrote. "Good reporters naturally fall into this classification [of investigative reporter]."[10]

Because such noted investigative journalists as Jack Anderson and David Burnham were included, the group gained immediate credibility. The steering committee's charge was to explore interest in a national organization and to plan a national conference, during which the organization could be established. In addition, the early organizers created an executive committee composed of Robert Peirce, Ronald Koziol, Paul Williams, Myrta Pulliam, Harley Bierce, Indianapolis media attorney Edward O. DeLaney, and Robert Friedly.

During the next few months, the steering committee met several times to plan the national meeting, write proposed by-laws, and apply for grants to fund the meeting and a permanent resource center, which members of the committee assumed would be located at Ohio State University, where Paul Williams could help set it up and manage it. The committee applied for incorporation as a not-for-profit organization under the laws of Indiana. Funding the organization, though, proved to be complicated and troublesome. Most service organizations are free to solicit start-up grants from various foundations. But IRE was different. Representing journalists who routinely investigate American institutions, including foundations, IRE would put itself in a delicate position by asking foundations for funds. Lilly Endowment, established by the pharmaceutical giant Eli Lilly, had provided the initial planning grant, and directors had plans to ask the foundation for $25,000 more. Nonetheless, the Lilly Endowment's contributions were seen as a possible conflict of interest for IRE, and its financial help represented the dilemma the organization faced. IRE needed funds, but it could not take money from just anybody. The steering committee set a final fund-raising goal of $90,000 after first proposing the unrealistically low figure of $20,000 and the

10. "Investigative Reporters Form Own Service Association."

overly ambitious amount of $250,000. Beirce, Pulliam, Williams, and other IRE organizers had initially hoped to raise enough money to pay for travel and accommodations for 250 reporters and editors to attend the first national conference. By paying the expenses, it was argued, IRE could attract "the very best" investigative reporters to the meeting. What they apparently failed to realize at the time was that selecting reporters and editors to invite to the meeting, all expenses paid, would restrict interest in the organization and artificially limit the number of members they could attract.

The organizers decided to seek funding from the American Newspaper Publishers Association Foundation, the Philip Stern Foundation, the Henry R. Luce Foundation, the 20th Century Fund, the Markle Foundation, and the Gannett Foundation, among others. Most declined to help. The Markle Foundation, for example, questioned the potential of the organization to offer anything unique to the profession of journalism. Moreover, the Gannett Foundation told IRE it should support itself on dues and fees. Consequently, by the end of 1975, IRE organizers had raised only slightly more than $5,000 of the $90,000 they had anticipated needing. That amount included the original $3,100 Lilly Endowment grant, as well as smaller donations from newspapers, newspaper corporations, and individuals. Indianapolis Newspapers, Inc., working home of Bierce and Pulliam, had given $1,000. In addition, donations had come from the *Omaha World-Herald*; Capitol Newspapers of Albany, New York; newspaper broker Bob Bolitho; publisher Eugene S. Pulliam of the Indianapolis newspapers; Muncie (Indiana) Newspapers; the *Huntington* (Indiana) *Herald*; and Les Whitten.

The organization's finances took a turn for the better in 1976. Several important donations arrived early in the year. The Stern Foundation, for example, provided $2,500, and financier Warren Buffet donated stocks to IRE that were sold, providing a cash donation of $787. More significantly, a "special projects fund" of $3,000 was donated by the New York Community Trust. By April of 1976, then, the steering committee had succeeded in putting together an operating budget of more than $18,000, including a new grant from the Lilly Endowment, about $700 in dues from the organization's sixty-eight members, newspaper company contributions, and other sources. But it was far from the $90,000 organizers had hoped for, and the idea of paying the expenses of those who came to the national meeting was abandoned. Complicating matters further, though, was the attitude of the general membership, which opposed soliciting funding from foundations. During the first annual conference, members roundly criticized the steering committee for taking funds from foundations such as the Lilly Endowment that might compromise the organization's image as an independent group. Additionally, some criticized organizers for approaching publishers for funding. One member chided them: "Where does IRE get off hoping to get seed money from publishers when publishers don't allow enough money for investigations now?" Consequently, members passed a resolution restricting fund-raising to foundations "which owe their existence to journalistic enterprise," or are educational or research entities. And if the organization had to go beyond those two sources, the group was to approach only foundations "not likely to compromise the integrity of IRE." The membership agreed to accept the Lilly Endowment money only if there were no strings attached.[11]

IRE's fund-raising soon acquired respectable support from two prominent newspaper publishers. Eugene S. Pulliam of Indianapolis and Barry Bingham, Jr., of Louisville co-signed a form letter that praised the young organization and urged newspapers and foundations to contribute to build the journalism profession's skills for investigative reporting. "IRE's goal of providing themselves [sic] with educational and information services seems a worthy undertaking," the letter states. "Such a service will, we believe, serve the papers for which they work and, even more important, the readers of those publications.... We urge you to join us in financial support of this venture until it [IRE] can stand on its own." Mr. Pulliam had already donated $1,000, and Bingham had promised $2,500.[12]

To IRE members' chagrin, however, a couple of donors proved to be an embarrassment when it was revealed (in a front-page *Wall Street Journal* article nonetheless) that IRE had accepted their contributions. At issue was the Louis Wolfson Foundation, whose creator was

11. "Minutes of the Meeting of the Membership of Investigative Reporters and Editors held on June 20, 1976," IRE files. Treasurer's Report, April 10, 1976, submitted by Harley Bierce, treasurer, IRE files.

12. Eugene S. Pulliam and Barry Bingham, Jr., letter, attached to August 10, 1976, memo from Tom Van Howe to Myrta Pulliam, IRE files.

imprisoned for securities violations, and attorney Julius Echeles of Chicago, who often represented Mafia clients. IRE leaders responded weakly that they couldn't know the background of all donors.[13]

Consequently, IRE would have to rely primarily on its members for funding. Harley Bierce sent out recruitment letters elaborating the goals of the new organization. He argued that a national organization could make investigative reporters "more efficient, more successful" and reduce the costs of investigations. Undeniably, facilitating cooperation among investigative journalists was a primary goal. In a letter to anticipated participants of the Reston, Virginia, meeting, Pulliam and Bierce stressed that "because areas which require investigative reporting are complex, reporters can save time by learning techniques and procedures used by colleagues. Awareness of outstanding models of investigative reporting can help reporters make their work more reliable and more useful to the public." They pointed out that cooperation among investigative reporters could provide a way for reporters to follow leads that require investigation outside their immediate geographical area, could help reporters avoid damaging pitfalls and costly mistakes, and could help reporters learn skills for particular types of stories. From the beginning, too, there was interest in establishing standards for investigative journalism. In another letter, Bierce wrote that a major goal of the organization would be to find a way to identify and encourage "standards that should be upheld." This would become a common theme of the organization during its early years.[14]

The organization quickly took shape as a group for working reporters and editors. Indeed, organizers decided at the first Reston meeting that IRE must not duplicate services provided by other journalism organizations, many of which were oriented toward management. API's seminars on investigative reporting techniques, for example, had promoted a systematic approach to investigative reporting developed by well-known investigative reporter Clark Mollenhoff of the Cowles Newspapers Washington Bureau. The seminars were an early means of training reporters and encouraging interest in investigative reporting. But API's representative at the Reston meet-

13. Jim Drinkhall, "Conflict-of-Interest, Censorship Charges Jar Unlikely Group," *Wall Street Journal*, February 23, 1977.
14. Myrta Pulliam and Harley Bierce to Stu Macdonald, February 13, 1975; Harley R. Bierce to J. Montgomery Curtis, February 6, 1975, IRE files.

ing, Malcolm Mallette, pointed out that API's priorities could change as interests among its members changed, suggesting that there was no guarantee that its seminars on investigative journalism skills would continue. In addition, other services, such as a directory of investigative reporters, a data bank of investigative stories, and an annual meeting open to all reporters interested in investigative journalism were not met by the API seminars. Questions about working with the Society of Professional Journalists, Sigma Delta Chi; The Reporters Committee for Freedom of the Press; and the American Newspaper Publishers Association also were expressed. Organizers agreed, however, that while coordination with other groups was important, independence from them would ensure perpetuation of the organization and also better serve to create a "community of temperament" among investigative journalists, to use Les Whitten's phrase. And, indeed, shortly after the Reston meeting, Stewart R. Macdonald, executive director of the ANPA Foundation, signaled what was an inherent conflict between working reporters and editors and the publishers for whom they work. Macdonald frankly stated that the American Newspaper Publishers Association should not be associated with a group such as IRE because it posed the possibility of becoming a reporters' group that could at times be at cross-purposes to newspaper management.[15]

The first national conference was held June 18–20, 1976, in Indianapolis. More than three hundred people attended, including approximately two hundred paying participants from thirty-five states, thirty speakers (who waived their speaking fees), and forty students. Jack Anderson provided the keynote address at the dinner. Workshop topics included the state of the art of investigative journalism, how to manage an investigation, how to work as a team, how to report specific topics such as crime, and how to deal with legal and ethical issues in investigative reporting. The membership voted to seek funds for establishing a resource center at Ohio State University by July 1, 1977. Rejecting earlier arguments that the IRE directory of investigative reporters should be limited to those who had been nominated to the directory because of outstanding work, the membership adopted a resolution that all members of IRE would

15. Pulliam notes, IRE files; Paul Williams, notes of Reston meeting, IRE papers; S. R. Macdonald, "Memorandum to the files," February 27, 1975, IRE files.

be included. Indicating interest in a topical issue of the time, the membership approved a resolution strongly urging reporters, editors, or news agencies working with the Central Intelligence Agency, the Federal Bureau of Investigation, or other law enforcement agencies to end their associations with the government agencies immediately because by "accepting payment from such agencies, news persons demean the principles of American journalistic independence." The membership also voted to establish an ethics committee "responsible for raising in a continuing way the ethical questions which confront journalists" and to be "responsible for examining the assumptions that underlie" investigative journalism. Finally, the membership voted to establish a committee of broadcast journalists to advise the board of directors about problems specific to broadcast investigations.[16]

"IRE has gotten off to a remarkably fast start with our help," Bob Friedly, the communications director for the Christian Church, Disciples of Christ, Indianapolis, and a former New Orleans reporter, reflected in a July 1, 1976, report to church officials. The church's Office of Communications had served as administrator of the planning grant from the Lilly Endowment, had designed the IRE logo, and had printed materials for the organization. However, Friedly was now bowing out of the organization so that it could continue as a reporter-editor group without the Christian Church's involvement. The Christian Church's general assembly had been remarkably supportive of news media freedom, and that had encouraged Friedly to get involved. In 1971, the assembly had condemned the Justice Department's subpoenaing of news reporters' notes, and two years later called for legislation to protect the anonymity of news sources. Harley Bierce and Myrta Pulliam had asked Friedly's office to sponsor the IRE group until incorporation could be obtained. Friedly was happy to do so because he saw the organization as a group that would provide journalists "some sense of community in their struggle with crime, corruption, consumer rip-offs, political shenanigans, money laundering and other public abuses..." In conclusion, Friedly summarized remarks that reporter Clark Mol-

16. The initial officers of the board of directors were Ronald Koziol, president; Paul Williams, vice president; and Edward DeLaney, secretary; "Minutes of the meeting of the membership," June 10, 1976, IRE files.

lenhoff made during his speech at the first conference's concluding luncheon: "The press is only a part of the check and balance system; there is no room for 'scoop happy opportunists'; it takes hard work, seriousness, responsibility and a genuine concern for the truth."[17]

Paul Williams's unexpected death in November 1976 brought the fledgling organization's first dilemma. The Ohio State journalism professor had been a leader in establishing IRE and had secured a working relationship between IRE and the university. After the first national conference, lawyers had drawn up an operating agreement between IRE and Ohio State. But with Williams out of the picture, Ohio State's journalism program could not be counted on to continue enthusiastic support for the organization. In the meantime, financial problems had forced the closing of temporary offices in Indianapolis in February 1977. A permanent home for the organization became even more important. Consequently, the executive committee decided to solicit offers from other universities. In addition to Ohio State, other universities showed interest: Michigan State University, Northwestern University, Indiana University, Boston University, the University of Missouri, and, later, Arizona State University. Most, including Ohio State, eventually decided not to make formal offers. Finally, in 1978, two proposals came to the IRE board of directors: one from Boston University, and one from the University of Missouri School of Journalism. Influential IRE board president Robert Greene of Long Island favored Boston University with its East Coast presence, and the executive committee had given Boston its tentative commitment.

Nevertheless, UMC School of Journalism Dean Roy M. Fisher stressed his school's tradition of service to professional journalists and its twenty-year affiliation with the Freedom of Information Center located at the school. He also tried to quiet the fears of IRE President (later, Chairman) Greene that IRE would get "overshadowed" by other UMC School of Journalism programs and that locating at Columbia, Missouri, would isolate the organization from urban centers outside the Midwest. Jim Polk of *NBC News*, chairman of the IRE executive committee, pointed out the advantages to the Missouri

17. Bob Friedly, "Summary Report of Involvement of Office of Communication with Investigative Reporters and Editors," July 1, 1976, IRE files.

offer in a letter to board members. "The Missouri proposal is very favorable in several aspects," he wrote. Missouri's School of Journalism, the oldest journalism school in the nation and rated among the best, agreed to provide free clipping services for IRE, pay the salaries of office staff members, and help IRE with fund-raising. Boston University's proposal was less attractive, and at their June 1978 annual meeting in Denver, IRE members unanimously chose the University of Missouri over Boston University for the site of the new IRE headquarters and named investigative reporter John Ullmann, a University of Missouri instructor, executive director.[18]

IRE's annual awards program criteria provide insight into the standards IRE wanted for investigative journalism. They establish that good investigative journalism is the product of the reporter's "initiative and efforts," meaning that reporting on the investigations of government agencies such as the Federal Bureau of Investigation would not be considered "investigative journalism." The topic should be original and of great importance to the publication's circulation area or the broadcast area. Moreover, it should reveal secrets that someone or some entity wants to keep hidden. Beyond that, it should be fair and accurate, with good documentation, and meet the "generally accepted standards" of the craft. It must be well-written and clearly presented. Reporters and their organizations should be willing to provide the necessary resources and to have the courage to face powerful opponents. Moreover, if the reporting has a significant social impact, that would be even better.

Among the first substantive issues was to adopt a definition of the practice. Organizers expressed early concern that the definition of investigative reporting should be as broad as possible. Adopting a definition written by Robert Greene of *Newsday*, IRE defined an investigative story as one that results from the initiative and personal work of a reporter (i.e., one that does not result from an inves-

18. Jack Nelson to IRE board members, May 28, 1978, IRE files; Roy M. Fisher, UMC School of Journalism dean, to Robert Greene, May 9, 1978, IRE files; Jack Nelson to John Ullmann, June 29, 1978, IRE files. Harley Bierce of the *Indianapolis Star* was IRE's first full-time executive director. He handled the day-to-day affairs of IRE from office space rented from the *Indianapolis Star*. His position as temporary executive director was eliminated and the office was closed February 11, 1977. Harley Bierce letter to IRE board members, February 3, 1977.

tigation by law enforcement or other institutions); that is important to readers/viewers; and that reveals information someone or some organization wants to keep secret. While the definition was controversial, particularly its emphasis on exposés of secrets, it represents the first time investigative journalists established an official and generally agreed-upon definition of their craft.[19]

Within two years, IRE founders had taken an informal group of interested people through incorporation into a fully constructed organization with by-laws, a board of directors with officers, an established funding structure, an identifiable community of interest, and a clearly established set of goals. Plans were in place for setting up a resource center, seeking funds from foundations and media companies, and providing a communication network among journalists interested in investigative reporting.

Perhaps the most important benefit of IRE was its creation of a community of interest among investigative journalists. Before Investigative Reporters and Editors formed, there had been little opportunity for investigative reporters to get together with one another, share techniques, debate standards. Magazine investigative reporter James Phelan, whose career spanned from the 1940s to the 1980s, recalled that his curiosity led him into investigative reporting. "I became an investigative reporter, on my own initiative and without anyone's urging or supervision, before I had ever heard of the term." Indeed, the investigative reporter of the 1950s and 1960s was like Mike Andros, protagonist of CBS's 1977 *The Andros Targets,* or Joe Rossi from the network's *Lou Grant* series and real-live reporters like the *New York Times*'s Nicholas Gage, from whom the fictional Mike Andros took his cues. While investigative reporters may have taken direction from their editors and enjoyed the occasional help of a couple of colleagues, more often than not they were on their own. Any one of the investigative reporters working before 1975 could have been the reporter journalism educators Peter Benjaminson and David Anderson had in mind when they described the myth that had developed around the character of the American investigative reporter by the mid-1970s:

19. John Ullmann to IRE board members, May 30, 1979, IRE files tabbed as "1979 Original awards criteria."

> Everybody knows what an investigative reporter is. He's the guy with the dangling cigarette, the grim visage, the belted trench coat, and the snap-brim fedora. He slinks in and out of phone booths, talks out of the side of his mouth, and ignores other, lesser reporters.
>
> He never had to learn his trade. He was born to it. He sprung from his mother's womb clutching a dog-eared address book and his real father's birth certificate. He has an interminable list of contacts. His job consists largely of calling the contacts and saying 'Gimme the dope.'... He appears in the city room only every two or three months to drop his copy on the desks of his astonished editors, mumble a few words, and disappear again into the night.

Anyone who has watched a television serial or Hollywood film or read a best-seller about a hero investigative reporter will recognize this description. *The Andros Targets* was roundly criticized, even by Nicolas Gage, as being overly and unrealistically dramatic — the lone reporter digging out corruption and crime and bringing justice to the city against outrageous odds. But the part about the investigative reporter being a loner was accurate.[20]

Investigative reporter Steve Weinberg recalled that it was not easy to know other investigative reporters or become familiar with their work during the early to mid-1970s. "I'd paid attention in journalism school to some of the contemporary investigative reporters — I guess you'd call them," he explained. "But I didn't know that many, by reputation or otherwise." He continued:

> I mean, I guess you'd put Jack Anderson in that category and Drew Pearson was still alive when I started out. Clark Mollenhoff at the *Des Moines Register* was somebody I'd heard about and occasionally got to read some of his stuff, and some of the stuff coming out of Vietnam, especially the work of David Halberstam, and, later, Seymour Hersh. So I was aware of that, but there weren't very many models...
>
> I didn't know very much about broader standards. I just hoped [my work] would be fair and accurate and thorough — those were kind of elusive words, elusive concepts, but ever since I became a journalist

20. Phelan, *Scandals, Scamps, and Scoundrels*, xii; Benjaminson and Anderson, *Investigative Reporting*, 3; Jimmy Breslin, "Breslin Walks Andros Beat: Reporter Show Found Lacking by Vet of Saloon Interview. Oh, What the Script Left Out!" *[MORE]*, April 1977, 48–49.

in high school, I followed fairness and accuracy and thoroughness. I don't know where it came from exactly.[21]

Another reporter remembered that he distrusted investigative journalism in the early 1970s because of what he later acknowledged was a misconception of the craft. Joe Rigert's experience suggests that the isolation of investigative reporters resulted from a lack of communication among those interested in investigative journalism. Rigert, a reporter for the *Minneapolis Star-Tribune*, was doing "in-depth" or "project" reporting in the mid-1970s, which essentially was investigative journalism, but he did not realize it. "I had kind of a dim view of investigative journalism," he said. "I felt that it was kind of a cult. [I considered them to be] reporters who had a cynical view about society, and they were probably making more out of these things than they were worth.... A lot of words about very minor things."[22] Rigert's misunderstanding was not unusual, for investigative journalists were isolated. Their contacts were haphazard and informal. They had not formally come together to agree on a definition of the craft or on what the standards should be. The closest reporters and editors doing investigative journalism had come to sharing information and educating one another had been seventy years earlier during the muckraking era. Camaraderie had developed among editor S. S. McClure and writers Ida Tarbell, Lincoln Steffens, Ray Baker, David Graham Phillips, and others centered around *McClure's Magazine* and, later, *American Magazine* and other publications. Tarbell, working on a critical history of John D. Rockefeller and Standard Oil, traveled to Rhode Island to get help from Henry Demarest Lloyd, who had investigated Standard Oil for his *Wealth Against Commonwealth* years earlier. Lloyd shared documents with Tarbell. For his part, McClure set standards for the articles in his magazine: name names, clearly designate the bad guys and the victims, write the nonfiction accounts as though they were literary short stories, fully document all accusations, and keep opinions of the writer out of the finished article. Other magazine editors copied McClure's approach, though informally.[23]

21. Steve Weinberg, interview with author, April 16, 1992, Columbia, Missouri.

22. Joe Rigert, interview with author, June 1992, Portland, Oregon.

23. Digby-Junger, *The Journalist as Reformer*, 167.

Additionally, teamwork among investigative journalists had existed before the 1970s, but it was usually among reporters for the same publication or news service. As early as the late nineteenth century there were investigative reporting teams set up by Frank Leslie, editor of *Frank Leslie's Weekly*, and by the *New York Times* and *St. Louis Post-Dispatch*. Moreover, the stars of Watergate in the early 1970s were Bob Woodward and Carl Bernstein, a team some referred to as "Woodstein." But these teams were individualistic, for each worked for a single newspaper or news organization and rarely communicated with muckrakers or investigative reporters beyond those on their own staff concerning story leads, background information, reporting techniques, proper standards, or other issues relating to the craft of ferreting out corruption and malfeasance.[24]

There was limited cooperation when two or more reporters happened onto the same story, but that, too, was rare. An informal organization of fewer than twenty reporters had been formed in the 1950s to foster cooperation in reporting information coming out of the Kefauver Crime Committee congressional investigation. The Senate launched the special committee in April 1950 to investigate organized crime after a Kansas City mobster was found murdered under a huge portrait of President Harry S. Truman in a Democratic club house. The Senate leadership chose Democrat Estes Kefauver, an ambitious freshman, to head the committee. Investigative reporter Clark Mollenhoff led the reporters' group and has written that the group "had been important to the success of the Kefauver Crime Committee." Other informal organizations of reporters were formed around labor racket inquiries in 1957, 1958, and 1959, according to Mollenhoff, though the full extent of the reporters' cooperation has not been documented. Jack Newfield of the *Village Voice* provided another example during an interview in the mid-1970s. He said he, John Hess of the *New York Times*, and Steve Bauman of New York City's WNEW-TV had cooperated informally during an investigation of New York City nursing home operator Bernard Bergman in 1974. The three reporters did not work together, Newfield said, but did exchange ideas. Because stories on Bergman were appearing in three

24. Warren T. Francke, "Team Investigation in the 19th Century: Sunday Sacrifices by the Reporting Corps," paper presented to Association for Education in Journalism and Mass Communication, annual convention, 1988; Downie, *The New Muckrakers*, 1–53.

local media outlets at the same time, the findings of Medicaid fraud could not be ignored by the power structure, Newfield said. Nevertheless, while the benefits of working together were recognized, there was no formal structure to encourage cooperation, and it was not common. "Too often," Newfield said, "if one paper breaks a story, rival papers will purposefully ignore it, or even make an effort to knock it down."[25]

Largely because individual investigative reporters were isolated, there was confusion about the practice. This was true even though some journalism educators and some journalists attempted to teach the skills of investigative journalism. A few schools of journalism included classes in investigative journalism, and the American Press Institute's periodic seminars offered training on investigative journalism techniques between 1961 and 1974. Yet, the response of one veteran reporter to Paul Williams was common in the profession. Williams recalls that one of his oldest newspaper friends "wrote to me after he heard I was teaching investigative reporting and asked: 'What's the difference between investigative reporting and just good reporting?' I was to hear a dozen variations of his question as I worked on this book." He was referring to the text he published in 1978, *Investigative Reporting and Editing*.[26]

Indeed, investigative journalism remained defined, like environmental reporting, travel reporting, and political reporting, as a "beat" within journalism and was not seen as a distinct and individual journalistic practice. The definition "investigative" defined the type of story that resulted, not the process used in doing the reporting. Consequently, most journalists believed investigative reporters used the same techniques and tools as the environmental reporter, the travel writer, or the political correspondent. The investigations of the Watergate scandal electrified a conference on public affairs reporting in 1973, and the speakers preached that investigative reporting was a reporter's "highest calling." But the conference participants viewed investigative reporting as an extension of public affairs reporting, as reporting that reporters did while they covered the state legislature, the environment, and education. Two years later, at another

25. Mollenhoff, *Investigative Reporting*, 340; Dygert, *Investigative Journalist*, 35.
26. API held seminars in 1961, 1963, 1969, 1971 (two), 1972, 1973, and 1974 (J. Montgomery Curtis letter to Harley Bierce and Myrta Pulliam, February 19, 1975, IRE Papers); Williams, *Investigative Reporting and Editing*, xi.

conference called to assess the "lessons of Watergate," investigative reporter Joe Heaney of the *Boston Herald-American* suggested that all reporters should be recognized as investigative reporters. And Robert Maynard, editorial writer for the *Washington Post*, urged his colleagues not to "get caught up in the business of thinking in terms of investigative reporters and the rest of us. I'm worried about the mystique of the term — it's what all of us are supposed to be all the time."[27]

At the height of the resurgence of investigative reporting after Watergate, even as scholars were beginning to study the work of early-twentieth-century muckrakers to unearth the roots of investigative reporting and prove a continuous history of the craft, and even as popular writers were declaring investigative reporters as the new American heroes, many journalists drew no clear distinction between what investigative reporters did and what all reporters did. The fact of the matter remained, however, that the stories that appeared routinely on a newspaper's front page, a TV news broadcast, or in the pages of a magazine were not investigative journalism. There is a quantifiable difference between coverage of a city council meeting or reporting on the latest political controversy and the type of reports that investigative journalists produce — the revealing of widespread political corruption or the exposure of illegal land transfers or the failure of regulatory agencies to protect the public from unsafe chemicals, faulty products, or unethical banking practices.

Lurking beneath the mythic vision of the investigative reporter as individual and folk hero, as well as the seemingly contradictory but ultimately compatible notion that investigative journalism is not a unique genre, was an institutional bias. The journalism profession saw investigative reporting as a product of a news organization staffed by individual journalists, not as the product of those individual journalists. For example, the main theme of one seminar on exposé writing in 1973 was that management is central to investigative reporting. Speakers, including the head of investigative teams for the *Los Angeles Times* and the *Riverside* (California) *Press-Enterprise*, stressed that all newspapers, whatever their sizes, can do investiga-

27. Bill Freivogel, "Public Affairs Reporting Assessed at Press Meeting," *Editor and Publisher*, November 3, 1973, 7; Bill Kirtz, "Investigative Reporters Relate How They Operate."

tions if management commits to the practice and assigns the necessary staff—any staff—to do them. No special skills, knowledge, or training are required. If all reporters are investigative reporters, then investigative reporters do nothing unique. Investigative journalism is not a genre in this view, but an extension of routine public affairs reporting.

Without a community of investigative journalists outside the institutional structure of the news media, though, the fate of the craft remained determined by the institutions. Without a focus on the practice, without recognition that investigative journalism was in fact a craft requiring specialized skills and producing stories and series of a different nature than other journalism, no sustained, systematic development of the craft could occur. Indeed, a study commissioned in 1975 by the Urban Policy Research Institute of Beverly Hills, California, to examine "the barriers to investigative reporting" concluded that the lack of a national service organization such as IRE was a significant obstacle to expansion and improvement of the practice.[28]

From 1976 to 1980, IRE established the resource center in cooperation with the University of Missouri School of Journalism, hired a permanent staff, founded a publication (the *IRE Journal*) to communicate with members, held annual and regional conferences, set up an annual awards program with detailed criteria that represent clearly delineated standards of investigative journalism, and adopted a definition of investigative journalism. The second national conference was held June 19, 1977, at Columbus, Ohio, in association with the journalism program at Ohio State University. The 1978 national meeting in Denver, though, amounted to a financial calamity for the organization, largely because of increased travel costs. While the organization paid higher costs to get speakers and board members to the Rocky Mountain state, many members chose to forgo the meeting because of the higher transportation costs. The meeting finished nine thousand dollars in the hole, a shortfall that was made up partially through gifts from *NBC News* and the *Denver Post*, as well as a three-thousand-dollar grant from philanthropist Stewart

---

28. "Notes from IRE executive committee meeting 3–22–75 at Bierce's house," IRE files.

Mott, who in the 1980s would become a benefactor of Fairness and Accuracy in Media (F.A.I.R.), a liberal media criticism group.

Remarkably, IRE quickly expanded into offering regional training conferences. The first was held in February 1978 at Eugene, Oregon, where more than 300 reporters and students gathered for training in investigative techniques, and resulted in a profit of about one thousand dollars for IRE. Later in 1978, a regional meeting in Palm Springs, California, drew 399 reporters, one in Indianapolis attracted 201 reporters, and one at Washington and Lee University in Lexington, Virginia, brought together 150 reporters and students. During 1979, meetings were held in San Mateo, California, and Portland, Oregon.

The 1979 national meeting in Boston did better financially than the 1978 meeting, and the organization itself was doing better with finances. By 1979, the organization was solvent with an annual cash-flow of about one hundred thousand dollars. Membership had steadily grown each year and had reached 675, and the solicitation of funding for specific projects from foundations and news media companies had brought the organization thousands of dollars to help set up its resource center and establish training programs. By 1980, IRE had 860 members, a functioning resource center at the University of Missouri, and solid financial resources for further growth.

But getting to the relative stability of 1980 took much effort. Between 1976 and 1980, IRE directors, staff, and members were preoccupied with the organization's noteworthy but controversial Arizona Project and the stormy aftermath that resulted. Members who had gathered in Indianapolis for the first IRE conference in June 1976 were shocked by the recent murder of one of their members, Don Bolles of the *Arizona Republic*. He had died after a bomb exploded beneath his car. His death was believed to be connected to his investigative work. Under the leadership of veteran investigator and board member Robert Greene of *Newsday*, IRE members resolved to respond to the killing with a unique project that would send reporters from multiple newspapers, magazines, and television news outlets — IRE members — into Phoenix to "finish the work Don Bolles was killed doing." The investigative project resulted in a series of jointly produced articles made available to participating newspapers and the Associated Press that detailed the web of political corruption and organized crime in Arizona. It was the first cooperative news-gathering project of its kind. The Arizona Project, conducted during IRE's first year, propelled IRE into national prominence, but in the process it nearly destroyed the organization. The project strained the young organization's finances, created internal conflicts that resulted in very public director resignations, and resulted in unflattering national publicity that raised questions about the organization's integrity.

The Arizona Project

IRE's Unique Contribution to American Journalism

Journalist Don Bolles, at forty-seven, had built a career exposing Arizona's political misdeeds and organized crime's activities in the state. During his fourteen years at the *Arizona Republic* in Phoenix, he had uncovered secret political slush funds controlled by the state patrol, bribery of state tax commissioners, land fraud, and Mafia influence in a national sports concession firm, Emprise Corporation, which was seeking control of Arizona's horse and dog racing tracks. Because of his reporting, the Arizona Legislature had in 1976 ordered Emprise to divest its racetrack investments in the state within five years. One of Bolles's stories revealed the names of nearly two hundred organized crime figures and associates who lived in Arizona and detailed their ties to legitimate businesses in the state. His impressive career earned him a Pulitzer Prize nomination and a solid reputation among investigative reporters throughout the United States. It also led to his murder.

Ironically, Don Bolles was no longer doing full-time investigative reporting for the *Republic* when he received the phone calls that lured him to his death. For various reasons, but primarily because of the stress from investigative reporting, Bolles had voluntarily moved to the *Republic*'s beat covering the city hall and then to the state legislature. He had not been doing investigative reporting for the past ten months when he was contacted in the late spring of 1976 by John Adamson, a local petty criminal who was a stranger to Bolles. Adamson promised to give Bolles proof of land fraud schemes involving Emprise Corporation and prominent Arizona politicians and business leaders. Bolles and Adamson had a brief meeting on May 27, and on June 1, Adamson arranged to meet Bolles in the lobby of Phoenix's Clarendon House hotel at 11:25 a.m. the next day. Adamson didn't show for the meeting, though. Bolles waited about ten minutes in the Clarendon House lobby before being summoned to the phone for a call from Adamson, who told him the meeting was off. Bolles returned to the hotel's parking lot, entered his 1976 Datsun, and was blown out its driver's side door by six pieces of dynamite planted under the car and detonated by someone nearby. His legs mangled and bleeding, he lapsed in and out of consciousness, but he managed to whisper to those trying to help him. "They finally got me," he said. "Emprise — the Mafia — John Adamson — Find him." He died eleven days later.[1]

The local police knew John Adamson, and they quickly arrested him. But nearly a decade would pass before the cases against him and others would conclude. Adamson readily confessed, but instead of ending the case, his confession outlined an intricate web of conspiracy. Hoping to strike a deal, he implicated others, including two prominent Arizona businessmen. His tale of intrigue took police and prosecutors months to work through, and the answers they got did not satisfy everyone.

Because the attack on Bolles came within days of IRE's first national conference in Indianapolis, the annual meeting was electrified. No doubt, someone had killed Bolles because of stories the reporter had written, or because of a story he was working on, and IRE leaders had been discussing for several days how best to respond. Violence against an American reporter was not new, but it was quite rare in the twentieth century. Veteran investigative reporter Clark Mollenhoff recalled that Bolles's murder shocked all reporters "and particularly

1. Michael F. Wendland, *The Arizona Project*, 3.

those of us in the field of investigative reporting. For years we had proceeded about our business ignoring threats to our lives and our job, more or less assuming that the bosses of organized crime and politics would 'be too smart' to kill a reporter or editor and stir up the whole journalistic community....I could not recall one incident of a reporter being an assassination target of organized crime since the blinding of Victor Riesel in April 1956."[2] Riesel, a syndicated columnist who specialized in labor issues, exposed organized crime's infiltration of the Teamsters Union and was scheduled to testify at a hearing when a mobster threw acid in his face. Before that, Alfred "Jake" Lingle, a reporter for the *Chicago Tribune* who used his ties to Al Capone and other mobsters to enrich himself, was shot and killed in 1930 by Chicago gangsters while on his way to the racetrack. Jerry Buckley, a popular crusader against corruption on radio station WMBC in Detroit, was gunned down by mobsters, also in 1930. And Carlo Tresca, the editor of an Italian-language newspaper in New York, was gunned down by New York mobsters in 1943, supposedly on the orders of Italy's dictator, Benito Mussolini, because of Tresca's attacks on fascism. Tresca was the last American journalist murdered because of his reporting—until Don Bolles was attacked in 1976.

Investigative journalists at the IRE convention were understandably shaken. They believed the attack on Bolles might embolden targets of other press investigations to strike out at journalists pursuing them. IRE members, reaching beyond their initial desire for revenge, viewed Bolles's murder as a lethal assault on America's press freedoms, and they decided they wanted to signal organized crime members and others that reporters could not be silenced through violence or threats of violence. The way to show that, they reasoned, was through a joint effort involving reporters throughout the country. Robert Greene was authorized to go to Phoenix on behalf of the organization and consult with editors and reporters at Bolles's newspaper, the *Arizona Republic*.

In a memorandum dated July 19, 1976, Greene outlined for IRE board members the conclusions he had reached after meeting with *Republic* staff members. He reported that a project involving reporters

2. Mollenhoff, *Investigative Reporting*, 340–41.

and editors throughout the country who would investigate Arizona corruption was "better than fifty percent" feasible. He concluded that

> The purpose of such an investigation would not have as its direct aim the solution of the Bolles assassination. The point would be to expose the political–land fraud–mob structure of Arizona with particular emphasis on Phoenix.
>
> The idea is to exert heavy pressure on every possible pocket of corruption whether it directly relates to the Bolles murder or not. An indirect result could be the solution of the Bolles murder.
>
> ...The community [Phoenix] and other like communities would reflect on what has happened, and hopefully would think twice about killing reporters. For all of us — particularly newspapers with high investigative profiles — this is eminently self-serving. We are buying life insurance for our own reporters.
>
> At the present time, an examination of land frauds and organized crime and the political connection with both seems to be the most promising path.[3]

The project team would work with the *Arizona Republic*, Green said, but would maintain its own headquarters. Greene, who had investigated organized crime for *Newsday*, implied in the memo that editors and reporters at the Phoenix dailies would be of limited value to the team's investigation, pointing out that the *Republic*'s understanding of organized crime in Arizona was cursory, at best.

The cost of the project, Greene estimated, would be twenty-five thousand dollars, not including the salaries of reporters and editors who would participate. He sorely underestimated what it would cost, however. The final bill amounted to more than seventy thousand dollars, not counting salaries. Funds were needed to rent rooms to board the reporters and for office space, to purchase or rent typewriters and other equipment, to rent cars, to photocopy records, to pay for phones, and to hire secretaries. Project organizers hoped news organizations would pay the salary of staff members sent to participate, or the reporters and editors would donate their vacation time to the project. Relying on his experience as a team leader at *Newsday*, where he had coordinated that paper's extensive Pulitzer

3. Robert W. Greene, "Memorandum RE: Bolles Affair," July 19, 1976, IRE files.

Prize–winning investigation of the heroin trade in 1974, Greene surmised that the investigation team in Phoenix could consist of a team leader, four reporters, two journalism graduate or undergraduate students, and two secretaries/stenographers. Greene noted that an alternative, which was eventually adopted, would involve several permanent team members with additional reporters and editors coming in for short stints. A structure in which reporters rotated in and out every one or two weeks, though, presented challenges not usually found on an investigative reporting team. The permanent reporters and editors would be constantly relying on new people, most of them unfamiliar with the lay of the political landscape and the law enforcement environment in Arizona, and most of them relatively unknown to the permanent staff. Being productive within such a framework required a well-planned infrastructure that would guarantee communication among reporters who might not have direct contact with one another. Greene devised a plan that relied heavily on daily memoranda and on a file system that was updated daily. He would set up teams of reporters that would partially overlap to maintain a continuity of investigation. And deputy team leaders would be appointed for each new team. Greene also planned to get help from reporters at newspapers in other cities for intermittent checking of records and interviewing of sources. On July 23, 1976, a letter on IRE letterhead and signed by IRE President Ron Koziol of Chicago went out to the organization's members outlining plans for the project and soliciting help.[4]

IRE maintained an office in Indianapolis during these first months of its existence. Financial demands for that office and other responsibilities, including the purchase of libel insurance to cover the Arizona Project stories, made it impossible for the organization to finance the project itself. Consequently, fund-raising for the Phoenix effort fell to Greene. Among the larger donations were five thousand dollars from eccentric philanthropist W. H. Ferry of New York; more than twenty thousand dollars from the Arizona Association of Industries; five thousand dollars from philanthropist David Hunter, executive director of the Stern Fund, which provided another three thousand dollars; and six thousand dollars from the New York Community Trust. Smaller donations ranging from twenty-five dol-

4. Greene, "Bolles Affair."

lars to five hundred dollars were obtained from a variety of people, news organizations such as guilds and associations, and newspaper companies.

The project began in October 1976 with plans for publication of its findings by March 1977. Greene set up headquarters in a suite of rooms on the nineteenth floor of Phoenix's Adams Hotel. Given the violence that had inspired the project, Greene hired a California security specialist. The full-time members of the reporting team included Greene; Tom Renner, his associate at *Newsday* and an organized crime specialist; Mike Wendland of Detroit, an acquaintance of Renner's who had reported often on organized crime stories; and three reporters from Arizona papers, the *Republic*'s John Winters, who had inherited the investigative beat from Bolles several months before Bolles's murder, and Alex Drehsler and John Rawlinson of the *Tucson Daily Star.* Committing a month to the project, Myrta Pulliam, one of the organizers of IRE and a reporter for the *Indianapolis Star,* also was an early participant. Most reporters arrived for shorter stays, usually a week or two, a few for a month each, and student interns from the state's major journalism programs worked shifts doing research and organizing files. Thirty-nine reporters and editors and an assortment of support staff came from Indianapolis, Detroit, Chicago, Boston, Kansas City, Denver, Riverside, California, Eugene, Oregon, Boston, Washington, D.C., Miami, and various cities in Arizona and other states. Reporters came from newspapers and television news outlets large and small, from the *Boston Globe, Chicago Daily News,* and *Miami Herald* to the *Elyria* (Ohio) *Chronicle, Seers Rio Grande Weekly,* and *Wenatchee* (Washington) *World.* Two television stations were represented, WEEI, the CBS affiliate in Boston, and KGUN in Tucson. Conspicuously absent, though, were the three largest urban newspapers, the *New York Times,* the *Washington Post,* and the *Los Angeles Times;* the three leading television networks, CBS, NBC, and ABC; and other prominent newspapers, including the *Wall Street Journal, New York Daily News, Philadelphia Inquirer, Dallas Times, San Francisco Chronicle, Seattle Times,* and *Atlanta Constitution.* Several reporters who couldn't go to Arizona contributed reporting from their hometowns, however.[5]

5. The professional journalists who officially worked on the project were Ross Becker, freelance; Lowell Bergman, no newspaper affiliation; Richard E.

The forty-eight-year-old Renner went undercover to dig for information. At the Adams Hotel, suite 1939 was transformed into a newsroom. Metal desks, typewriters on stands, and filing cabinets replaced the usual bedroom furniture, and Greene had four private phone lines installed. He hired two secretaries. Greene, a forty-seven-year-old, rotund stevedore of a man with the accent of a native New Yorker, commanded the operation, arriving early each morning after having worked late reading the voluminous memoranda from the previous day's reporting efforts and planning the team's next moves. Greene handed out assignments each morning, sending reporters to collect copies of public documents, photocopy previously published news stories, and interview sources. Each evening, team members would reassemble in the office suite to type memoranda detailing the information they had collected during the day. The memoranda were cross-indexed and filed, with copies routed by Greene to reporters who were working on related matters. The complex file system involved use of a microfiche system and the efforts of several file clerks. Reporters tape-recorded interviews when possible, took photographs, and filed their notes. When reporting ended in December 1976, a team of writers working in Phoenix assembled the stories throughout January and February 1977, and Tony Insolia, a *Newsday* man-

---

Cady, *Indianapolis Star*; Don Devereux, *Seers Rio Grande Weekly*; Alex Drehsler, *Arizona Daily Star*; Jack Driscoll, *Boston Globe*; Dave Freed, *Colorado Springs Sun*; Robert Greene, *Newsday*; Bill Hume, *Albuquerque Journal*; Anthony Insolia, *Newsday*; Susan Irby, *Gulfport* (Mississippi) *Herald*; Harry Jones, *Kansas City Star*; Dick Johnson, *Kansas City Star*; Ron Koziol, *Chicago Tribune*; Larry Kraftowitz, Jack Anderson Associates; Doug Kramer, *Elyria* (Ohio) *Chronicle*; Dick Levitan, WEEI, Boston; Dick Lyneis, *Riverside* (California) *Press*; Ken Matthews, *Idaho Statesman*; Jack McFarren, Reno Newspapers; Bill Montalbano, *Miami Herald*; Phil O'Connor, *Chicago Daily News*; Dave Offer, *Milwaukee Journal*; Dave Overton, KGUN, Tucson; Myrta Pulliam, *Indianapolis Star*; John Rawlinson, *Arizona Daily Star*; Tom Renner, *Newsday*; Ed Rooney, *Chicago Daily News*; Mike Satchell, *Washington Star*; Ray Schrick, *Wenatchee* (Washington) *World*; Bob Teuscher, *St. Louis Globe-Democrat*; Norm Udevitz, *Denver Post*; Jerry Uhrhammer, *Eugene* (Oregon) *Register Guard*; Bob Weaver, *San Jose Mercury*; Mike Wendland, *Detroit News*; Steve Wick, *Colorado Springs Sun*; Jack Wimer, *Tulsa Tribune*. (List provided by IRE, attached to Eugene S. Pulliam letter to Senator Barry Goldwater, March 28, 1977, IRE files.) Two *Arizona Republic* reporters, John Winters and Chuck Kelly, also worked on the IRE team, according to participant Michael Wendland. Their names were left off the list IRE provided to Pulliam, though, perhaps in recognition of *Arizona Republic* top management's denial when the IRE series came out that the newspaper had participated (Wendland, *The Arizona Project*, 294).

aging editor, arrived to edit the series. A New York libel attorney donated his services to read the finished stories, and project managers invited participating newspapers to send reporters, editors, or libel attorneys to review file cabinets full of documentation. Only the *Kansas City Star* sent a representative. Unfortunately, the controversies began before the project was finished.

Never before had reporters from different news organizations worked together in a noncompetitive situation to produce a single report. IRE had pioneered a new concept in investigative reporting: direct cooperation among reporters. In an article previewing the March 1977 series on Arizona distributed by IRE, Tom Collins of *Newsday* called the project "an unusual experiment in collective journalism." Team members told Collins that the reporters worked closely and without ego clashes. "Cooperation has been tremendous," Jack Driscoll of the *Boston Globe* told Collins. Not all journalists agreed with the idea of collective journalism, however, and the project took abuse from some of the more prominent newspapers in America. Ben Bradlee, the editor who had shepherded the *Washington Post*'s Watergate coverage, A. M. Rosenthal, managing editor of the *New York Times*, and Otis Chandler, publisher of the *Los Angeles Times* and one of the owners of Robert Greene's newspaper on Long Island, *Newsday*, all publicly opposed the project and would not allow their reporters and editors to participate. Bradlee argued outside reporters were arrogant to assume they could do a better job of reporting on Arizona than local reporters could. Chandler said he would resent a team of reporters from other cities coming into his city to investigate matters his newspaper could cover. And Rosenthal, perhaps the most respected editor in America, questioned whether such cooperation hurt journalism by removing its competitiveness and diversity. "If a story is worth investigating, we should do it ourselves," he said. Charles Seib, ombudsman for the *Washington Post*, condemned the project and all investigative journalism as a "journalistic fad."[6]

The criticism in the press, and subsequent internal bickering among board members, kept potential members away from the organization and interfered with IRE's ability to raise funds. Harley Bierce, acting executive director, reported in February 1977, one month before the series would be released, that foundations backed away

6. Quoted in Mollenhoff, *Investigative Reporting*, 342.

from funding proposals because of criticism from the journalists who would have been expected to support IRE. The program officer of the Markle Foundation reported to Bierce that IRE's problems were coming from "very loud, very opinionated, sometimes idiotic, opposition" from journalists that board members of the Markle Foundation had queried about IRE's grant proposal. Board members of the Stern Fund also were backing away, and IRE was facing bankruptcy. Fortunately for the organization, Bierce and others successfully turned around opposition within the Lilly Endowment and the foundation eventually assured IRE of a twenty-five-thousand-dollar grant for 1977, and another seventeen thousand dollars for 1978.[7]

Adding to IRE's financial and image problems were internal controversies growing out of the Arizona Project that resulted in public embarrassment for the organization. One of the first controversies erupted in December 1976, as the reporting phase of the project was wrapping up, when IRE board members found out that team participant Michael Wendland of the *Detroit News* was writing a book about his experiences as one of the team members for the project, and board members thought IRE President Ron Koziol might be a co-author. The Wendland book threatened IRE's own plans for a sanctioned book and possible movie and, Greene argued, violated an agreement reporters on the project signed not to personally profit from their work on the project.[8]

At a January 1977 board meeting, Koziol was confronted about reports that he was helping Wendland write the book, but he refused to answer the allegations. During the same meeting, a second controversy flared over a proposal to sell movie rights to David Susskind, a TV producer, without giving Susskind full access to IRE files. Nevertheless, a majority of the board supported restricting access to the Arizona Project files to outsiders and prevailed. In protest, board member Jack Taylor of the Oklahoma City *Daily Oklahoman* resigned, saying he would not participate in censorship. Other directors were unhappy enough to threaten their resignations as well, and the acrimonious meeting split up without fully resolving the controversy.

7. Harley Bierce, untitled letter to IRE board members, February 2, 1977, IRE files.
8. "Minutes of Meeting of Board of Directors of IRE held on 3 March 1977," IRE files; "Minutes of a Meeting of the Executive Committee of IRE held 14 March 1977," IRE files.

On February 23, 1977, IRE's dirty laundry unceremoniously aired on the front page of the *Wall Street Journal* when IRE member Jim Drinkhall, a *Journal* reporter, published a lengthy article about the board controversies and exposed questionable donations to the organization from a convicted securities broker and a lawyer who had represented members of organized crime families. The article's headline cut to the chase: "Conflict-of-Interest, Censorship Charges Jar Unlikely Group." In retaliation, Greene and others associated with IRE filed a complaint with the National News Council that accused the article of misrepresenting the organization, but they later decided not to pursue it.

In March, battered by the swirling controversies over the proposed book rights to the Arizona Project story, board president Ron Koziol, the person who had inspired creation of IRE by publishing an article in *Editor and Publisher* suggesting that investigative reporters meet to discuss common issues and reporting techniques, sent word to the board that he was resigning. But the relationships between the former colleagues had grown poisonous, and other members of the board defiantly rejected his resignation and voted to publicly oust him from office. (Further weakening the board, David Burnham of the *New York Times* and Len Downie of the *Washington Post,* two of the original IRE organizers, also resigned from the board at this time, though the board controversies apparently were not their primary motivation.)

Another controversy whirling within and outside the organization centered on Robert Greene's willingness to share the team's files with law enforcement agencies. The appearance of working for law enforcement can cripple an investigation, causing some sources to shy away from reporters. Greene defended the practice as it was handled in the Arizona Project, acknowledging that he shared information with police and FBI agents when doing so seemed to help the team get information from law enforcement. He stressed that no confidential sources were ever revealed. The IRE board accepted Greene's explanation, but board members stressed they did not sanction the practice beyond its limited use in the Arizona Project investigation.

Even before the series was published, IRE board members knew that the team's experiences while reporting the story could be a lucrative tale to sell. As Robert Greene was setting up the team for the investigation, a major book publisher, MacMillan, and TV producer Norman Lear expressed interest in telling the story of the project. Amid complaints from some IRE members that the group should not exploit Don Bolles's death by selling the team's story for a book, movie, or TV program, the IRE board secured the services of the Sterling Lord Agency of New York to represent the organization. Magazine rights were sold to *New West* for two thousand dollars. The *New West* article, which appeared after the series was released, focused on the revelations about Senator Barry Goldwater and his family. Book rights were sold to Prentice-Hall in April, and IRE stood to gain at least fifteen thousand dollars if the book was published. Ben Bagdikian, a freelance writer at the time but previously an editor and ombudsman for the *Washington Post*, signed on as author. Prentice-Hall provided a ten-thousand-dollar advance, with slightly more than two thousand dollars going to IRE. In June, however, Bagdikian withdrew from the book project after accepting a full-time teaching position at the University of California–Berkeley and the publisher suggested as his replacement the author James Dygert, who had published a book about investigative reporting in 1976 with Prentice-Hall. Closely tied to the book rights was the possible sale of movie rights, which could generate considerably more money for IRE. But by August, the Prentice-Hall agreement was falling apart because of a notice by Sheed, Andrews and McMeel, a Kansas City, Missouri, publisher, that a book on the Arizona Project by Michael Wendland was forthcoming.[9]

IRE, through attorney Edward DeLaney, attempted to stop the Wendland book by threatening legal action against Wendland and his publisher. DeLaney argued that the IRE series was copyrighted and that Wendland, who had been a permanent member of the investigative team, had not obtained permission from IRE to use its files. Greene and DeLaney argued that participants signed statements promising that they would not personally profit from the information being collected. Wendland claimed he had never signed the form, which read, in part, that "IRE alone will have the right to use, sell, or rent these files [collected during the investigation] for any

9. "Minutes of the Meeting of the Executive Committee of IRE held 19 March 1977," IRE files. Edward O. DeLaney letter to Myrta Pulliam, May 13, 1977, IRE files; Sterling Lord letter to Robert Greene and Edward O. DeLaney, August 5, 1977, IRE files.

purpose consistent with its articles of incorporation. This includes any use for written publication, broadcast or film production in any form." DeLaney said Wendland had signed the form. Nevertheless, the legal threats failed to dissuade Wendland or Sheed, Andrews and McMeel, and *The Arizona Project* was published. Prentice-Hall then canceled its contract with IRE and Bagdikian, and the book advances were returned. Consequently, there would be no official book about the project, and with no book, IRE would have trouble selling the movie rights to the story.

In the ensuing years, several movie and television producers expressed interest in filming the story of the Arizona Project. From 1977 through 1983, nine producers, including NBC Entertainment, Paramount, Columbia Pictures, and DPL Productions, entered into or attempted to enter into agreements with IRE to produce a movie, a TV special, or a TV series about Don Bolles, the Arizona Project, and IRE. IRE stood to make at least fifty thousand dollars if a production went forward. At least one producer stressed the need to have sex appeal in the story, suggesting that a love interest be manufactured between Myrta Pulliam, the only prominent woman on the team, and one of the male reporters to add spice to the story line. The suggestion was not well received at IRE, though, and underscored to everyone involved that a TV or Hollywood film that fictionalized the story would necessarily corrupt the facts. One by one, the producers came and went without committing to the project. Even when advances were paid (DPL, for example, paid IRE five thousand dollars and entered into consulting agreements while exploring the possibility of a production), the producers eventually walked away from the story. In addition to the problems of writing an acceptable script and getting a production contract, producers were concerned about legal liabilities because IRE had no book in hand, which would have run interference should anyone decide to sue over the way they were portrayed. Moreover, lingering libel actions growing out of the project made use of the IRE material questionable. Ultimately, no film or series was produced.[10]

The Arizona Project reporters completed their investigation of Arizona in December 1976, and the eighty-thousand-word series was

10. Specific memorandum and minutes of board of director meetings between August 1977 and May 1986, IRE files.

written and edited during January and February 1977. More than thirty reporters and editors, representing twenty-eight newspapers and television stations, had worked on the project. Forty thousand memoranda had been collected, filed, and cross-indexed. Hundreds of people had been interviewed and thousands of public and private records had been studied. The out-of-pocket expenses had overrun Greene's initial estimate of twenty-five thousand dollars by forty-seven thousand dollars, plus reporter salaries. In addition, important services, such as those of the libel lawyer who read the stories prior to publication, were donated. Donated professional services and reporter salaries paid by their news organizations as salary or vacation compensation were estimated to reach $250,000. In March 1977, the series was ready for distribution.

IRE editors divided their mountain of research into a twenty-three-part series outlining the structure of organized crime activity in Arizona; the tradition of land-development fraud in the state; drug-dealing, gambling, and prostitution throughout the state; problems in the administration of justice; and ties between Arizona politicians and members of organized crime. The series began with a story about the IRE investigation that outlined the general themes that would be pursued in the following installments. The IRE team reported it had been harassed by "a shotgun-toting guard" when team members tried to interview illegal Mexican farm workers employed by a citrus ranch partially owned by Senator Barry Goldwater's brother, Robert. They told of interviewing the confessed killer of Don Bolles, John Adamson, who asked the reporters to take messages to prosecutors that he wanted to strike a deal—his testimony for leniency. IRE reporters crossed the Mexico-Arizona border with drug smugglers and interviewed top mobsters in the state and prostitutes who worked for organized crime–controlled massage parlors. They "talked with both honest and corrupt public officials, with arrogant and concerned politicians, with honest cops, dope dealers and worried civic leaders." The conclusion, the IRE team reported, was that the state of Arizona "is in deep trouble." They reported there was a tolerance among the power structure and law enforcement for lawlessness. "The state has become a haven for white-collar swindlers," the first story reported, "who sit in plush mountainside homes and skyscraper offices and direct intricate frauds that span the nation and have fleeced small investors and buyers out of more than one billion dollars." Often, the reporters said, the con artists and other criminals are encouraged "by officials of both political parties who have joined them in attractive business deals and itchy-palmed public officials eager to look the other way for a price."[11]

The team also reported in the first article that law enforcement agencies were understaffed and underfunded and agencies with over-lapping jurisdiction often competed and ended up working at cross-purposes to one another. Even if the state wanted to go after white-collar crime, it didn't have the law enforcement infrastructure to accomplish the task, the reporters concluded.

Republican Barry Goldwater, the senior U.S. senator from Arizona and 1964 presidential nominee, had been one of the targets of the IRE investigation. His only quoted response in the article, though, was a lame comment that denied the accusations. He said he had lived in Arizona for sixty-eight years, and he was unaware of any white-collar or organized crime activities in the state.

In the second day's story, the IRE team revealed the Goldwater family's dominance of Arizona politics and the state's Republican Party, as well as its considerable influence in Arizona business circles. The story outlined the Goldwater family's business dealings, includ-ing part ownership in a ranch that exploited illegal alien workers, and focused on the Goldwaters' friendships and business associa-tions with known gangsters such as Gus Greenbaum of Las Vegas, a former lieutenant in Meyer Lansky's criminal organization, Moe B. Dalitz, and racketeer Willie Bioff, who was killed by a car bomb in 1955 after reportedly angering mobster Peter Licavoli, Sr.

On day three of the series, the IRE team detailed Harry Rosen-zweig's connections to mobsters. Rosenzweig, a wealthy jeweler and Phoenix political boss, was a business partner of Robert Goldwater and a key political backer of Barry Goldwater, according to the series. He also apparently used his jewelry store as a front for controlling prostitution in the city, according to the IRE series.

Day four continued the team's investigation into Rosenzweig's political and business dealings. The Phoenix Advertising Club's "Man of the Year" and longtime chairman of the Arizona Republican

11. All references to the Arizona Project series were taken from a tabloid reprint of the series, "Arizona Project: Reprint of a 1977 Series," Investigative Reporters and Editors, undated.

Party, according to IRE's investigation, "built a quiet record of behind-the-scenes influence brokering in state and local justice and profited in a real estate transaction in which nationally known land fraud 'godfather' Ned Warren, Sr., was hidden in the background."

The series' fifth story documented Robert Goldwater's political powerbroking and the ties he "maintained...directly and indirectly, with organized crime figures." On day six, the series detailed his partnership in the Hobo Joe's restaurant chain with an associate of Mafia underboss Peter Licavoli, Sr., Herbert L. Applegate, and Phoenix businessman Joseph F. Martori. The story revealed that in a twenty-one-month period, the Hobo Joe's chain was looted of more than $1.5 million to help finance "a corporate love nest featuring wild parties with former Playboy bunnies," a $350,000 mansion for Applegate, fancy Las Vegas parties, and equipment and supplies that vanished. Southwestern Research Corporation, a publicly held company and owner of slightly more than one-fourth of the Hobo Joe's stock, was forced to take the financial loss, the story said.

On day seven, the series examined the Del E. Webb Corporation of Phoenix, a developer of shopping centers, office buildings, and retirement communities. The story reported Del Webb's alleged links to organized crime and Las Vegas gambling casinos at a time when the Mafia controlled the casinos.

Day eight's story was dedicated to detailing the exploitation of illegal Mexican workers on the Arrowhead Ranches, a citrus farm partially owned by Robert Goldwater and the Martori family. The hiring of illegals, which the story asserts Senator Barry Goldwater was aware of, was not against the law. Nevertheless, the story reported that IRE investigators "found women and children sleeping on the ground without blankets. One family of five, including a pregnant woman, lived in a packing crate. A six-month-old baby lay on a blanket, his dirty face covered with flies."

The IRE story on the ninth day examined the business dealings of Arizona Governor Raul Castro and his ties to millionaire Kemper Marley, the liquor distributor who had been implicated in Don Bolles's death by John Adamson. On day ten, the series detailed Marley's business and political dealings.

Day eleven stories dealt with Ned Warren, Sr.'s business dealings. His various schemes, which until 1975 eluded Arizona authorities, earned him the nickname "godfather" of land fraud. "I was a thief,"

Warren told IRE reporters. "And I was a good thief." Day twelve continued the saga of Warren's rise to riches and included details of his corruption of government officials. Day thirteen's story raised questions about Warren's influence on the criminal justice system, which until recently had left him untouched, but suspiciously heaped punishment upon his accusers.

On the fourteenth day, the IRE series examined organized crime's infiltration into Arizona's neighbor, New Mexico.

Stories on the fifteenth and sixteenth days described how mobsters Joseph (Joe Bananas) Bonanno, Sr., and Peter Licavoli, Sr., used the lack of serious law enforcement in Arizona to set up criminal operations, including turning Arizona into a corridor for heroin, cocaine, and marijuana smuggled from Mexico. Day seventeen's story fleshed out the extent of mob infiltration in Arizona. Day eighteen's article examined the unincorporated, policeless resort town of Lake Havasu City, Arizona, described by IRE reporters as "an important western outpost for organized crime figures and a safe haven for thugs and thieves" as well as for drug traffickers and prostitutes.

Drug smuggling over the Arizona-Mexico border is detailed in the nineteenth installment, including a first-person account by IRE reporters describing their travels across the border with drug smugglers. "It soon became obvious to both drug traffickers and law enforcement agencies alike that Arizona provided the shortest direct route between the United States and the opium poppy and marijuana fields of Mexico," the story reported, adding that there were at least twenty-three major smuggling rings operating throughout the Mexico-Arizona corridor and "as many as eight hundred pilots, 550 of these in the Phoenix area alone," making their livings by flying drugs from Mexico into Arizona. The tales of smuggling continued on day twenty, concentrating on the drug-smugglers' influence in Tucson, Arizona's second-largest city. On day twenty-one, the story focused on drug dealing in Phoenix.

The series' final two stories concerned organized crime influence found within Arizona's criminal justice system. "As guardians of the quality of justice, judges and lawyers, knowingly and otherwise, have contributed to an atmosphere in which organized crime seems to flourish, members of prominent families get lenient treatment" and other questionable practices appeared routine, according to the story on day twenty-two, which documented the allegations. The story on day twenty-three told how "wiretaps tying the president-elect of a national bar association to the planned formation of a large call girl operation in Phoenix have been destroyed by state authorities under strange circumstances."

A sidebar to the final day's story recalled incidents and statements "that reflected a strange sense of ethics and public responsibility on the part of state and local officials." Among them was a quote from a former Tucson police chief, who wrote in an official state investigative report on organized crime influence in his city that "Mafia money [is] as good as anybody's."

Once the stories were published, the alleged connections between organized crime members and Arizona Senator Barry Goldwater, his brother, Robert Goldwater, and their business and political associate, Harry Rosenzweig, a former Arizona state Republican chairman, captured the most public attention. Even Robert Greene played up that part of the story. When a Phoenix radio executive asked him what the team members had found that so impressed them, Greene responded:

> The senior senator of your state [Barry Goldwater] is up to his ass in association with top organized crime figures. We're impressed with that.
>
> The Hobo Joe's restaurant operation was a three-million-dollar mob [organized crime] steal involving Barry Goldwater's brother [Robert]. We're impressed with that.
>
> There are 550 licensed pilots in Phoenix alone who make their living flying drugs into Arizona from Mexico. We're impressed with that.
>
> We named twenty-three organizations that move all the heavy narcotics through your state. Ninety-six percent of the heroin in the U.S. comes from Mexico. The most concentrated corridor of entry comes through your state. We're impressed with that.[12]

To place such contemporary events into a cultural and historical context, however, the articles included much information about past events, most of which were already known. Tracing the connection between the Goldwaters and organized crime figures, for example, the IRE reporters took readers back to Goldwater's maiden Senate

12. Tom Lewis, "Have Reporters Become Sitting Ducks?: The Story Behind the Goldwater/Arizona Expose," *Mother Jones*, June 1977, 30–32.

campaign in the early 1950s, when convicted extortionist, pimp, and organized crime associate Willie Bioff, known in Phoenix as William Nelson, was a social acquaintance of Goldwater and a major contributor to his campaign. An anecdote typical of the techniques used to tell the story of Arizona crime and corruption is the Arizona Project story about Barry Goldwater, Harry Rosenzweig, and Willie Bioff: "A month before Bioff was killed [in November 1955], Rosenzweig, Sen. Goldwater and his family and Bioff and his wife took a vacation together in Las Vegas, staying at the Riveria. Rosenzweig made the arrangements. Goldwater and Rosenzweig maintained that at first they had not known Bioff's true identity. But they continued to associate with him after they knew who he really was. Goldwater later said he had used Bioff to get information about labor racketeering."[13] Such techniques, used throughout the series, were criticized by some journalists, who cited the lack of direct attribution of information, associations made between people showing that they knew each other but not that one endorsed the behavior of the other, and the compilation of considerable information that was history in 1976 and 1977.

Granted, the series did not reveal shocking news, except in the aggregate; its impact comes instead from its framing of the issues. It weaves bits and pieces of news items—some many years old, others gathered or documented by the IRE team—into a tapestry that meets the investigative journalism value of "telling the whole story" in much the same way the turn-of-the-century muckrakers plied their craft. In the tradition of muckrakers Lincoln Steffens and Ida Tarbell, the IRE team presented its evidence not as lawyers building a legal indictment, but as journalists wanting to tell the story of corruption in public affairs. When Steffens was confronted with the fact that his articles on corruption in city governments across the country included information that was already well-known in the communities he studied, he replied, "The exposition of what people know and stand for is the purpose of these articles, not the exposure of corruption." Steffens's "what people know and stand for" was, for press critic Melvin Mencher, "an essential ingredient" of the IRE series. The fact that organized crime affects the quality of life in any state in the United States is not news to most people. Indeed,

13. IRE Team, "Arizona Project," 6–10.

the story of organized crime's influence in public affairs could have been told about almost any state in the nation, with only the names and dates different, and not always even that. Tom Renner of *Newsday*, the organized crime specialist who participated full-time in the Arizona Project, pointed out in 1981: "To be successful in this field of investigation [of organized crime], it is necessary to arm yourself with history, names, files and documents that must be preserved to prepare for the inevitable truth—history always repeats itself." The IRE series, however, compellingly narrated the intricate relationship between crime, politics, and the criminal justice system. It named names, and it exposed facts about specific crimes and malfeasances that many within the power structures of Arizona and New Mexico did not want revealed.[14]

After libel lawyers had reviewed the team's work, twenty-six newspapers, three television stations, United Press International, and the Associated Press were sent ten-pound packages containing the stories and artwork to accompany them. Each participating news organization paid a $125 duplication cost for the materials. Debut of the series was set for Sunday, March 13, 1977.

Response from the nation's press, though, was lukewarm, at best. Three newspapers that had participated in the Arizona Project initially declined to run the series, in whole or in edited versions. They were the *St. Louis Globe-Democrat*, which argued that the series was too massive to allow its staff to adequately fact-check it; the *Chicago Tribune*, the employer of reporter Ron Koziol, who had been ousted as IRE president; and, surprising to most people, including many on its staff, the *Arizona Republic*. A statement published by the *Republic*'s publisher, Nina Pulliam—Myrta Pulliam's grandmother—argued that the stories reported much that the paper had already published and the new information in them could not be verified. The *Republic* and other participating news organizations, however, had been invited to review the IRE team's documentation of allegations in the stories if they had any questions. The *Republic*'s city editor, Bob Early, who had headed his paper's extensive coverage of the Bolles murder and its aftermath, was stunned. "I genuinely thought we should run the

14. Melvin Mencher, "The Arizona Project: An Appraisal," *Columbia Journalism Review*, November/December 1977, 38; Tom Renner, "Investigating the Mob," *IRE Journal*, Spring 1981, 17.

series. I wanted to run it, if just to show support for the group effort. We tried to run the downsized AP (Associated Press) version, but then word came down that we would not even run that." Indeed, the *Republic*'s top editors distanced themselves from the IRE team, saying the newspaper had not participated with the investigation, though two *Republic* reporters had worked on the project.[15]

"If the *Republic* wanted to run the story, if they didn't like the writing, all they had to do was rewrite and cut," Robert Greene told *Mother Jones* in 1977. "If they wanted documentation, all they had to do was lift the phone. They have some great reporters, but from the beginning to the end, the higher management at the *Republic* has been essentially gutless."[16]

Public reaction to the *Republic*'s decision to withhold the series was dramatic. Some Phoenix residents expressed outrage. They wrote letters to the editor to protest and snatched up out-of-town papers carrying the series, including the *Tucson Sun* and the *Denver Post*. In addition, protesters picketed the offices of the *Arizona Republic* to publicly criticize the newspaper's decision. Succumbing to the pressure, *Republic* editors began running heavily edited Associated Press versions of the story on March 18, five days after the first stories had been released.[17]

In April, one month after the Arizona Project series began running, Behavior Research Center, a Phoenix-based public opinion polling service, surveyed one thousand heads of households throughout the Rocky Mountain states and found that the IRE series had "strong impact" throughout Arizona and the rest of the states. Awareness of the series averaged 80 percent among Arizona residents and 64 percent throughout the Rocky Mountains states. "The impact of the IRE reports on westerners' attitudes regarding whether land fraud and organized crime problems in Arizona are more or less serious than elsewhere in the nation is unmistakable," the authors of the study reported. The study showed that 41 percent of the Arizonans surveyed and 28 percent of the people surveyed throughout the Rocky Mountain region said that after the series ran they believed

15. Kenneth C. Killebrew, "Don Bolles: News Martyr of the 1970s Enigma of the 1990s," paper presented to the History Division, Association for Education in Journalism and Mass Communication 1995 annual meeting, 22.

16. Lewis, "Have Reporters Become Sitting Ducks?" 28.

17. Mencher, "The Arizona Project," 39.

that the problem of organized crime was more serious in Arizona than elsewhere in the country. In addition, 67 percent of the respondents from Arizona thought land fraud was more serious in Arizona than elsewhere in the country and 42 percent of all Rocky Mountain area respondents thought it was more serious in Arizona than elsewhere in the country. To test whether the perceived seriousness of organized crime activities and land fraud in Arizona was related to the IRE series, the researchers compared the answers of those who were aware of the IRE series with the answers of respondents who were unaware of the published articles. They found that those who were unaware of the series took a substantially less serious view of these problems. "Without question, the IRE reports have had a negative impact on the image of Arizona among residents of the Rocky Mountain region," the researchers concluded.[18]

This "negative impact" led to changes in Arizona, according to Arizona politician Bruce Babbitt, who by John Adamson's account was also targeted for assassination on behalf of Kemper Marley. Babbitt had been attorney general when Bolles was murdered and, five years later, was governor when he offered an assessment of what the Arizona Project meant to Arizona. When IRE's team appeared in Arizona in October 1976, "the public had gone to sleep, the press was on the sidelines, law enforcement was demoralized," Babbitt recalled. "The citizens of this state were aroused [by IRE's work] to a level of indignation that was truly awesome." Public outrage pressured the legislature to increase funding for law enforcement and regulatory agencies, he said. "And public agencies began to respond," the governor recalled. "The legislature acted; they picked up an agenda that law enforcement had had in front of them for a long, long time. The land laws of this state were revised from A to Z.... The blind trust laws were amended. We created for the first time in the history of this state, effective state level law enforcement, integrated from intelligence."[19]

Noted press critic David Shaw of the *Los Angeles Times* issued one

18. Behavior Research Center, "IRE Reports Had Strong Impact in Arizona, Western States," undated press release, IRE files.

19. Bruce E. Babbitt, quoted in "Arizona Report Has Stood Test of Time," *The Arizona Report—Plus Five*, University of Arizona Department of Journalism, March 26–27, 1982, 8.

of the more scathing critiques of the Arizona Project reports. He wrote that the project "smacked of elitism and vigilantism," that the stories lacked sufficient documentation, were "vague, unproven, filled with innuendo and guilty by association," and "instead of proof, the Arizona team too frequently offered unsubstantiated surmise, syllogistic reasoning and hyperfervid language."[20]

And, indeed, the project's handling of documentation deviated from the accepted norms of modern investigative journalism just as much as the concept of journalism-by-collective threatened established practices. Serious charges were being made about powerful people and, in some cases, documentation had to be abbreviated. Robert Greene, in a November 1977 letter to Melvin Mencher, explained the team's predicament. Unlike Shaw, Mencher had written a favorable review of the project for the *Columbia Journalism Review,* and Greene was responding to Mencher's article: "I prefer to write an indictment type story. I like to set out my conclusions and then step-by-step lay out the evidence that led to that conclusion. This makes for a long story. It also gives you little room to demonstrate a scintillating writing style.... The biggest critics of stories written this way are within the industry... They say such stories are too long and that people won't read them.... This is precisely the problem we faced in Arizona." Even story editor Tony Insolia's editing failed to shorten the articles enough, and the IRE editors pared the stories even more by leaving out much of the detailed documentation of evidence. "Part of the rationale justifying the shorter stories was that we constituted an investigative force and as such we had the right to state flatly what we had found," Greene said. "As such, we could eliminate some of the cliché-type attributions.... Much of the criticism came from editors who insist on using: 'police said' at least twice in every lead and four times in every succeeding graph." In essence, the IRE team offered a new standard for documenting evidence within the text of investigative reports that some journalists were unwilling to accept.[21]

Mencher, though, agreed with critics who said that even the shortened series was longer than most papers could handle and that some

20. Richard Cady letter to David Shaw, April 14, 1977, IRE files.
21. Robert Greene letter to Melvin Mencher, November 28, 1977, IRE files.

of the writing was uneven and too often "hyperfervid." Yet, Mencher wrote, the IRE team was a worthwhile journalistic experiment. Specifically, Mencher said, it demonstrated the practicality of the investigative team concept, which could be used in the future, especially among smaller newspapers and broadcasting outlets desiring to report on a project that would overwhelm individual papers or TV news operations.[22]

In contrast to the earlier criticism, after the project was completed most of the media and media organizations praised the project. *Time* magazine said the Arizona Project was "extraordinary," and called it "the most remarkable journalistic effort since Woodward and Bernstein." The Society of Professional Journalists gave IRE its 1977 Public Service Award. Moreover, the project won the University of Arizona's John Peter Zenger Award for Freedom of the Press and the People's Right to Know. The American Society of Journalists and Authors awarded Don Bolles and the IRE project its Conscience in the Media Gold Medal Award and called the Arizona Project "the finest hour in American journalism."[23]

The response from some of the people reported on in the Arizona Project series, however, was acrimonious. Senator Barry Goldwater, in a letter on U.S. Senate stationery to Eugene S. Pulliam, publisher of the *Indianapolis Star,* demanded the names of all reporters who participated in the project and a list of financial contributors to IRE. Pulliam complied. The newspaper publisher denied, correctly, that his family had been "one of the sizable contributors to the so-called Phoenix project." While Pulliam family and newspaper donations had gone to IRE, neither the family nor its newspapers provided any funding for the Arizona Project. Goldwater threatened a libel suit but never filed one. Others, however, did file suits that dragged IRE into a morass of financial and legal tangles for several years.[24]

Six suits were filed naming IRE, various media outlets, and individual reporters as defendants. The suits alleged libel, invasion of privacy, and emotional distress. While IRE had purchased libel insurance to cover the organization, individual reporters, and editors

22. Mencher, "The Arizona Project," 39.
23. "Arizona Invasion Force," *Time,* October 18, 1976, 61; Mollenhoff, *Investigative Reporting,* 344.
24. Barry Goldwater letter to Eugene Pulliam, March 18, 1977, IRE files.

who worked on the Arizona Project, the insurance policy included a fifteen-thousand-dollar deductible, which the company initially insisted meant IRE would have to pay the first fifteen thousand dollars of each suit, or a possible total of ninety thousand dollars.[25]

Suits were filed by:

—Peter Licovoli, Jr., the son of reputed mob leader Peter "Horseface" Licovoli, Sr., who had moved to Arizona from Detroit. The series alleged that Peter Jr. was a drug dealer operating out of a Tucson discotheque, The Living Room.

—Michael Licovoli, Peter Licovoli's brother, who, the IRE reporters said, "is usually found sitting at the bar [The Living Room] in the afternoons, talking to small-time drug dealers." That is the only mention of Michael Licovoli in the series.

—Jaime Ostler Robles, a Mexican national implicated by the IRE series in drug trafficking.

—Jerry Colangelo, general manager of the Phoenix Suns, who, the IRE report alleged, frequented a Phoenix bagel shop that served as the gathering spot for "much of the gambling fraternity" in Phoenix.

—Alfred Gay, an Arizona and Alaska businessman that the IRE series implied might be running drugs, but for certain was allowing the town he controlled on the Arizona-Mexico border to be used as a haven for drug smugglers.

—Kemper Marley, Sr., the multimillionaire Arizona businessman linked to the death of Don Bolles by the confessed murderer, John Adamson. The IRE series alleged that Marley had ties to organized crime, as well as to the powerful politicians in the state.

Another person mentioned in the series sought revenge against IRE in a unique way. He wrote a novel, *Street Fights*. Attorney Joe Martori's former wife wrote the novel for him, which was published under his by-line by a vanity press ten years after the IRE series was published. Martori paid $125,000 of his own money to publish the book, which he said showed the sloppiness and unprofessional behavior of the IRE reporters. Martori was mentioned in the series as a

25. Edward O. DeLaney letter to Arthur B. Banson, Esq., re: IRE Deductible, August 5, 1981; Jerry Uhrhammer letter to IRE board members, July 30, 1981, IRE files.

business partner of and attorney to Robert Goldwater, Senator Barry Goldwater's brother, and was implicated in some of the questionable business relationships and dealings associated with his and Robert Goldwater's corporation, Goldmar, Inc.[26]

Only one suit, that by Kemper Marley, went to trial. Lawyers settled the other suits out of court. IRE paid no damages and claimed victory in each case, although board members agreed to some corrections to the Alfred Gay story. The Marley trial, held in Phoenix, lasted five months, and the jury found that the stories IRE wrote did not libel him or invade his privacy. However, the jury awarded Marley fifteen thousand dollars for emotional distress because of the colorful language used to tell the story. This award was later set aside during out-of-court negotiations.

Even so, the legal victories came with a pricetag. The burden of fighting the lawsuits tied up IRE funds and personnel so that the organization's progress was stymied. The last suit, Marley's, was not concluded until July 1981, four and a half years after the series was published. Board President Jerry Uhrhammer, in a letter to board members in 1981, wrote, "Ever since the Arizona Project, IRE's development as a service and educational organization for professional journalists has been hampered by our commitment to pay off that legal obligation, a task that was necessary but, given our nickel-and-dime finances, one that would seemingly take forever." A saving financial grace came in August of that year, however, when IRE's libel insurance carrier decided that all of the suits arising from the Arizona Project would be considered as a single incident. IRE would have to pay only one fifteen-thousand-dollar deductible instead of six. This erased a thirty-five-thousand-dollar legal fee IRE still owed and reimbursed more than twenty-five thousand dollars in legal fees the organization had already paid.[27]

Tellingly, two years after Don Bolles's murder and fifteen months after release of the Arizona Project stories, the *Arizona Republic* published a sixteen-page special section essentially validating and expanding the conclusions of the IRE series. Carrying the headline "Mob crime is flooding the state," the story package sensationalizes the

26. Deborah Laake, "One Italian's Revenge against the IRE," *New Times*, June 17–23, 1987, 25.
27. Jerry Uhrhammer letter to IRE board members, July 30, 1981, IRE files.

story of organized crime influence in the state much more than the Arizona Project series did. Its front page contains a lurid black-and-white drawing depicting an exploded car in a residential area and a man lying dead, his legs blown off. The word "Crime!" is stamped in large, red, capital block letters across the scene. Much of the section is taken up by photographs and profiles of swindlers, drug smugglers, and organized crime figures who operated in the state. The section's back page is taken up by large crime-scene photos of people murdered in suspected mob hits, including Mr. and Mrs. Gus Greenbaum, shot to death in their home twenty years before, and a photo of the bombed-out car of Don Bolles. Noticeably absent from the special section are stories detailing the connections between gangsters and swindlers and Arizona's politicians, bureaucrats, and business leaders.[28]

During and immediately following the Arizona Project, some commentators suggested the project would be recorded in journalism history, to be studied by student reporters, emulated by modern investigative journalists, and analyzed by historians. Yet, for the most part this hasn't happened. Journalism survey histories written for college students rarely give the project even a footnote. Studies that focus on muckraking or investigative journalism have usually overlooked the project's contributions to the craft. Even more discouraging, the Arizona Project has not entered the collective memory of investigative journalists, much less other journalists, to the level that Watergate, President Kennedy's assassination, or even the *Chicago Sun-Times*'s 1978 Mirage Bar escapade have entered it. The Arizona Project is rarely talked about, examined, or even referred to except by those who participated in it, perhaps because the project toppled no president, or even governor, or maybe because leaders of the news industry, including the *Washington Post* and the *New York Times*, roundly criticized the project. Michael Wendland, the project participant from Detroit who wrote an insider's account of the event, concluded in a postscript to a 1988 reprint of *The Arizona Project* that the project was a failure, arguing that it changed little or nothing in the way Arizona conducted itself.[29] But if documented political

28. "Mob Crime Is Flooding State," *Arizona Republic*, Special Section R, June 25, 1978.
29. Wendland, *Arizona Project*, 266.

change were the single criterion for the success of investigative journalism, very few projects could be considered successful.

To the contrary, there is much to commend the Arizona Project to contemporary journalists. It was a defining moment in the history of journalism, particularly investigative journalism, for it was a rare case when normally competitive investigative journalists set aside their egos and worked together on a story that was too big for any one of them alone. It was a time when reporters and editors, acting as members of the community of journalists, stepped outside their respective newsrooms to report a story that was bigger than any individual newspaper or broadcast news operation. Furthermore, it was an instance when American journalists stood up for freedom of the press, taking up the reporting agenda of one of their fallen colleagues to show those who killed him that the press will not be silenced by violence. IRE responded most appropriately to the killers of Don Bolles and the Arizona community that fostered the violence, for it did not try to supplant the criminal justice system by investigating the murder itself. Instead, the IRE reporters reacted by digging, prying, uncovering, and reporting stories important to the public — the essence of what investigative journalism is all about. And the citizens of Arizona, or at least a vocal faction of them, were informed, engaged, and inspired by the series, which is what good journalism is supposed to do. Moreover, the project validated the investigative team concept, suggesting methodology for doing investigations by showing through example how to organize a project, how to report a story of sweeping historical and contemporary implications, and how to document and write the results without overwhelming publications or readers.

While IRE's financial and legal travails relating to the Arizona Project lasted more than four years, it took nearly a decade for the wheels of justice to turn on John Adamson and others connected with the murder of Don Bolles. Adamson, who had a criminal record for less violent crimes, confessed to setting up Bolles and sought leniency by naming names. He implicated wealthy contractor and developer Max Dunlap, a protégé of millionaire Kemper Marley, Sr. Marley had been forced off the Arizona racing commission after Bolles published an account of his checkered past performance on state commissions and his ties to Arizona Governor Raul Castro. Adamson also fingered

James Robison, a local down-on-his-luck plumber, as the triggerman who manually exploded the bomb under Bolles's Datsun. Allowed to plead guilty to second-degree murder with the prospect of a twenty-year sentence, Adamson testified against Dunlap and Robison, both of whom were convicted of first-degree murder. Yet, on appeal Adamson's guilty plea and both convictions were thrown out. Trying to leverage an even more lenient deal than he had received the first time, Adamson refused to testify again against Dunlap and Robison under the same terms he had initially received. Prosecutors called his bluff, though, and he was convicted of Bolles's murder. This time, he carried the full blame for the murder and a judge sentenced him to die in the gas chamber. The cases against Dunlap and Robison went nowhere for nearly a decade, until Adamson agreed to testify against them in exchange for getting off death row. In November 1993, Dunlap was convicted of conspiracy in Bolles's murder and sentenced to life in prison. Robison was found not guilty of triggering the bomb but he returned to prison anyway to finish serving a sentence for conspiring to hire a hit man to kill a prosecution witness in the Bolles case.

Numerous theories of the Bolles killing have been ventured. Some point the finger at Dunlap and Marley. Others say both men were Adamson's fall guys. The people who hired Adamson to kill Bolles have never been conclusively identified or punished, and the reasons behind the killing have never been satisfactorily revealed. In 1991, the year Marley died, Arizona Attorney General Grant Woods said new evidence existed that supports the contention Marley was a key player in Bolles's murder. Even so, Marley's name now graces the Arizona Historical Society's new museum complex in Phoenix to honor him for a generous donation his estate gave to the society.[30]

The Arizona Project had been the best of times and the worst of times for IRE. It brought national attention to a struggling organization and ultimately attracted members to the organization. From 1976 to 1981, the membership grew from about 200 to 1,029. And yet, the project caused internal dissension and threatened the organization's financial well-being. But IRE came out of the experience

30. G. Robbins, "A Friend and Colleague of Don Bolles Remembers," *Editor and Publisher*, June 19, 1993, 67, 76.

stronger and better organized. Its association with the University of Missouri School of Journalism was in place, membership numbers were up, and finances were stabilized.

While IRE might have prospered without the Arizona Project, its growth in membership and influence probably would not have been so rapid. At a critical time when the organization needed national exposure and needed to motivate journalists to join, the dramatic Arizona Project was a magnet drawing valuable attention to the organization.

6

IRE and the Mainstreaming of Investigative Journalism

In 1984, reporter Charles Shepard and his colleagues at the *Charlotte* (North Carolina) *Observer* were onto one of the biggest scandals of the decade. Sources were coming forward with astonishing tales about celebrity televangelists Jim and Tammy Bakker and life behind their multimillion-dollar PTL ("Praise the Lord") facade. Eventually, the sources told of illicit sexual behavior, hush-money payments, huge paychecks and bonuses for the Bakkers and other top PTL executives, mismanagement of the ministry, personal use of ministry funds, and fraud. The fraud allegation consisted of accusations that Jim Bakker and his associates were selling tens of thousands more "lifetime partnerships" through their popular television show, *The PTL Club*, than the PTL resort had lodging to accommodate. *The PTL Club* enjoyed the loyalty of tens of thousands of viewers and members who came to the defense of the religious organization, and three years passed before the full facts and ramifications of the scandal were realized. Because of the sensitivity of the topic and the power of PTL, *Observer* editor Richard Oppel insisted that any story about Jim and Tammy Bakker, especially about Jim Bakker's sordid sexual encounter with secretary Jessica Hahn, had to come from on-the-record sources and documents—proper standards for any investigative project.[1]

While apprehensive about the possible backlash from PTL supporters, the reporters and editors of the *Observer* did not shy from their responsibility to commit the resources necessary to expose the Bakkers' misuse of donated ministry funds—including the payment of $265,000 to Jessica Hahn to keep her quiet about having sex with Jim Bakker. Like many members of the press in the 1980s, those at the *Observer* saw investigative journalism as a natural part of what any good newspaper would do—an acceptance largely brought about through the work by Investigative Reporters and Editors, Inc.

Seeking advice and the necessary skills, metro editor Jeannie Falknor and reporter Charles Shepard, in the midst of digging into the PTL scandal, took time out to attend an IRE national conference. One of the workshops they attended talked about the use of public records to document allegations and to ferret out information that people do not necessarily want to talk about. They were energized by their experience at the IRE convention—by the workshops and by the conversations they had with other reporters. Falknor and Shepard returned to Charlotte "with a determination to push for better use of public records in all kinds of reporting, especially in following the PTL."[2] Putting his IRE training to use, Shepard filed a request for FCC documents under the federal Freedom of Information Act, asking the Federal Communication Commission for records of its investigation into the Bakkers' television show, *The PTL Club*. The paper trail documented the fraudulent operation run by the Bakkers, and it showed that federal officials had taken no action to stop or punish the Bakker ministry, although there was ample reason to do so. The FCC records provided important documentation for a key step in the *Observer*'s investigation of the Bakkers—to prove that what the ministry was doing included fraudulent fund-raising practices. Later, when Jim Bakker learned that the *Observer* also had evidence of his sexual encounter with Hahn and his use of ministry

1. Andrew Radolf, "Pressure from the Preacher," *Editor and Publisher*, October 31, 1987, 14.
2. "Public Service," *Knight-Ridder News* 3, no. 2 (Summer 1988): 11.

funds to keep her quiet—and that the paper planned to run the story—he called Oppel to announce his resignation from the PTL leadership. The Rev. Jerry Falwell, former head of the Christian Coalition, moved into PTL headquarters and took over from the Bakkers. Over the next few months, basing their stories on extensive interviews and examination of documents, and often with assistance from Falwell and the new PTL management, Shepard and other reporters at the *Observer* disclosed the sexual encounter that brought down Jim Bakker. They exposed the $265,000 payment to Jessica Hahn to buy her silence. And they detailed a host of other financial and moral misdeeds by the Bakkers and others in the old PTL management. The *Observer* also was able to reveal the power struggle that resulted within the evangelical Christian community because of the leadership vacuum the Jim Bakker scandal left.

The reporters and editors of the *Observer* had shown considerable courage going up against the extensive power of the PTL organization, for the Bakkers had access to 180 television stations across the country and had launched a massive campaign to discredit the newspaper. Moreover, throughout their investigation, the *Observer* staff adhered to high standards, backing every accusation with "demonstrable fact," to use editor Oppel's words. In the best tradition of investigative journalism, the *Charlotte Observer* and Charles Shepard toppled the Bakkers' corrupt church empire, sparked a national debate over television evangelicalism, and took home a 1988 Pulitzer Prize for Public Service.[3]

However, the *Charlotte Observer* was far from alone in its willingness to undertake investigative reporting when the circumstances called for it. And, indeed, many in the press went looking for the right circumstances, seeing the exposure of corruption and mismanagement as their public duty. The 1970s and 1980s saw a commitment to investigative reporting unmatched since the muckraking era of the early twentieth century. In a number of ways, IRE led that revival by spreading the principles and practice of investigative journalism to thousands of American journalists.

The Arizona Project had transformed Investigative Reporters and Editors from a small, elite group associated with the *Indianapolis*

---

3. Garry Boulard, "Keeping the Spotlight on PTL," *Editor and Publisher*, May 23, 1987, 17.

Star into an organization of national range and reputation. By succeeding on a number of levels, the Arizona Project had raised IRE's profile and legitimized the organization. Moreover, establishment of an endowment helped resolve the volatile financial problems that had plagued the group from its inception, and praise for the publication of the IRE team's remarkable investigation overshadowed the negative publicity that internal problems had brought. By the mid-1980s, IRE had positioned itself to grow its numbers and expand its services.[4]

IRE existed during the early 1980s with a membership that fluctuated but ultimately grew from 900 in 1980 to 3,000 in 1985. (The group had begun with a mere 177 in 1976.) The largest segment of the membership worked for newspapers, because most American journalists worked for newspapers, and newspapers did most of the investigative journalism in the United States. To be precise, the membership in July 1984 consisted of 1,036 newspaper reporters and editors; 239 television reporters and producers; 39 radio reporters, producers and editors; 97 journalism students; 95 journalism educators; 58 freelance writers and editors; and 20 magazine reporters. Additionally, there were 10 newspaper publishers, a magazine publisher, 11 wire service journalists, and a book author. The actual membership was higher, but other members had not listed their affiliations.[5]

By the fall of 1984, IRE reached a membership of 2,000. And in October 1985, the membership neared 3,000. Tellingly, few were full-time investigative reporters. Most were young reporters interested in investigative reporting, evidence that the growth and influence of IRE was directly tied to the founders' early decision to keep the organization open to all journalists, and not just to established investigative journalists. Some of the better-known investigative reporters in America had attended the meeting in Reston, Virginia, when organizers decided to form IRE, and they continued to be prominent as speakers at national and regional conferences. But many of them found little use for the organization as members. They had succeeded in investigative journalism; they knew how to practice it. James Polk of *NBC News* recalled trying to interest these prominent

4. M. L. Stein, "IRE Continues to Help Teach Investigative Reporters," 11.
5. IRE Board of Directors meeting minutes, July 15, 1984, IRE files.

practitioners in joining the organization. "I once sent around letters to all our national speakers who were not members or who had let that [sic] lapse," he informed IRE's executive committee. "There were scores. I included personal notes to the ones I knew rather well. The response to that membership appeal was abysmally low. A lot of them, I guess, were people who already had such accomplishments they saw little need to belong to us. Condescending, yes, but also prevalent." While the failure to attract many of the foremost practitioners of the craft as active members disappointed many in the organization's leadership, by reaching out to all reporters rather than to the few journalists who considered themselves full-time investigative reporters, IRE grew to a membership that allowed it to influence journalism by spreading the skills of investigative reporting to beat and general assignment reporters in hundreds of newsrooms.[6]

In February 1984, the IRE board of directors reaffirmed the organization's commitment to all reporters when it decided to add to IRE material the motto: "Every reporter can be an investigative reporter." This was especially important for IRE's growth because few news organizations kept full-time investigative reporters on staff. A survey conducted by IRE and the University of Missouri School of Journalism in 1985 found that 98 percent of newpaper editors and television producers reported that investigative reporting was either a regular or occasional newsroom activity, but only 19 percent of the newspapers and 21 percent of the television stations that were surveyed had more than one full-time investigative reporter on staff; and many (64.3 percent newspaper and 43.7 percent television) had no full-time investigative reporter.[7]

IRE's focus during the 1980s under executive directors John Ullmann and, after 1983, Steve Weinberg included the resource center at the University of Missouri School of Journalism; an annual conference held at locations throughout the United States; regional and student conferences designed to reach more reporters and editors and student journalists; the IRE Journal, a quarterly magazine that carried how-to articles, case studies, and discussions of law and ethics;

6. Jim Polk letter to Steve Weinberg, undated response to Weinberg letter to Polk, January 31, 1989, IRE files.
7. "Investigative Reporters Form Own Service Association," 10; IRE Board of Directors meeting minutes, February 24, 1984, IRE files; Stan Abbott, "National Survey Charts Growth of Investigative Reporting."

the annual awards program; the popular *Reporter's Handbook* published by St. Martin's Press; and an occasional skills book or pamphlet on specific topics. The thrust of the organization, then, was education and community-building. Funding came from annual dues, donations from foundations and news organizations, profits made from registration fees paid by participants at the national and regional conferences, and the sale of books and other resource materials.

The resource center, which included a depository of print and broadcast investigative reports, received three to five calls a day from journalists seeking advice or information. The center was supported through membership dues, grants, and subsidization by the University of Missouri School of Journalism. By the end of 1981, its library of published investigative reports contained 970 categories with almost 10,000 individual stories. By maintaining the center's library, IRE preserved the history of late-twentieth-century investigative journalism in the United States.

Attendance at the annual conferences slowly grew through the years. The first conference, held in Indianapolis in 1976, attracted slightly more than 200 journalists and academicians. The 1980 national conference, held in Kansas City, Missouri, drew 375 attendees. In 1982, 525 journalists and journalism educators attended the annual meeting in Washington, D.C. Regional and student conferences attracted a widely varying number of participants; some of the conferences proved quite profitable for IRE, while others lost money. For example, a regional conference specializing in agricultural issues, held at the University of Missouri in 1981, earned a profit of $2,588; but a 1980 conference on broadcasting lost between $2,000 and $2,500. From 1980 through 1990, IRE held regional conferences throughout the country, including in Dallas (1981), Minneapolis (1981 and 1985), Palm Springs, California (1983), Richmond, Virginia (1984), New York City (1984), Jacksonville, Florida (1985 and 1987), Philadelphia (1985), Columbia, Missouri (1985), San Antonio (1986), Hartford, Connecticut (1988), San Jose, California (1989), Baton Rouge, Louisiana (1989), and Indianapolis (1990). Because most regional conferences covered a range of topics, they were essentially mini-national conferences; others covered special topics, such as the New York City conference, which covered political reporting; the Jacksonville conferences, which covered sports reporting; the Indianapolis conference on computer-assisted reporting; and the Columbia, Missouri, conference on agriculture. IRE also held conferences for journalism students in Los Angeles (1983), Ames, Iowa (1983), Columbia, South Carolina (1983), New Haven, Connecticut (1983), Washington, D.C. (1983 and 1989), Indianapolis (1984), Chicago (1988), Portland, Oregon (1988), Baton Rouge, Louisiana (1989), and Columbia, Missouri (1990).

The training had immediate and direct influence on journalists. Joe Rigert of the *Minneapolis Star Tribune*, an investigative reporter who was active in IRE and would serve two terms as president, was impressed with the organization's progress. "It's just kind of unbelievable what IRE has done in the way of educating people on how to do investigative reporting," he said during an interview. "Not just in projects, but in everyday reporting: How to get records. What's out there. What the records are. How to get sources. How to develop the sources. How to manage a project. How to put the stuff all together into stories and how to write them. I mean just every aspect of it. I periodically ask for articles from the resource center to see what other people have done on the subject matter I'm going to be investigating."[8] Likewise, Windsor Ridenour, who was managing editor of the *Tulsa* (Oklahoma) *Tribune*, recalled attending an IRE national conference and returning convinced that his reporter, Mary Hargrove, had to learn how to use public records. Consequently, Hargrove attended IRE conferences to learn from experienced investigators how to research records, a skill that paid off in 1982 when she and her fellow reporters on the *Tribune* broke the story of how poor management and unsecured loans to high-rolling clients had bankrupted the Penn Square Bank in Oklahoma.[9]

Another source for working journalists was the *IRE Journal*, which maintained communication among IRE members and disseminated how-to articles about investigative journalism. A typical issue would include one or two case studies, a column on a legal issue, book reviews, and information about upcoming conferences and other news about the IRE organization. Volume 4, Number 1, in the winter of 1981, for example, included news of IRE's successful conclusion

8. Joe Rigert, interview with author, Portland, Oregon, June 1992.
9. Alan Prendergast, "Best in the West: Tulsa Troubleshooter Mary Hargrove," *Washington Journalism Review*, July/August 1987, 23.

of a libel suit filed by Arizona businessman Kemper Marley that arose out of the Arizona Project; a case study of Don Barlett's and James Steele's series for the *Philadelphia Inquirer* on how U.S. oil companies manufactured the oil scarcity of the late 1970s; a how-to article on investigating how a state administers its criminal pardons; a how-to article on how to discover who is responsible for a failed bank; a profile of a citizens' group in Chicago, the Better Government Association, which was active in investigating political corruption; a report of a survey on how many journalism schools offer courses that teach investigative journalism skills; an article on how to pry government documents out of an agency; and articles on the upcoming national conference in San Diego and on the recently concluded regional conference in Dallas.

Other issues of the *Journal* carried lengthy discussions of ethics, articles about what investigative reporting was and who investigative reporters were, and profiles of historically important investigative journalists. This reinforced the practice's self-conception. IRE directors saw the magazine as an important service to working journalists. And members benefited from the journal. A survey of IRE members by Executive Director John Ullmann in 1981 found that 98 percent of the respondents found the magazine to be "very" or "somewhat" valuable to their reporting and 99 percent found it to be interesting. Additionally, in 1980, IRE agreed to a partial merger with the University of Missouri School of Journalism's Freedom of Information Center, which resulted in the *IRE Journal's* assuming the publication of the FOI Center's state FOI reports, which added 594 institutional subscribers to the magazine.

Furthermore, the annual awards program, approved in 1979 and beginning in 1980, provided a means of identifying and disseminating the better work of U.S. investigative journalists. It also served as a means of collecting important examples of investigative journalism for IRE's resource center collection. While there were other awards programs for journalism, the most prominent being the Pulitzers, in the early 1980s the IRE awards were the only contest that specifically showcased investigative journalism. Executive Director Steve Weinberg acknowledged in a 1988 issue of the *IRE Journal* that there were legitimate questions about creating another contest, but he defended IRE's decision. "Why another? . . . It is the only contest specifically for investigative work judged under stringent guidelines by experienced investigative journalists. Our definition of investigative journalism is imperfect, but it is specific and more carefully constructed than that of any other contest. In a sense, the IRE awards are a consumer's guide to authentic, first-rate investigative journalism."[10]

The importance of the IRE awards contest as an arena for a continuing discussion about the definition of investigative journalism is significant. It is the only forum within IRE that gives a definition of the practice, making it the standard-bearer for defining the practice. When the awards program was first established, IRE adopted investigative reporter and editor Robert Greene's definition of investigative journalism: it is work that is substantially the product of the reporter's own initiative and uncovers facts or events that somebody or some organization tried to keep secret. It must be about matters of public importance to the publication's circulation or broadcast area. It must be fair and accurate; it must contain sufficient documentation; it must be well written and effectively presented; it must be followed up. In addition, the amount of difficulty and the resources available to the news organization are to be considered. The impact and scope of the story also are important. And, finally, it must meet "all generally accepted craft standards." This definition of investigative journalism was the first established through the consensus of practicing investigative journalists. The definition, in essence, outlines the internal goods and general standards of excellence for the practice. However, a sticking point in the definition was the requirement that investigative journalism must reveal secrets. At a special meeting of the IRE executive committee in November 1980, this particular issue was discussed. James Polk of NBC News asked that the judging criteria be altered so that revelation of secret facts or events would be considered by contest judges, but would not be a mandatory part of the definition for investigative journalism. Norm Udevitz of the Denver Post, who had worked with Robert Greene and Jay Shelledy to develop the original definition, argued that he still agreed with Robert Greene. Investigative

10. Steve Weinberg, "The Triumphs of Good Reporting," IRE Journal, Spring 1988, 3.

journalism, by definition, discloses secret information, he argued, and stories on previously unreported subjects are simply enterprise reporting. However, Shelledy agreed with Polk that the original definition was too restrictive.[11]

This disagreement over the definition of investigative journalism reflected a broader and longer-lasting issue among investigative journalists. Whether it has to reveal secrecy has been the most divisive issue in settling on a common definition. The issue had been debated in the mid-1970s and would continue to be debated in the 1980s. A judge for the IRE awards contest, University of Missouri faculty member George Pica, objected to IRE's limited view of investigative journalism as a revelation of secret facts and events. In a memorandum to the IRE board, Pica wrote that Donald Barlett's and James Steele's series on nuclear waste management failed IRE's definition because of the secrecy requirement, but was investigative journalism nonetheless. "They invested days and weeks identifying the points in seemingly unrelated documents, then connecting those dots to produce a powerful picture of nuclear waste in America," he argued. "It is precisely this type of thoughtful, sometimes grueling, analytical reporting that runs the risk of being overlooked by the IRE if the rules as we understand them continue to be the gauge against which entries are measured." In response to the concerns of Pica and others, the IRE board altered the awards criteria slightly to reaffirm that disclosure of secret facts and events would only be a consideration, not a requirement.[12]

The IRE board also altered the requirement that the work be the reporter's own to read that the work be "substantially" the product of the reporter. This change reflected a second, though less controversial, sticking point in the definition of investigative journalism. Indeed, most definitions of investigative journalism used by textbook authors and others focus not on secrecy, but rather on independent discovery by the journalist. It is the original digging for information beyond the routine collection of information common to most journalism that separates investigative reporting from other forms of

11. IRE Executive Committee meeting minutes, November 19, 1980, IRE files.
12. Frederick R. Blevens, "Introduction: Shifting Paradigms of Investigative Journalism," 257; George Pica memorandum to Steve Weinberg, March 1984, IRE files.

n-depth journalism. It is what separates modern investigative journalism from much of the exposure journalism that has occurred in U.S. history. James Callender, for example, did not dig up on his own the 1802 allegation that President Thomas Jefferson was having an affair with his slave Sally Hemings. Partisan scandalmongers whispered the information to him. Callender, as a Virginia newspaper editor, simply revealed the information that others had collected. And that characterizes much of the exposure journalism in America's past. This distinction also distinguishes the investigative work on the Watergate scandal from the publication of the Pentagon Papers. The *New York Times* and the *Washington Post* went to great lengths to acquire and prepare the Pentagon Papers for publication, even fighting in court against the Nixon administration's attempt to suppress their publication. As researcher Fred Blevens has observed, "One [the Watergate coverage] was a crusade to extract information from those who conspired to lie and keep secrets, while the other [the Pentagon Papers publication] was a legal fight to publish the contents of an investigation conducted independently of the press." The Pentagon Papers were compiled by researchers at the Rand Corporation under contract to the Pentagon. The press's role involved condensing and analyzing the information, not discovering it. In contrast, the Watergate reportage included a series of astounding press revelations about corruption, extortion, obstruction of justice, and other high crimes and misdemeanors in the highest office in the land. "Spy Funds Linked to GOP Aides," read one of the famous Watergate headlines in the *Washington Post*. While few scholars or working journalists would label the Pentagon Papers "investigative reporting," nearly all would recognize the Watergate reportage as a classic example of investigative journalism.[13]

As it evolved, the IRE definition found strong support among working journalists. When IRE and the University of Missouri School of Journalism surveyed journalists in 1986, respondents largely agreed with IRE's definition of the practice. Slightly more than 98 percent of the respondents agreed that investigative journalism is in-depth reporting that discloses something significant that someone wants

13. IRE Board of Directors meeting minutes, October 12, 1984, IRE files; Blevens, "Shifting Paradigms," 257–58.

to keep secret, and is largely the reporter's own work. The benefit o
an officially sanctioned definition contributed to the cohesion of the
practice; it provided a common understanding of investigative jour
nalism to which practitioners could relate.[14]

IRE began publishing pamphlets and books in 1979 with its pub
lication of reporter David Burnham's pamphlet on the interpreta
tion of crime statistics. Then, in 1983, with an advance of more than
$11,500 from St. Martin's Press, IRE published its first edition of *The
Reporter's Handbook: An Investigator's Guide to Documents and Techniques*, which has become the standard reference for investigative
reporting used in classrooms and in newsrooms. In addition, the organization published a collection of the best articles from the *IRE
Journal*, summaries of IRE award-winning articles, an index to the
IRE article collection, and a reprint of a supplement from the *IRE
Journal* about evaluating electronic data bases. These publications
became an important source of income for the organization and
extended the organization's educational role.[15]

Even with funding coming from membership dues, fees for conferences, sales of books and pamphlets, and foundation grants, as
well as basic support from the University of Missouri School of Journalism, financing was still a continuous struggle for IRE during the
1980s. The organization, which earlier had been criticized for receiving grants from nonjournalism foundations, resolved to seek outside funds only from news organizations and journalism-related
foundations. By the mid-1980s, IRE was operating on a budget of
approximately $100,000 to $125,000 a year, not including subsidization from the University of Missouri, which provided office space,
one-half of the executive director's salary, printing of the *IRE Journal*, and other contributions. The journalism industry's financial
support of IRE was not overwhelming, but was substantial nonetheless. Gannett Foundation, for example, was providing $5,500 a year
for the IRE awards program by 1985. In addition, one-time contribu-

14. Abbott, "National Survey," 6.
15. David Burnham, "Crime Statistics: How Not to Be Abused," Investigative
Reporters and Editors, Inc., 1980. John Ullmann and Steve Honeyman, eds., *The
Reporter's Handbook: An Investigator's Guide to Documents and Techniques* (New
York: St. Martin's Press, 1983); IRE Board of Directors meeting minutes, Febru-
ary 24, 1984, IRE files. In 2004, *The Reporter's Handbook* was in its sixth edition.

tions were routine from individual newspapers and broadcast news operations for regional and national conferences. The *Los Angeles Times*, for example, donated $1,000 for the 1983 national conference in St. Louis; the Richmond, Virginia, newspapers offered $500 for a regional conference in their area in 1984; and for the national conference in Washington, D.C., in 1982, the Philip L. Graham Fund, which is associated with the *Washington Post*, donated $2,500, and $1,000 each came from the *Los Angeles Times* and *NBC News*.[16]

During the early 1980s, IRE carried out educational and community-building activities with honesty, courage, justice, and a sense of tradition in the MacIntyrean meaning of those terms. Concerned with the maintenance and extension of the practice's standards of excellence, IRE established the resource center, the awards program, and a conference schedule to provide examples of and a forum for discussion of the best investigative journalistic techniques, methods, and products. It founded the *IRE Journal* to spread information about skills, ethics, law, and tradition to its members. And it adjusted its fund-raising activities to insulate itself from appearances of conflicts of interest. The IRE board not only decided to no longer solicit grants from nonjournalism foundations but also had to resolve a controversial situation with an anonymous donor. Investigative reporters are used to dealing with anonymous sources, of course, but the problem of accepting money from people not known to the IRE board members was a different situation altogether. In 1983, the anonymous donor provided $5,000 to IRE through the Fiduciary Trust Company of New York. It was much-needed funding, but the anonymity of the donor caused appropriate concern. Fiduciary Trust would not reveal the identity of the donor, but assured IRE that the person would not be an embarrassment to IRE nor would the donation compromise the organization if his identity was ever revealed. In 1984, the same donor once again made an anonymous $5,000 gift to the organization, and once again the board

16. Jim Drinkhall, "Conflict-of-Interest, Censorship Charges Jar Unlikely Group," *Wall Street Journal*, February 23, 1977; "Investigative Reporters Form Own Service Organization"; IRE Board of Directors meeting minutes, June 26, 1983, and February 24, 1984, IRE files; IRE Board of Directors meeting minutes, June 22, 1983, and June 26, 1983; "IRE Detailed Schedule of Contributions for the Year Ended Dec. 31, 1982," IRE files.

accepted it. But the danger of accepting such donations was not lost on the board members, and the acceptance of such gifts, needed though they were, was halted the following year.

Reaching beyond its immediate concerns of education and community-building, IRE's board of directors in the early 1980s also showed what scholar Edmund Lambeth has called "stewardship" of the First Amendment, which he lists as one of the necessary guiding principles of journalism. Lambeth writes that stewardship involves "the notion of a commitment to trusteeship which a journalist is free to assume in a constitutional democracy.... Journalists — reporters, editors, publishers, media owners — are in a unique position to help keep the wells of public discourse unpoisoned, if not wholly clean.... As special beneficiaries of the First Amendment, journalists have a material motive to protect a protection meant for all." In 1981, for example, IRE membership approved a resolution opposing congressional amendments designed to narrow access to government documents under the federal Freedom of Information Act. James Polk presented the resolution to the House Government Information and Individual Rights Subcommittee on July 14, 1981. And in 1983, IRE gave testimony to the Consumer Products Safety Commission in opposition to closed government records.[17]

IRE entered the second half of the 1980s with a solid reputation. On July 4, 1987, *Editor and Publisher*, a leading industry magazine directed at management, published an editorial praising IRE for bringing investigative journalism into the mainstream of journalism: "There is no doubt that the organization has raised the professional level of investigative reporting.... It [investigative reporting] has developed as an accepted, important and responsible facet of newspaper reporting and IRE gets the credit for providing the guidance and the guidelines." An important industry observer, in other words, saw IRE as having set the standards for investigative journalism and as having shown journalists how to meet those standards. Moreover, *Editor and Publisher* saw IRE's work as elevating the performance of all journalism. The magazine's editors editorialized in 1986 that "... newspaper reporting is getting better. Investigative reporting set the goals. At the start it [investigative journalism] was the epitome

17. Lambeth, *Committed Journalism*, 32.

of what newspaper reporting should be. It emphasized techniques that had been mislaid in many newsrooms. Once rediscovered they are now having a beneficial effect on all reporting." The growth of IRE, according to *Editor and Publisher*, was "symptomatic of the expansion of in-depth reporting throughout the newspaper industry."[18]

And, indeed, the growth of IRE was substantial. From 1985 to 1990 it became a well-run, relatively financially secure service organization. Its national and regional conferences attracted more and more journalists through the years and became important sources of revenue for the organization. IRE's 1987 national meeting in Phoenix brought in revenues of $71,451, an additional 223 new members, and turned an $8,834 profit, plus added $7,075 in membership dues. The next year, its national conference in Minneapolis had revenues of $73,091, brought in 275 new members, and turned a $12,172 profit, plus adding $9,800 to the organization's coffers in additional membership dues. The 1989 Philadelphia national meeting attracted more than one thousand participants, operated on revenues of $98,510, and resulted in a profit of $6,912. It attracted more than four hundred new members and added $13,425 in membership fees to IRE's income.[19]

An additional money-maker for IRE started in the 1980s: in-service training seminars for individual news organizations. The executive director and/or board members offered to present a one-day seminar for a newspaper or television newsroom at a cost based on the size of the news organization, plus expenses. In 1987, for example, IRE presented a seminar for the *Christian Science Monitor*'s staff for a two-thousand-dollar honorarium. David Winder, assistant managing editor for the *Monitor*, wrote in a letter to Executive Director Steve Weinberg that "the IRE workshop has been one of the highlights of our year.... A recurring comment was how much your background helped ... [us] learn the finer points of how to really dig into a story. Now we just need to put into practice what we learned." As of June 6, 1990, Director Weinberg had presented thirty-six newsroom seminars, and board members had presented twelve. The seminars were

18. "To Better Inform," *Editor and Publisher*, July 4, 1987, 6; "Investigative Reporting," *Editor and Publisher*, July 12, 1986, 8.
19. IRE Board of Directors meeting minutes, June 6, 1990, IRE files.

presented for news organizations of varying size throughout the United States, evidence that the organization had achieved national appeal among a range of publications. Less interest was shown by smaller television stations and radio stations, however. Seminars were presented for the *Memphis Commercial Appeal;* the *Los Angeles Times;* the *Virginia-Pilot* in Norfolk, Virginia; Harcourt Brace Jovanovich magazines of Cleveland; the Worcester County, Massachusetts, newspapers; the *Capital Times,* Madison, Wisconsin; the *Birmingham* (Alabama) *News;* the Jackson Newspapers, New Haven, Connecticut; *St. Louis Business Journal;* ABC News' 20/20, New York; the *Macon* (Georgia) *Telegraph and News;* the *Roanoke* (Virginia) *Times and World News;* the *Saginaw* (Michigan) *News;* the *Fort Lauderdale* (Florida) *News and Sun-Sentinel;* and the *Columbia* (Missouri) *Tribune,* among others. These seminars further extended IRE's influence into newsrooms across the country and trained hundreds of journalists in the basic skills of investigation.[20]

IRE's growth during the late 1980s also can be seen in its operating budget. Total operating revenues, which came mainly from membership dues, conferences, contributions, and sales/services, more than doubled in six years, growing from $124,893 in 1984 to $291,157 in 1990. Operating expenses, however, often were more than the growing revenues. Expenses for staff and equipment for the resource center; printing expenses for the *IRE Journal,* a cost once covered by the University of Missouri but which IRE had assumed; and the cost of presenting conferences grew along with the organization's revenues. Expenses went from $122,461 in 1984 to $312,329 in 1990, outstripping operating revenues in 1987, 1989, and 1990. Underscoring how financially stable the organization had become, reserves in the operating budget were available to cover the shortfall in the years when expenses exceeded revenues. The organization was not in danger of bankruptcy. But efforts to reverse the trend were clearly needed.[21]

During the late 1980s, IRE concentrated on improving the services it had initiated during the late 1970s and early 1980s. It computerized the resource center for better retrieval of information for mem-

---

20. David Winder letter to Steve Weinberg, December 16, 1987, IRE files.
21. Audited IRE financial reports for 1984, 1985, 1986, 1987, 1988, 1989, 1990, IRE files.

ɔers; it extended its services to include electronic database searches
ʿor members; it expanded its skills-training effort by adding to its
ɔonference seminars one of the few advances in investigative report-
ɪng techniques—the use of computers to analyze large amounts of
electronic data, which is referred to as computer-assisted reporting;
and it began a minority recruitment program, recognizing that investigative reporting had attracted few minority reporters. To further
stabilize IRE's finances, the board in 1988 established an endowment
with a goal of $1.1 million. The purpose of the endowment was to
provide funds to offer programs that could increase minority partic-
ipation and enhance IRE workshops with special attention to science, business, and agriculture; to expand the organization's existing
professional education programs; to provide fellowships in investigative reporting; and to possibly establish a distinguished professor-
ship in investigative reporting at a school of journalism. In addition,
the endowment could provide funds so that IRE might pay the full
salary of its executive director to free the director from teaching
duties at the University of Missouri School of Journalism. In 1989,
the endowment had garnered actual and pledged contributions from
Cox News Service ($15,000), the *Minneapolis Star-Tribune* ($50,000),
the Knight Foundation ($75,000), Central Newspapers of Indianapo-
lis ($22,000), Phillip Graham Foundation ($15,000), the *Chicago Tribune* ($2,000), and the *Tulsa Tribune* ($1,000), as well as individual
contributions from board members. Total contributions to the endowment by February 1989, including a $17,000 transfer of funds
from IRE's operating revenues, were $197,900. By June 1990, the en-
dowment had grown to more than $250,000.[22]

In November 1989, other universities were courting IRE's resource
center. The University of Maryland, Indiana University, and Louisiana
State University expressed interest in having IRE move its resource
center to one of their campuses. The most tempting offer was from
LSU, which offered to raise funds for the IRE endowment to support one and perhaps two distinguished professorships in investigative journalism, as well as to match other accommodations and
funding being provided by the University of Missouri School of Journalism. However, LSU withdrew its offer after the IRE board discussed

22. IRE Board of Directors meeting minutes, June 6, 1990, IRE files.

the matter and unofficially agreed to stay at the University of Missouri.[23]

But the offer from LSU and other universities caused some soul-searching by board members who set the agenda for decision-making within the organization as it moved into the 1990s. Fredric Tulsky of the *Philadelphia Inquirer*, president of the board of directors in 1990, sent his fellow board members a letter prior to the meeting at which the LSU offer would be discussed. In it, he laid out the issues confronting the organization. After more than a decade of operation, IRE had offered training in the basics of traditional American journalism to a generation of journalists. Would it continue training the younger journalists, or should it offer more for the experienced reporters and editors? Tulsky summed up the issue:

> When I joined the board I thought that we had the conferences, in large part, to introduce ourselves to new members and to retain old members; to get people coming and signing up to be members and, in the process, to teach them what we can about reporting.... Are the conferences our most important service? Are the publications? Are newsroom seminars?
>
> Should our main efforts be spent keeping our longtime members, and servicing what they want by new innovations? Should our main effort be to continue doing what has worked, since we continue to attract new members, and to focus on educating the young reporter? Should we make the focus of our efforts innovations, such as a worldwide investigative reporting network? Should we do more to promote investigative reporting within the industry, so that the media treats [sic] us as a force?

These questions confront a mature organization, one that has met its original goals of creating a community of interest, promoting high standards, and pushing for the mainstreaming of a practice that was once thought of, at least by one reporter, as "kind of a cult...a lot of words about very minor things."[24]

23. Louisiana State University Manship School of Journalism letter to IRE Board of Directors, September 17, 1990, IRE files. The issue of moving the resource center arose again in 1996 when the University of Maryland sweetened and renewed its offer, and some board members felt that the University of Missouri was ignoring IRE's needs. The board split on the issue after heated debate and decided, once again, to stay at Missouri.
24. Rick Tulsky letter to IRE Board of Directors, August 28, 1990, IRE files; Joe Rigert, interview with author, Portland, Oregon, June 1992.

During the 1980s, investigative journalism moved into the mainstream of American journalism, developed and expanded computer-assisted reporting, battled for its share of shrinking newsroom budgets, saw the emergence of the investigative book as a financial and journalistic blockbuster, and weathered embarrassing libel trials that caused the practice to reflect on its techniques and values.

If the Watergate investigations (led by the *Washington Post*) and the Arizona Project (conducted by IRE) provided the outstanding events for investigative journalism during the 1970s, the collective work of the *Philadelphia Inquirer* exemplified the possibilities of investigative journalism during the 1980s. The paper's significance does not come from any single investigative project—although there were several outstanding examples of individual efforts—but from the overall commitment and achievement of the newspaper under the direction of editor Eugene Roberts.

When Knight-Ridder purchased the *Inquirer* from Walter Annenberg in 1972, it had the reputation of being one of the worst urban papers in the United States. It competed poorly with the *Philadelphia Bulletin*. Knight-Ridder executives coaxed Roberts from the *New York Times* national desk to head the *Inquirer*, which he systematically upgraded. He improved the paper's hard news coverage by encouraging "take-outs"—the *Inquirer*'s term for long, in-depth, investigative pieces. In the eighteen years Roberts ran the paper (he retired in 1990), the *Inquirer* won seventeen Pulitzer Prizes, several of which were for investigative-style reporting. Eleven of the seventeen Pulitzers were garnered between 1985 and 1990. Seven were for in-depth reporting, a phenomenal record in the journalism business. One of those Pulitzers went to Bill Marimow in 1985 for revealing the Philadelphia Police Department's canine unit was out of control and its dogs were harming people. In 1986, Arthur Howe took home a Pulitzer for exposing the Internal Revenue Service's deficiencies in processing tax returns, a report that led the IRS to apologize to the American people. The paper won two investigative Pulitzers in 1987, one for John Woestendiek's reporting that freed from prison an innocent man convicted of murder, the other for Daniel Biddle, H. G. Bissinger, and Fredric Tulsky's series "Disorder in the Court," which led to federal and state criminal investigations into Philadelphia's court system. In 1988, Tim Weiner won a Pulitzer for his series on a secret Pentagon budget used to fund an arms buildup. Donald Barlett and James Steele, the *Inquirer*'s legendary investigative team, took a Pulitzer in 1989 for their classic exposé of the Tax Reform Act of 1986, which was loaded with special tax breaks for politically connected individuals and businesses. And in 1990, the *Inquirer* won the Pulitzer's Public Service award for Gilbert Gaul's exposé of companies that collect and distribute the nation's medical blood supply. Roberts and his staff built a national reputation for the *Inquirer* primarily on the strength of vigorous in-depth coverage on a wide range of topics. Moreover, the *Inquirer* showed that investigative reporting can build circulation and, hence, provide a financial benefit for urban papers. This position was underscored when the *Bulletin*, battered in its head-to-head newspaper war with the *Inquirer*, folded in 1982 after its circulation dropped from 619,113 daily to 397,397.[25]

For Gene Roberts, investigative reporting was a newspaper's duty. During his 1988 Otis Chandler Lecture at the University of Southern California, he explained that "the finest reporting—whether short or long—is always investigative in that it digs, and digs, and digs.... [I]nvestigative reporting means freeing a reporter from the normal constraints of time and space and letting the report really inform the public about a situation of vital importance. It means coming to grips with a society grown far too complex to be covered merely with news briefs or a snappy color graphic. Some papers fail their readers by refusing to do any investigative reporting at all." The belief that the American press is obligated, by virtue of operating within a democracy, to do investigative reporting—a message that IRE had been sending since 1976—was accepted by most of the better newspaper editors and television news directors by the mid-1980s. The two decades between 1970 and 1990 were a heyday for investigative reporting in a variety of formats.[26]

Former *New York Times* man Bill Kovach became editor of the *Atlanta Journal-Constitution* with a game plan similar to the one Gene Roberts had sketched out at the *Inquirer*. From 1986 to 1989, Kovach worked to make the *Journal-Constitution* "world-class" by adding hard-hitting, in-depth coverage. Kovach would later become

25. Edmund B. Lambeth, "Gene Roberts: A Case for Leadership," *Quill*, June 1991, 14–25; Paul Taylor, "Gene Roberts: Down Home Editor of the Philadelphia Inquirer," *Washington Journalism Review*, April 1983, 35–41.

26. Eugene Roberts, "The Finest Reporting Is Always Investigative," *IRE Journal*, Winter 1988, 12.

curator of the Nieman Foundation for Journalism at Harvard and the founding director of the Committee of Concerned Journalists. His view, shared by many of his peers, is that investigative journalism is a mark of quality for a newspaper or TV news operation. One of the more remarkable stories done at the *Atlanta Journal-Constitution* under his watch was an investigation of mortgage red-lining by Atlanta's banks. Reporter Bill Dedman produced one of the first investigative series based on a computer analysis of public records and showed that Atlanta banks routinely discriminated against blacks when making mortgage loans. Because of Dedman's reporting, the *Atlanta Journal-Constitution* took home a Pulitzer Prize in 1989, the year Kovach left the paper over a disagreement with his bosses. When Cox Communications executives wanted less hard-hitting investigative journalism, Kovach and the newspaper parted ways. Nevertheless, many publishers and editors at weeklies and small dailies also believed that investigative journalism was essential to serve a paper's readers. In 1984, a thirty-one-year-old Kansan, Angelo S. Lynn, moved to Vermont and bought the *Addison County Independent* because he "wanted to own a paper that would be far more than a bulletin board" and found success in the community weekly world by introducing investigative journalism to a ninety-five-hundred-circulation twice-weekly. And in 1988, a Pulitzer Prize for General News Reporting went to the staff of the *Alabama Journal of Montgomery*, a weekly in the state's capital city, for its investigation of Alabama's unusually high infant mortality rate.[27]

In television, local stations such as WBRZ-TV in Baton Rouge, Louisiana, pushed for aggressive, investigative reporting during the 1980s. WBRZ hired investigative reporter John Camp and gave him free rein to pursue stories, even when they caused advertisers to withdraw their accounts. "WBRZ seems too good to be true," a Louisiana State University journalism professor told a trade magazine in 1988.

---

27. Peter J. Boyer, "Atlanta Burns," *Vanity Fair*, February 1989, 136–41, 173–78; Bill Cutler, "Trying to Make Atlanta's Papers 'World-Class,'" *Columbia Journalism Review*, March/April 1988, 40–45; Terry A. Dalton, "Boat Rockers, Please Apply: A Twice-Weekly Commits Itself to In-Depth Reporting," *Quill*, November 1989, 30–33. The *Alabama Journal's* history stands as evidence that honored investigative reporting cannot necessarily financially reward a publication. After decades of operation, the *Journal* merged with the *Montgomery Advertiser* in 1993, the victim of economic losses.

"I think the only people who are critical are the ones who have been the subject of their exposés." John Camp captured national attention at WBRZ when he exposed the sins of his hometown televangelist, Jimmy Swaggert, in 1988. "Television used properly can be the most effective medium there is for investigative reporting," Camp explained. "In a newspaper article you can't capture the little nuances when someone who is lying to you is explaining the unexplainable." In 1990, Camp moved to CNN in Atlanta to do investigative reporting.[28]

At the networks, CBS continued strong in the 1980s with 60 Minutes, the nation's first TV magazine that mixed investigative reports with celebrity profiles, and added 48 Hours in 1988 as a vehicle for longer documentary investigations. ABC copied the 60 Minutes format when it launched 20/20, and NBC got in the game with Exposé. Cable News Network hired veteran investigative reporters from the Wall Street Journal, the Associated Press, the New York Times, and other publications and local television stations for its Special Assignment team, and the Public Broadcasting System established its investigative documentary series Frontline. Radio stations such as WTIC in Hartford, Connecticut, and WSM in Nashville, Tennessee, produced documentary and news investigations, too, and National Public Radio brought investigations to the national airwaves.[29]

Among magazines, Mother Jones, under the editorship of Mark Dowie, led the pack in breaking investigative stories. In 1977 it revealed that Ford Pintos would burst into flames on impact because of a faulty fuel tank design that Ford Motor Company executives knew about. Dowie revealed that the defect could have been fixed for a mere ten dollars per car, but the company chose not to spend the money. The magazine also revealed that Dalkon Shield intrauterine devices, which company executives knew could cause deadly

28. Lou Prato, "Keeping Baton Rouge Honest: WBRZ-TV Reports All the News — Even When It Hurts," Channels, November 1988, 70; Ron Chepesiuk, Haney Howell, and Edward Lee, Raising Hell: Straight Talk with Investigative Journalists, 30.

29. William M. Carley, "As TV News Reporting Gets More Aggressive, It Draws More Suits," Wall Street Journal, January 21, 1983; Robert Goldberg, "CNN's Crack Investigative Team," Wall Street Journal, October 29, 1990; "NBC News Is 'Ready for Prime Time' Player," Broadcasting, December 23, 1990, 45, 48; Dana Kennedy, "David Fanning of 'Frontline': Telling Stories for PBS," Washington Journalism Review, November 1988, 39–41.

infections in some women, were kept on the market anyway—what *Mother Jones* called the "Corporate Crime of the Century" in 1979. Throughout the magazine industry, investigative reporting was being done at the newsmagazines (*Time, Newsweek,* and *U.S. News and World Report*), in periodicals as varied as *Vanity Fair,* the *New Yorker, Playboy, Penthouse,* and the *Progressive,* as well as by some trade magazines, including *Fleet Owner,* which serves the trucking industry. James Phelan plied the investigative beat for a number of magazines beginning in the 1960s as a staff writer for the *Saturday Evening Post.* He investigated a wide variety of subjects, including medical malpractice, the Mafia, and reclusive billionaire Howard Hughes for the *Post, Collier's, Life, Look,* the *Reporter, True, Playboy, Penthouse,* and others. "The reluctance of newspapers to support my curiosity habit propelled me into writing for magazines," he recalled in the introduction to a 1982 compilation of his magazine work. "I found them [magazines] a much more congenial home for the overly investigative reporter. There one could work on a story for weeks or even months without cocking the right eye on the clock and the left on an unhappy bookkeeper."[30]

Book publishers rediscovered the investigative book as well in the 1970s and 1980s, sometimes providing six-figure advances for book-length exposés. Jonathan Kwitny's *Vicious Circles: The Mafia and the Marketplace,* published in 1979, led the way. Robert A. Caro's *The Power Broker,* about New York public works czar Robert Moses, and his *The Path to Power,* about Lyndon Johnson, melded biography with investigative journalism. Seymour Hersh built his reporting career with muckraking books such as *The Price of Power: Kissinger in the Nixon White House,* published in 1983. In 1990, Bryan Burrough and John Helyar, *Wall Street Journal* reporters at the time, published the best-seller *Barbarians at the Gate: The Fall of RJR Nabisco,* perhaps the most successful investigative book about the business world since 1904, when Ida Tarbell published the *History of the Standard Oil Company.*[31]

30. "Best Magazine for Investigative Journalism: Mother Jones," *Washington Journalism Review,* March 1990, 33; Jan Colbert, Bruce Moores, and Steve Weinberg, eds., *Top 100 Investigations: Investigative Reporters and Editors Selected 1989 Contest Winners,* 111–23; Phelan, *Scandals, Scamps, and Scoundrels,* xiv.

31. Robert A. Caro, *The Power Broker: Robert Moses and the Fall of New York* (New York: Knopf, 1974); Robert A. Caro, *The Years of Lyndon Johnson, Vol. 1, The*

Indeed, throughout the media industry, investigative reportage came to be seen as a duty and became a standard of excellence for journalism. The survey of editors and news directors by Stan Abbott, IRE, and the University of Missouri in the mid-1980s concluded, in fact, that investigative reporting had increased "substantially" in newspapers and on television during the 1980s. The study found that 42 percent of the newspaper respondents said that investigative reporting is a "regular activity" for their papers; 55 percent said it was "occasional." Of the television respondents, 47 percent said investigative reporting was a regular activity and nearly 39 percent said it was an occasional activity. In addition, 71 percent of the newspaper editors said their reporters were using more investigative techniques during routine reporting. Thirty-two percent of the television news directors said their stations had more commitment to investigative reporting.[32]

In addition, the Abbott survey also found that most editors and news directors saw investigative journalism as a responsibility of the press. Forty-three percent of the newspaper editors said it was "journalism's role," while another 33 percent said it was a "community service." Among the television news directors, 31 percent saw investigative reporting as journalism's role and 45 percent saw it as a community service. Fifty-one percent of the newspaper editors said their newspapers were doing more investigative reporting than they had done five years before; more than 62 percent said they were doing more than they had done ten years before. Fifty-six percent indicated they would maintain their current level of investigative reporting in the coming year, and about 31 percent said they would

Path to Power (New York: Knopf, 1982); Seymour Hersh, *The Price of Power: Kissinger in the Nixon White House* (New York: Summit Books, 1983); Brian Burrough and John Helyar, *Barbarians at the Gate: The Fall of RJR Nabisco* (New York: Harper Collins, 1989); Michelle Osborn, "A Million-Dollar Advance for Burrough," *USA Today*, November 7, 1990.

32. C. David Rambo, "Excellence in Small Dailies," *presstime*, November 1984, 16–22; Jon Katz, "Memo to Local News Directors: Re: Improving the Product," *Columbia Journalism Review*, May/June 1990, 40–45; Ron Ridenhour, "Between the Lines at the Times-Picayune," *New Orleans*, November 1990, 94; Abbott, "National Survey," 5. Abbott sent questionnaires to the editors of the five hundred largest-circulated newspapers and to news directors of television stations in the forty primary market areas. Thirty-five percent of the newspapers and 30 percent of the television stations responded.

increase it. Fifty-six percent of the news directors said their television stations were doing more investigative reporting than they had done five years before, and 47 percent said they intended to maintain their current level; 35 percent said they planned to increase the amount their stations did.

But the institutions supporting investigative journalism — the newspapers, magazines, book publishers, and broadcast news divisions — are always susceptible to the pressures of profits. Hence, unlike the practice itself, they cannot be depended on to maintain, nurture, and expand investigative work. And in the late 1980s, an economic slump hit the newspaper and television industry, causing some news operations to curtail expensive investigative practices. While interest in investigative reporting and editing was growing among journalists, as witnessed by the increased attendance at IRE conferences and membership in the organization, publishers, editors, and news directors faced budgetary constraints that caused a restriction of the practice at some news organizations. The networks cut back their commitment to investigative reportage, and some local television stations and newspapers noted for investigative reporting eliminated or cut back investigative efforts as well.[33]

Having become part of mainstream journalism, however, investigative journalism continued to be supported by many news organizations despite their revenue problems. Cutbacks in budgets for investigative projects occurred, but — in most cases — they only caused editors to become more selective of the projects they undertook, rather than eliminating the practice altogether. In fact, one area of investigative reporting saw considerable advancement during the late 1980s. That was the use of computer analysis to produce in-depth, investigative stories.

Donald Barlett and James Steele of the *Philadelphia Inquirer*, with help from Philip Meyer, who pioneered the use of social science techniques in journalism, showed investigative reporters the uses of computer analysis in 1983, when they published their ground-breaking

33. Neal Rosenau, "After the Cutbacks: What's the Damage to Local TV News?" *Columbia Journalism Review*, September/October 1988, 46–50; Staci D. Kramer, "Investigative Reporting in the '90s: The *Wall Street Journal* Managing Editor Sees Tough Times Ahead," *Editor and Publisher*, July 21, 1990, 17, 41; Mark Lagerkvist, "Owner Makes Millions, News Takes a Beating: On Quitting WZZM-TV, Grand Rapids," *Washington Journalism Review*, December 1988, 38–41.

study of criminal justice in Philadelphia. It was the type of innovative, in-depth reportage that Gene Roberts encouraged at the *Inquirer*.

Meyer, who had studied social science methodology at Harvard University during a Nieman fellowship, gained experience with survey research and data analysis during a study of the 1967 Detroit riots for the *Detroit Free-Press*. Barlett and Steele, wanting to study the criminal court system in Philadelphia but lacking the background with computers and social science methodology, enlisted Meyer's help in the design of the study. It was an early journalistic attempt at such a comprehensive study, and their methods were, by today's computerization standards, a bit primitive. The data had to be gleaned laboriously by hand from thousands of printed documents, then had to be transferred by key-punch operators onto IBM cards. The cards were then fed into the computer for analysis. The reporters backed their public records data with in-person interviews of hundreds of people who worked in the justice system or who had gone through it, either as crime victims or defendants, and showed that justice was not meted out equally in Philadelphia's courtrooms. But it was the computer analysis that set their study apart from previous journalistic efforts and set a new standard for investigative journalists.[34]

After the personal computer became widely available in the late 1980s, computer-assisted reporting became more accessible. By 1985, the trade press was reporting — based on a panel presentation at the IRE annual conference — that computers had become investigative tools and "journalists are crunching numbers to handle data-filled stories that they once considered too complex to tackle." A year later, *Time* magazine reported that computers were "revolutionizing investigative reporting," quoting IRE Executive Director Steve Weinberg on the computer's impact. Computer analysis was used to report on campaign contributions given to local government officials in Alaska; arson prosecutions in Rhode Island; inordinately long jail terms for undefended, indigent people convicted of misdemeanors in Milwaukee; and state contracts for highway construction in New York. By the end of the 1980s, with help from IRE, the University of Missouri School of Journalism, Philip Meyer at the University of North Carolina School of Journalism, and Indiana University's Na-

---

34. The series is discussed and reprinted in Meyer, *Precision Journalism*, 366–89; Weinberg, *Telling the Untold Story*, 111–12.

tional Institute for Advanced Reporting, computer-assisted investigative journalism was mainstream journalism. In 1989, the University of Missouri School of Journalism, in collaboration with IRE, founded the Missouri Institute for Computer-Assisted Reporting to train working journalists. To head the institute, which would later merge with IRE, the university chose Elliot Jaspin, who had gained national recognition for a computer-assisted investigation of school-bus drivers in Rhode Island for the *Providence* (Rhode Island) *Journal-Bulletin*.[35]

The decade of the 1980s also saw the practice of investigative journalism stumble badly. While computer-assisted reporting techniques were pushing investigative reporting forward, a series of embarrassing libel lawsuits resulted from reporting that did not meet established standards for investigative reporting. As early as 1982, investigative journalist James Phelan noted that the threat of libel lawsuits was imperiling the vitality of investigative journalism. Full-time investigative reporters, Phelan noted, "work in a high-risk specialty, akin to the people who make a living walking a tightrope across Niagara Falls or defusing bombs. A single bad error and one disappears into a maelstrom of libel or is blown out of the business."[36] Four libel suits in particular, filed against prestigious news organizations by prominent people for reports published or broadcast during the late 1970s and early 1980s, dragged the press through ten years of high-profile trials that raised serious questions about the techniques and standards of investigative reporters.

William Tavoulareas, president of Mobil Oil Company, sued the *Washington Post* for reporting in 1979 that he had used his corporate position to set up his son in the shipping business. Las Vegas singer Wayne Newton sued NBC and its noted investigative team of Ira Silverman and Brian Ross for reporting in 1980 that Newton had ties to organized crime. General Ariel Sharon of Israel sued *Time* magazine for reporting in 1982 that he had encouraged a Phalangist massacre of Palestinian refugees in Lebanon. And U.S. Army General William Westmoreland sued CBS, including 60 *Minutes* anchor Mike

35. George Garneau, "Computers as Investigative Tools," *Editor and Publisher*, November 9, 1985, 30–31; Exra Bowen, "New Paths to Buried Treasures," *Time*, July 7, 1986, 56; Dorothy Bland, "Computers Can Turn Ordinary Reporters into Super Sleuths," *ASNE Bulletin*, January/February 1991, 11–15.
36. Phelan, *Scandals, Scamps, and Scoundrels*, xii.

Wallace, for reporting in a 1982 CBS *Reports* documentary that he had ordered his subordinates to cover up the extent of the enemy's strength when he was commander of American forces during the Vietnam War. The cases, taken together, showed a new aggressiveness on the part of business executives and public figures and officials to counterattack investigative reporting, and they also showed the vulnerability of the investigative press when its reporting falls short of established standards.[37]

The Tavoulareas case resulted from a November 30, 1979, *Washington Post* report that William Tavoulareas had used Mobil Oil resources and influence to create an opportunity in the shipping business for his son, Peter. William and Peter Tavoulareas, after failing to convince the *Post* to print a retraction, sued the newspaper and its executive editor, Ben Bradlee, its metropolitan editor, Bob Woodward, its reporter, Patrick Tyler, a freelance reporter, Sandy Golden, and Dr. Philip Piro, Jr., the former son-in-law of William Tavoulareas and the *Post*'s initial source for its story.[38]

For the most part, the investigative techniques and standards used in reporting the Tavoulareas story cannot be faulted. In fact, Woodward testified at the trial that Tyler's reporting and the newspaper's editing met established standards for investigative journalism and resulted in "the best obtainable version of the truth." And the story was substantially correct. William Tavoulareas's position with Mobil Oil was at least indirectly responsible for Peter Tavoulareas's being made a partner of the Atlas shipping company, which had an exclusive contract to operate Mobil Oil tankers. However, William Tavoulareas did not use Mobil Oil resources and did not ask that his son Peter be made a partner of Atlas. In addition, Mobil Oil was not required to report Peter Tavoulareas's position with Atlas to the Securities and Exchange Commission, although the *Post* story said it was.

These relatively inconsequential errors were enough, given the jury's mind-set, for a finding of fault and an awarding of a $2.05 million judgment against the *Post* and the other defendants. The jury was convinced that the *Post* had been unfair to the Tavoulareases,

37. *Tavoulareas v. Washington Post*, 13 Med.L.Rptr. 2377, 817 F.2d 762 (D.C. Cir. 1987); *Newton v. NBC*, 14 Med.L.Rptr. 1914 (D.Nev. 1987); *Sharon v. Time*, 609 F.Supp. 1291 (S.D.N.Y. 1984); *Westmoreland v. CBS, Inc.*, 596 F.Supp. 1170 (S.D.N.Y. 1984); Clurman, *Beyond Malice.*

38. Steven Brill, "The Lawsuit and the Trial," *IRE Journal*, Winter 1983, 11.

that defendant Golden had surreptitiously and wrongly tape-recorded conversations with his source Piro, and that Golden was using the *Post* story as a stepping stone to a better newspaper job than the one he held with a Rockville, Maryland, newspaper. In addition, the jury was unimpressed with the revelations in the story—a father helping a son become established in the business world was not considered of major public importance. Nonetheless, the jury's verdict and award were eventually overturned on appeal. The higher court ruled that the story was basically correct and the errors it contained were not the result of malice. However, the incident left the impression that the *Post* had been unfair and mean-spirited, investigating and publishing a story that held little public importance because, as reporter Tyler had suggested to Golden, it was not every day that the press got a chance to "knock off one of the Seven Sisters (oil companies)."[39]

The reporting of the Wayne Newton story by *NBC News* was more clearly questionable. On October 6, 1980, NBC broadcast Ross and Silverman's report that Newton had made phone calls to mobster Guido Penosi and had denied a relationship with Penosi when he [Newton] testified before the Nevada Gaming Commission. Newton was applying for a gaming license to purchase the Alladin Hotel in Las Vegas, and the NBC report implied that Penosi would be a secret partner. The facts were correct, the implication was not. Newton showed during the resulting libel trial that he had contacted Penosi not for financing the hotel deal but for protection after a Penosi associate had made threats against Newton's family. In addition, the NBC broadcast had left out a segment of Newton's testimony to the gaming commission when he stated that if Penosi had mob ties, Newton would sever his friendship with him. The jury found that NBC had libeled Newton and awarded Newton damages totaling $19.2 million, the largest libel verdict up to that time against a news organization. When NBC appealed, the entire damage award was eventually thrown out. The appellate judges ruled that actual malice and damage to reputation had not been proved.[40]

Gaining even more publicity, however, were the libel suits against CBS and *Time* magazine by Generals Westmoreland and Sharon,

39. Ibid.
40. John A. Jenkins, "Newton's Law: How Mort Galane Fought NBC and Won," *ABA Journal*, April 1989, 70.

respectively. In 1982, CBS Reports broadcast "The Uncounted Enemy: A Vietnam Deception," which argued that Westmoreland had conspired with his subordinates to mislead President Lyndon Johnson, the Joint Chiefs of Staff, the Congress, and the American public about the strength of the North Vietnamese and Viet Cong troops. Westmoreland claimed his honor had been impugned and sued the network for $120 million, which he offered to donate to charity if he won. The resulting libel trial and an internal investigation by CBS showed that the documentary producers and reporters had violated CBS's own standards as well as the standards of investigative journalism. The internal CBS investigation by executive Burton Benjamin found, for example, that the broadcast treated witnesses against Westmoreland sympathetically while it was harsh on witnesses supporting Westmoreland. In essence, the show did not give Westmoreland and his supporters an opportunity to refute the accusations. In addition, some of the editing of the videotape misled viewers, the internal study found. Westmoreland, who received legal help from the conservative Capital Legal Foundation, decided during the trial that he would have difficulty proving the broadcast contained false accusations and withdrew the suit before the case was given to the jury. In return, CBS issued a statement that the network had never intended to suggest that Westmoreland was dishonorable. But the larger issue for the media and the public, as Benjamin pointed out in his internal report and the book he wrote about the case, was the ethical issue of fairness. CBS had not been fair to Westmoreland, Benjamin asserted. This was not a legal issue, as the judge in the libel trial pointed out repeatedly, but it was a stinging indictment of the CBS producers and reporters given the importance that the practice of investigative journalism places on the value of fairness.[41]

In a New York courtroom in the same building and at the same time that Westmoreland's case was being heard, Ariel Sharon was building his libel case against another media giant, Time magazine. On February 1, 1983, Time had published a cover story on the report of a secret Israeli tribunal that had investigated the massacre of more than five hundred Palestinian women and children in two refugee

41. Burton Benjamin, *Fair Play: CBS, General Westmoreland, and How a Television Documentary Went Wrong*, 74–87.

camps in Lebanon. Christian Phalangists had carried out the massacre—during Israeli occupation of Lebanon—in revenge for the assassination of Lebanon's president-elect, Bashir Gemayel. The *Time* report said that Sharon, Israel's minister of defense at the time of the report, had "reportedly discussed" the need for revenge with the Phalangists immediately before the massacre. Sharon, the tribunal reported, had given the Phalangists permission to go into the refugee camps to look for armed guerrillas. Moreover, the tribunal had accused Sharon of "indirect" responsibility for the massacre.[42]

Time correspondent David Halevy, however, reported that an unpublished appendix to the report confirmed beyond a doubt that Sharon had collaborated with the Phalangists in the massacre. Halevy reported that a confidential source had told him the contents of the secret appendix. During the resulting libel trial, however, Halevy admitted from the witness stand that he had only "inferred" that the damning information about Sharon was in the appendix and that he had no direct knowledge that it was there. He also was forced to admit under questioning that he had no documentation that Sharon had communicated to the Phalangists that their need for revenge could be acted upon. The case went to the jury, which had been instructed by the judge to consider falsity, actual malice, and damages separately. The jury concluded during its first segment of deliberations that *Time* had libeled the Israeli general and returned to the jury room to decide whether the magazine had reported the falsehoods "with malice," which libel law required before damages could be awarded. Unsure that malice had been proved, Sharon called off the trial before the jury returned a second time. Nevertheless, he declared his reputation had been vindicated. The trial was concluded, but the proved lack of fairness in the use of a confidential source and *Time*'s lesser standard for documentation left the investigative press tainted.

Even though the Tavoulareas, Newton, Westmoreland, and Sharon libel cases were eventually won by the press—from the standpoint that the news organizations did not have to pay damages in any of the cases—the investigative press was still shaken. The cost of defending the lawsuits had been high. The *Washington Post* paid more than $1.8 million in its defense. CBS reportedly spent more than

42. Clurman, *Beyond Malice*, 84.

$10 million to defend itself against Westmoreland. And the Sharon suit cost *Time* and Sharon more than $3 million each. But more than the money spent in defending itself, the press was left battered by allegations that investigative reporting is sometimes sloppy, sometimes done with less-than-pure motives, and often done by an arrogant press. The investigative press, which had made great strides during the 1980s, was forced to confront its tactics and behavior to protect its reputation.

The facts of the prominent libel cases are indicative that IRE, which influenced the setting of standards among investigative journalists, could not police the practice. Unlike a profession, which has disciplinary powers over its practitioners, journalism organizations can only influence through education and peer pressure. During the 1980s, because of the high-profile libel cases as much as anything, the discussion of ethics became pronounced in the popular and trade press. Television reporters rethought their use of ambush interviews, selective editing, and hidden cameras. And the entire press reconsidered its use of unnamed sources, undercover reporting, and the invasion of people's privacy in the interest of getting a story. The increased interest in press ethics can be seen throughout the trade and popular press, but IRE contributed directly to discussions of investigative press ethics by providing a forum for such discussions in the *IRE Journal* and at annual and regional conferences. By the end of the 1980s, IRE staff and most members understood that the continued progress of investigative journalism was intimately tied to the work of ethical reporters and editors.[43]

43. "Investigative Reporting Roundtable: Challenges and Obstacles," *IRE Journal*, Winter 1987, 14–19; Jack W. Fuller, "Can We Be Bold and Not a Bully?: To Be Credible, Depth Reporting Must Meet the Needs of Our Time," *IRE Journal*, Spring 1987, 5–7; Jim McGee, Tom Fiedler, and James Savage, "The Miami Herald's Story on Gary Hart: How It Happened," *IRE Journal*, Summer 1987, 12–18.

7

A Social Practice

When Paul Williams, one of the original founders of IRE, talked with a fellow member about how the Arizona Project should be carried out, he argued that IRE should extend its reach and do more than go to Phoenix in anger to find the criminals who had murdered their friend, Don Bolles, a reporter for the *Arizona Republic*. "... The intent should not be to bring Don Bolles's killers to justice per se," Williams told IRE president Ron Koziol. "The cops and the local papers are doing that right now. Instead, we should go into Arizona and describe the particular climate that caused his death." That is to say, to extend the practice of investigative journalism, journalists had to seek truth and go beyond the immediate personal outrage over the death of Don Bolles. The reporting could only be accomplished by the proposed team effort and it could not be a duplication of what the local press would routinely accomplish anyway.[1]

1. Wendland, *The Arizona Project*, 30.

In this regard, Williams intuitively understood that IRE's response to the killing of one of its own must extend the practice of journalistic investigations, something that a team investigation of Arizona could accomplish, and avoid being seen as simply a biased act of vengeance. His suggestion came from a perhaps unarticulated desire to sustain and strengthen the practice of investigative journalism rather than to damage it by carrying out a project that would violate the principles of objectivity and fairness that, by the mid-1970s, were highly valued by investigative journalists. According to moral philosopher Alasdair MacIntyre, sustenance and strengthening occur through the exercise of the virtues, which he defines as justice, truth, courage, and an adequate sense of the traditions of a social practice. In each particular case, he asserts, individual practitioners must apply the virtues that are most relevant.[2]

MacIntyre explains that a social practice is "any coherent and complex form of socially established cooperative human activity" which achieves "internal goods" as practitioners pursue standards of excellence "which are appropriate to, and partially definitive of" the practice. "External goods" are those benefits that are not inherent in the practice itself, including such advantages as money, celebrity, or status that might be endowed on an investigative journalist who wins a top prize from the profession. But these goods, external to the practice, do not benefit other journalists and the work they do. A social practice such as investigative journalism progresses when the practitioners apply and live the virtues while carrying out the practice. Moreover, through this virtue-based practice, investigative journalism can be "systematically extended" in ways that allow future practitioners to do the work even better.[3]

The evolution of modern investigative journalism has progressed as journalists have sought the internal goods peculiar to investigative journalism. Such goods include "telling the whole story," reporting on matters of public importance, truth-telling, originality, and "making a difference." They must be willing to fulfill the practice's standards of excellence, which include having the courage to confront the powerful, being independent, documenting their assertions, doing a thorough job of reporting, presenting their findings

2. MacIntyre, *After Virtue*, 207.
3. Ibid., 175.

vividly and in proper perspective, and doing follow-up stories. When journalists do their work, if they abide by the virtues, meet the standards of excellence, and seek the practice's internal goods, the practice will be systematically extended. The Arizona Project is exemplary. The manner in which IRE carried out the Arizona Project deserves closer scrutiny, for it is an instance when journalists, using the resources of IRE, systematically extended the practice of investigative journalism.

Had members of the IRE team that went into Phoenix only concentrated on the superficial aspects of Bolles's killing—who did it and why?—they would not have done enough. The project would not have risen above the "kind of wild justice" of revenge discussed in the seventeenth century by Francis Bacon, and perhaps if that was what they only hoped to do, they should have followed Bacon's advice to consider "passing it over." Discovering the identity of the persons responsible for the killing of Bolles would have benefited the internal good of "telling of truth" but would not have necessarily strengthened the practice of investigative journalism. The police department and the local newspapers could have done as much. More would be required to justify the unusual and dramatic step of sending a high-profile team of reporters from different newspapers, magazines, and TV news stations into Arizona.[4]

An ethical press, scholar Edmund Lambeth argues, will monitor society's institutions to determine whether justice is being served; in other words, how a society's fundamental rights and duties are assigned and whether economic opportunities and social conditions are justly distributed. If social justice is a goal of society, then the fundamental role of an ethical press is to identify, expose, and publicize the manner in which the major social institutions carry out their responsibility to be just. If journalists detect situations void of justice, they are obligated to expose them, to avenge the wrongs of society, to seek reform-by-exposé.[5]

The investigative journalists who worked on the Arizona Project, inspired by the murder of a fellow journalist, operated under this duty to expose injustice, to right the wrongs—by way of publicity—

4. Francis Bacon, "Of Revenge," *The Essays or Counsels, Civil and Moral, of Francis Ld. Verulam* (Mount Vernon: Peter Pauper Press, 1963), 21.
5. This is a concept of social justice from John Rawls, *A Theory of Justice* (Cambridge, Mass.: Belknap Press, 1971), 7.

of institutions in Arizona. In anticipating the project, Robert Greene of *Newsday*, the team's leader, said he wanted to "exert heavy pressure on every possible pocket of corruption." The team's targets ultimately included organized crime operations in Arizona, narcotics and illegal-alien trafficking, political corruption, and land fraud. Institutions examined included the criminal justice system, the legislature, the state executive branch, and private businesses.[6]

The ethical dimension of investigative reporting comes not from the initial decision to be spurred to action by some injustice. In fact, most, if not all, investigative journalism springs from a reporter's or a news organization's outrage toward some injustice, whether committed against the practice of journalism or against some segment of society. The determining factor, then, is within the nature of the response.

First and foremost, journalists should heed the age-old advice of Bacon: "The most tolerable sort of revenge, is for those wrongs which there is no law to remedy." The Arizona Project team was not concerned with finding the killers of Don Bolles. The law against murder backed by a system of criminal justice was sufficient to satisfy that need. If the criminal justice system was inefficient or corrupt, that is to say, was not carrying out justice, there would be occasion to seek Bolles's killers. The IRE team, however, wisely understood that the local media would, and should, monitor the performance of the local criminal justice system. However, there is no law and no formal system of justice capable of responding to the larger social issue of protecting free expression and none, at least in Arizona at that time, capable of or willing to respond to the social problem of systemic corruption and criminality. On these two issues, then, the team rightly set its sights.[7]

Second, journalists should follow Bacon's further admonishment, ". . . but let a man take heed, the revenge be such as there is no law to punish; else a man's enemy is still before hand, and it is two for one." In other words, journalists bent on avenging a wrong must follow other ethical obligations not to harm innocent people (the principle of humaneness, in Lambeth's terms) and not to break just laws or ethical principles.[8]

---

6. Wendland, *Arizona Project*, 34.
7. Bacon, "Of Revenge," 22.
8. Ibid.; Lambeth, *Committed Journalism*, 30–32.

Another of the principles that must be applied is truth-telling. Accuracy can never be abandoned no matter what the cause; otherwise, trust between news media and the public will be damaged. The Arizona Project team understood this and consequently set high standards for its reporting. Not only did Greene and other editors carefully monitor all reporting and writing, but three attorneys also reviewed the stories before publication. They spent five days combing the stories, and their challenges led to one entire story being killed and others being altered. The standard used: Can the facts be proven? In addition, the IRE team adhered to the more substantial meaning of truthfulness defined by Lambeth as "social truth." Participants of the project sought to tell the whole story, not just a portion of it. They worked through extensive document searches, in-depth interviews, and other techniques to establish the larger truth of the circumstances in Arizona.[9]

Journalists also must consider the principle of justice. While what inspires the reporting may be a desire for personal justice, what must complete the reporting is a desire for social justice. The IRE team members wanted justice for Bolles, but their reporting sought justice for all residents of Arizona by exposing criminal, corrupt, and inefficient practices that benefited the criminal few rather than all of society. The virtue of justice, likewise, had to extend beyond the immediate and personal goal to bring Bolles's killers to justice. To be virtuous, then, the justice sought had to be the type of social justice described by philosopher John Rawls, wherein fundamental rights and duties—the basic structure of social institutions—are examined. Consequently, the Arizona Project was not designed to ask, "Who killed Don Bolles and have they been brought to justice?" but, rather, to ask, "Are the social institutions operating properly in Arizona?" As Williams suggested, "Let's respond as journalists, the only way we know how. Professionally." By taking a systemic, Rawlsian approach to the question of justice, the team members extended the concept of investigative journalism from a practice that seeks out individuals who have committed crimes and corruption to a type of reporting that examines the underlying social factors that give rise to social problems such as crime.[10]

Reporting that results from a sense of outrage also must adhere to

9. Wendland, *Arizona Project*, 254; Lambeth, *Committed Journalism*, 26.
10. Wendland, *Arizona Project*, 30.

the principle of freedom as described by Lambeth. The act of reporting must further the protection of freedom of expression. This can be done by adhering to the principles of justice and truth and thereby strengthening the audience's trust in the news organization. This increases appreciation for the First Amendment. In addition, reporting must be free—autonomous or independent. This means that reporters must be free of malice and the appearance of malice as well as other compulsions that would color the trustworthiness of their stories. "A free press is free from compulsions from whatever source, governmental or social, external or internal," the 1947 Hutchins Commission on Freedom of the Press counseled.[11]

In a case of journalistic outrage, meeting this requirement is not easy. It requires soul-searching and honesty about one's motives and careful attention to goals. The IRE reporters masterfully accomplished this by refusing at the outset to go after Bolles's killers but, instead, to seek to protect the greater value of freedom of expression.

Moreover, to be morally robust, the virtue of courage must entail more than the endurance of long hours, low pay, and occasional physical risk. It had to begin with the conceptualization of the project, with the IRE members' willingness to stand up not just to Bolles's killers but also to all who would stifle free expression. Lambeth expands on this principle of stewardship: "A journalist ... is in a unique position to *help* keep the wells of public discourse unpoisoned, if not wholly clean. . . . As a special beneficiary of the First Amendment, the journalist has a material motive to protect a protection meant for all. It is his responsibility to do all of this, for he is a steward of free expression" (italics in original). Recognizing and accepting this responsibility at the outset of the Arizona Project showed IRE members had recognized the moral dictates of the traditions embedded in the history of investigative journalism. "The killing of a reporter is one hell of a way of depriving him of his First Amendment rights," Robert Greene told the Overseas Press Club in justification of the Arizona Project after the project concluded.[12]

Practicing the virtues turned what could have been a melodramatic crime series into a "MacIntyrean moment," to use Lambeth's

11. Lambeth, *Committed Journalism*, 29–30; Commission on Freedom of the Press, *A Free and Responsible Press*, 128.

12. Lambeth, *Committed Journalism*, 32; John Consoli, "IRE Execs Vow: No More Collective Investigations," *Editor and Publisher*, March 8, 1975, 12.

phrase, wherein journalists have reconceptualized, transmuted, and extended the goods of the practice. The social practice of investigative journalism was strengthened and systematically extended. Editors and reporters who supported the project explained that the Arizona Project expanded the existing tradition of shared resources such as combined news wires and "is an example of how newspapers can combine their resources for the public good in an investigation that they could not individually afford and which otherwise would not take place."[13]

The Arizona Project was an important event in the history of investigative journalism and a pivotal episode in the history of Investigative Reporters and Editors, Inc. It provided the vehicle for modern investigative journalism to become a defining characteristic of the press and to systematically extend the work of all journalists.

An examination of the work of investigative journalists published from 1960 to 1975 shows that there developed an understanding of the practice's important internal goods and the standards of excellence that should be applied. Investigative journalists also understood they must live the virtues of courage, justice, honesty, humaneness, freedom, stewardship, and sense of tradition. In essence, investigative journalism had already acquired many of the characteristics of a social practice when journalists suggested the creation of IRE. The organization, though, would complete the evolution of investigative journalism into a fully developed social practice. In a sense, IRE was a natural outgrowth of the process that was moving the practice toward an independent existence within the profession of journalism.

While the internal goods were understood and the standards of excellence were in place, investigative journalism was in danger of imploding from its own successes. It was characterized by fragmentation, isolation of practitioners, and unhealthy control by the institutions that supported the practice — the news organizations, which, in their pursuit of profits, would lead the practice in a frivolous and sensationalistic direction. Investigative journalism evolved like a social practice under MacIntyrean terms from 1960 to 1975, but it was not a social practice until the formation of IRE. Investigative Reporters and Editors provided the structure of a community of

13. Lambeth, "Waiting for a New St. Benedict," 103–4; Tom Collins, "Uniting Journalists for a Common Cause," 173–74.

interest for investigative journalists and a forum for investigativ journalists to discuss and to learn the internal goods and standard of excellence of the practice.

A sense of community is essential for a social practice, according to MacIntyre. IRE provided that community for investigative jour nalists. It allowed the practice to separate itself from the newsroom and other press institutions and allowed the practice to move for ward. MacIntyre explains that institutions, which are nevertheles essential for the support of social practices, are necessarily concernec with "external goods," such as profits, prestige, status, and socia power. But if a practice allows itself to be controlled by the institu tions that support it, the practice will ultimately be corrupted by the institutions' pursuit of these external goods. The body of journal ism is replete with examples of practices usurped for the purposes of the news institutions. Automotive, real estate, and sometimes health care reporters, for example, largely because these specialties have not successfully separated themselves from the institutions that support them, have been co-opted in many newsrooms, relegated to producing fluff news for the benefit of advertisers. IRE, in contrast, encouraged investigative journalists to see investigative journalism as an activity with goods internal to it and standards of excellence that must not be violated. This conceptualization allows an inves tigative reporter such as Joe Bergantino at Boston's WBZ-TV to dis tinguish between investigative journalism and stories that only ap pear to be investigative. "There's been a lot of scandal reporting passed off as investigative," he told an interviewer. His sense of what is "investigative journalism" separates reports that meet the standards and values of the practice from those like the news reports of Presi dent Bill Clinton and his affair with intern Monica Lewinsky and the reports about the congressional intern Chandra Levy's murder that do not.[14]

IRE's founders expressly sought to protect the standards of inves tigative journalism, to provide help to investigative journalists in the researching of stories, and to train journalists to use investigative techniques. The organizers rejected suggestions that IRE become an elite group of prominent investigative journalists and opted instead to welcome into the organization all journalists interested in using

14. MacIntyre, *After Virtue*, 178–79, 181; Hough, "Truth Be Told."

the techniques and methods of investigative journalism. The result was a broad-based organization capable of spreading investigative skills — public document use, in-depth interviews, and story conception that goes beyond reporting public-official announcements and acts — among beat journalists. This allowed the organization to upgrade the standards of journalism across the board. IRE encouraged reporters on daily assignment to use investigative techniques and methods and to search public records or ask questions that probed beneath the service. In this manner, investigative tools were taken into the mainstream of American journalism. "Local TV seldom has the staff or resources to do the longer in-depth pieces," IRE executive director Brant Houston explained to *Electronic Media*, "but there are times that the visualization of the story makes it much more powerful and compelling."[15] The same could be said about print media.

In addition to affecting American journalism, IRE has also contributed directly to the success of individual projects involving investigative reporting. Reporters could access IRE's substantial holdings of prior investigative reports to see what others might have done before on a topic similar to the one they were working on. Members received the *IRE Journal*, which disseminated information about skills and techniques of investigative journalism and provided a forum for discussion of the practice's values. Additionally, IRE brought reporters and editors together annually to network, to learn new skills, and to discuss issues important to the craft.

In the late 1980s, IRE grew into a financially stable organization firmly established within the American journalism industry. It continued to educate new reporters while at the same time providing more experienced reporters with training in the emerging technology of computer-assisted reporting. It continued to carry forth the basic standards of hard-news reporting to journalists throughout the United States and began to reach out to international journalists. Granted, lapses in the standards of investigative journalism led during the late 1980s and in the 1990s to embarrassing libel suits and other journalistic scandals, underscoring not that IRE had failed but that IRE is a service organization, not a policing organization

15. "Investigative Reporters and Editors Form Own Service Association," 10; "To Better Inform," *Editor and Publisher*, July 4, 1987, 6; Lee Hall, "Local News Must Dig Deeper Than the Hype," *Electronic Media*, October 21, 2002, 13.

for the craft. Journalism is not a profession. The law has the American Bar Association and state bar associations and medicine has the American Medical Association and affiliated state organizations to oversee the performance of their professionals. IRE could not develop into a regulator of investigative journalism in the same way the ABA and the AMA enforce standards in their professions. On the other hand, investigative journalism has become a social practice that supports and protects standards that all journalism can be held to. IRE has evolved into a clear and convincing standard-bearer and a leading educator for all journalists.

The MacIntyrean social practice paradigm ties together sociology and ethics and emphasizes the connection between the ethical performance of individual practitioners and the health of a practice. MacIntyre acknowledges that internal goods "are indeed the outcome of competition to excel" but stresses that an internal good is an end that, when achieved, "is a good for the whole community who participate in the practice." When Donald Barlett and James Steele produced their study of the Philadelphia criminal justice system through the use of computer analysis of court records in 1972, they advanced all investigative journalists by setting new standards of documentation and thoroughness for the practice. When Robert Greene and his *Newsday* team faced down organized crime–connected drug dealers and corrupt government officials to detail the heroin trail that existed between Turkey, France, and New York in 1974, the public was served and the practice benefited through the advancing of standards for investigative projects and investigative team management. In both cases, individual journalists propelled the entire practice forward. Similarly, the shameful mistakes of the few investigative reporters who have failed to live up to the standards of excellence and internal goods of the practice have tarnished the reputation of all journalists. When *Time* magazine published reporter David Halevy's unsubstantiated and incorrect report about Israeli General Ariel Sharon in 1983, its failure to require acceptable standards of the practice damaged not only its own reputation but the reputations of all investigative journalists as well. The examples of investigative missteps are many. The *Cincinnati Enquirer* paid Chiquita Brands well over ten million dollars in 1998 and ran a front-page apology after its top investigative reporter had illegally obtained information from the corporation's voice-mail system that he used in what was meant to be a blockbuster report on the sordid behavior of one of Cincinnati's largest companies. While the fourteen-page investigative report was factually solid, the reporter's illegal behavior destroyed its credibility. Likewise, *Time* and CNN, in connection with the début of their joint program, *NewsStand*, ended up paying substantial out-of-court settlements to libeled individuals after CNN investigators bungled an exposé and erroneously accused the U.S. Army of using sarin nerve gas on American deserters in Laos during the Vietnam War. Unfortunately, U.S. networks issued a number of botched investigations during the 1990s, including NBC *Dateline*'s rigged explosion of a General Motors truck to "expose" its unsafe gas cap in 1993, and the reporting that led to supermarket chain Food Lion's successful lawsuit in 1997 against ABC's *Prime Time Live* for fraud and lying on job applications. High-profile goof-ups, bald-faced frauds and thefts, and shoddy reporting wracked the practice of investigative journalism during the 1990s. Only by counterbalancing such indefensible blunders with the numerous ethically reported investigative stories that appeared in newspapers, magazines, and on television and cable during the 1980s and 1990s can the health of American investigative journalism be accurately gauged. Although the practice stumbled too often, it remained vibrant and healthy through the 1990s. As Douglass K. Daniel, a journalism professor at Kansas State University, observed for a 2000 book on the condition of investigative journalism, "[t]here has been a Dickensian quality to investigative reporting and the American press since Watergate, a mixture of the best of times and the worst of times. Great stories and embarrassing errors. New media that has brought promise and problems.... Time and time again, journalism had brought balance to society, and society had brought balance to journalism, as only a free society could." Taking the longer view of the practice as Daniel does fits well with the MacIntyrean paradigm, for MacIntyre offers an understanding of the role of tradition in the continuing progress of a practice. It explains the link between past practitioners and past examples of investigative journalism with contemporary investigative reporters and their work. "Practices of course ... have a history," MacIntyre has written. "We have to learn to recognize what is due to whom.... To enter into a practice is to enter into a relationship not only with its contemporary practitioners, but also with those who have preceded us in the practice, particularly those whose achievements extended the reach of the practice to its present point." In other words, a practice can progress only if it recognizes the standards established by past practitioners. Contemporary journalists must strive to meet and exceed those standards for investigative journalism to move forward. "For not to accept these," MacIntyre warns, "so far bars us from achieving the standards of excellence or the goods internal to the practice that it renders the practice pointless except as a device for achieving external goods."[16]

IRE has provided the means for investigative journalism to evolve into a viable social practice. It has built a community of interest among journalists interested in investigative reporting. Its resource center collects the history of investigative journalism so it can be shared with new practitioners and studied by veterans.

To MacIntyre, such cooperation is central to furtherance of a practice: "...[G]oods can only be achieved by subordinating ourselves to the best standard so far achieved, and that entails subordinating ourselves within the practice in our relationship to other practitioners....Every practice requires a certain kind of relationship between those who participate in it." L. Gregory Jones, writing of MacIntyre's notion of community, says this relationship among members of a practice is a "communion that exists through the time spent...sharing in practices." Out of this shared communion comes a shared vision and understanding of goods.[17]

Before the formation of IRE, a social practice of investigative journalism did not exist because there was no communion among practitioners wherein goods could be decided upon. IRE, through its annual meetings, regional conferences, monthly magazine, and annual contest, generates a continuing dialogue among practitioners.

MacIntyre's definition of a practice requires that practitioners establish and maintain standards of excellence, and when one enters

---

16. MacIntyre, *After Virtue*, 177–88; Clurman, *Beyond Malice*, 161; Douglas Frantz, "After Apology, Issues Raised in Chiquita Articles Remain," *New York Times*, July 17, 1998; "CNN Retracts Tailwind Coverage," July 2, 1998, http://www.cnn.com/US/9807/02/tailwind.johnson/, May 25, 2004; David Zurawik and Christina Stoehr, "Money Changes Everything," *American Journalism Review*, April 1993, 26–30; Scott Andron, "Food Lion versus ABC," *Quill*, March 1997, 15–21; Douglass K. Daniel, "Best of Times and Worst of Times: Investigative Reporting in Post-Watergate America," 31.

17. MacIntyre, *After Virtue*, 188; L. Gregory Jones, "Alasdair MacIntyre on Narrative, Community, and the Moral Life," *Modern Theology*, 4, no. 1 (1987): 63.

a practice he or she must "accept the authority of those standards" and be willing to have one's own work judged in relation to those standards.[18] IRE, through its awards presentations, its seminars, and its publications, teaches, assesses, and rewrites the standards of excellence for investigative reporting. Standards existed before the founding of IRE, of course, but they were informal standards not sanctioned by a national organization dedicated to the improvement and maintenance of the craft. From the beginning of IRE's founding, its goal was to identify and promote standards of excellence. At IRE's first national conference in 1976, in fact, the program was designed to educate investigative journalists on standards of excellence, as well as on specific skills. In addition, creation of the IRE awards program in 1980 further contributed to the establishment of standards by holding up the best work as examples of how the craft should be carried out.

Throughout its existence, IRE has worked to create the social practice of investigative journalism. It has contributed to a self-consciousness among investigative reporters and editors that allows a conceptualization of the practice that is separate from the news organizations. Consequently, instead of looking to the institutions for leadership in the skills and ethics of investigative journalism, reporters and editors look to IRE for the guidance, and through this communion of practitioners, investigative journalism is extended and refined, and therein, the practice continues to define the qualities of great journalism.

18. MacIntyre, *After Virtue*, 178.

Selected Bibliography

Books

Anderson, Jack. *The Anderson Papers.* New York: Random House, 1973.
———, with James Boyd. *Confessions of a Muckraker.* New York: Random House, 1979.
Anonymous. *More Washington Merry-Go-Round.* New York: Horace Liveright, 1932.
Anonymous. *Washington Merry-Go-Round.* New York: Horace Liveright, 1931.
Armstrong, David. *A Trumpet to Arms: Alternative Media in America.* Boston: South End Press, 1981.
Aronson, James. *The Press and the Cold War.* Indianapolis: Bobbs-Merrill, 1970.
Baker, Russell. *The Good Times.* New York: William Morrow, 1989.
Baughman, James L. *The Republic of Mass Culture: Journalism, Filmmaking, and Broadcasting in America since 1941.* Baltimore: John Hopkins University Press, 1992.
Bayley, Edwin R. *Joe McCarthy and the Press.* New York: Pantheon, 1981.
Behrens, John C. *The Typewriter Guerrillas: Closeups of 20 Top Investigative Reporters.* Chicago: Nelson-Hall, 1977.
Benjamin, Burton. *Fair Play: CBS, General Westmoreland, and How a Television Documentary Went Wrong.* New York: Harper and Row, 1988.
Benjaminson, Peter, and David Anderson. *Investigative Reporting.* Bloomington: Indiana University Press, 1976.

Bent, Silas. *Newspaper Crusaders: A Neglected Story.* Westport, Conn.: Greenwood, 1970.

Bernstein, Carl, and Bob Woodward. *All the President's Men.* New York: Simon and Schuster, 1974.

Blum, John Morton. *Years of Discord: American Politics and Society, 1961–1974.* New York: W. W. Norton, 1991.

Brasch, Walter M. *Forerunners of Revolution: Muckrakers and the American Social Conscience.* Lanham, Md.: University Press of America, 1990.

Broder, David S. *Behind the Front Page: A Candid Look at How the News Is Made.* New York: Simon and Schuster, 1987.

Brown, Charlene J., Trevor R. Brown, and William L. Rivers. *The Media and the People.* New York: Holt, Rinehart and Winston, 1978.

Carey, James. *Communication as Culture: Essays on Media and Society.* Boston: Unwin Hyman, 1989.

Chafee, Zechariah, Jr. *Government and Mass Communications.* Vol. 2. Chicago: University of Chicago Press, 1947.

Chalmers, David Mark. *The Muckrake Years.* Huntington, N.Y.: Robert Krieger, 1980.

Chepesiuk, Ron, Haney Howell, and Edward Lee. *Raising Hell: Straight Talk with Investigative Journalists.* Jefferson, N.C.: McFarland, 1997.

Clurman, Richard M. *Beyond Malice: The Media's Years of Reckoning.* New York: New American, 1990.

Colbert, Jan, Bruce Moores, and Steve Weinberg, eds. *Top 100 Investigations: Investigative Reporters and Editors Selected 1989 Contest Winners.* Columbia, Mo.: Investigative Reporters and Editors, Inc., 1990.

Dicken-Garcia, Hazel. *Journalistic Standards in Nineteenth-Century America.* Madison: University of Wisconsin Press, 1989.

Digby-Junger, Richard. *The Journalist as Reformer: Henry Demarest Lloyd and* Wealth Against Commonwealth. Westport, Conn.: Greenwood Press, 1996.

Donovan, Robert J., and Ray Scherer. *Unsilent Revolution: Television News and American Public Life 1948–1991.* Cambridge, England: Cambridge University Press, 1992.

Downie, Leonard, Jr. *The New Muckrakers.* New York: New American, 1976.

Dygert, James H. *The Investigative Journalist: Folk Heroes of a New Era.* Englewood Cliffs, N.J.: Prentice-Hall, 1976.

Emerson, Thomas I. *The System of Free Expression*. New York: Random House, 1970.

Epstein, Edward Jay. *Between Fact and Fiction: The Problem of Journalism*. New York: Vintage, 1975.

Ettema, James S., and Theodore L. Glasser. *Custodians of Conscience: Investigative Journalism and Public Virtue*. New York: Columbia University Press, 1998.

Ewen, Stuart. *Captains of Consciousness: Advertising and the Social Roots of the Consumer Culture*. New York: McGraw-Hill, 1976.

Fitzpatrick, Ellen F. *Muckraking: Three Landmark Articles*. Boston: Bedford Books, 1994.

Forer, Lois G. *A Chilling Effect: The Mounting Threat of Libel and Invasion of Privacy Actions to the First Amendment*. New York: Norton, 1987.

Garment, Suzanne. *Scandal: The Culture of Mistrust in American Politics*. New York: Times Books, 1991.

Gitlin, Todd. *The Sixties: Years of Hope, Days of Rage*. New York: Bantam, 1989.

———. *The Whole World Is Watching: Mass Media in the Making and Unmaking of the New Left*. Berkeley: University of California Press, 2003.

Glessing, Robert. *The Underground Press in America*. Bloomington: Indiana University Press, 1970.

Goldstein, Tom. *The News At Any Cost: How Journalists Compromise Their Ethics to Shape the News*. New York: Touchstone, 1985.

Greenwald, Marilyn, and Joseph Bernt, eds. *The Big Chill: Investigative Reporting in the Current Media Environment*. Ames: Iowa State University Press, 2000.

Halberstam, David. *The Powers That Be*. New York: Alfred Knopf, 1979.

Hallin, Daniel C. *The "Uncensored War": The Media and Vietnam*. New York: Oxford University Press, 1986.

Heath, Jim F. *Decade of Disillusionment: The Kennedy-Johnson Years*. Bloomington: Indiana University Press, 1975.

Hersh, Seymour. *My Lai 4: A Report on the Massacre and Its Aftermath*. New York: Random House, 1970.

Hess, Stephen. *The Washington Reporters*. Washington, D.C.: Brookings Institute, 1981.

Hodgson, Godfrey. *America in Our Time: From World War II to Nixon, What Happened and Why*. New York: Vintage, 1978.

Hume, Brit. *Inside Story*. New York: Doubleday, 1974.

Johnson, Michael L. *The New Journalism: The Underground Press, the Artists of Nonfiction, and Changes in the Established Media.* Lawrence: University Press of Kansas, 1971.

Johnstone, J. W. C., E. J. Slawski, and W. W. Bowman. *The News People.* Urbana: University of Illinois Press, 1976.

Kutler, Stanley I. *The Wars of Watergate: The Last Crisis of Richard Nixon.* New York: W. W. Norton, 1990.

Lambeth, Edmund. *Committed Journalism: An Ethic for the Profession.* 2d ed. Bloomington: Indiana University Press, 1992.

Leamer, Laurence. *The Paper Revolutionaries: The Rise of the Underground Press.* New York: Simon and Schuster, 1972.

Lears, T. J. Jackson, and R. Fox, eds. *The Culture of Consumption.* New York: Pantheon, 1983.

Leonard, Thomas C. *The Power of the Press.* New York: Oxford University Press, 1986.

Lewis, Anthony. *Make No Law: The Sullivan Case and the First Amendment.* New York: Vintage, 1991.

Lubars, Walter, and John Wicklein, eds. *Investigative Reporting: The Lessons of Watergate.* Boston: Boston University, 1975.

MacIntyre, Alasdair. *After Virtue: A Study in Moral Theory.* Notre Dame, Ind.: University of Notre Dame Press, 1981.

Marchand, Roland. *Advertising the American Dream: Making Way for Modernity, 1920–1940.* Berkeley: University of California Press, 1985.

Marion, George. *Stop the Press!* New York: Fairplay Publishers, 1953.

Matusow, Allen J. *The Unraveling of America: A History of Liberalism in the 1960s.* New York: Harper, 1984.

McQuaid, Kim. *The Anxious Years: America in the Vietnam-Watergate Era.* New York: Basic, 1989.

Meiklejohn, Alexander. *Free Speech and Its Relation to Self-Government.* New York: Harper and Bros., 1948.

Mencken, H. L. *Newspaper Days.* New York: Alfred A. Knopf, 1941.

Meyer, Philip. *Precision Journalism: A Reporter's Introduction to Social Science Methods.* Bloomington: Indiana University Press, 1973.

Miraldi, Robert. *Muckraking and Objectivity: Journalism's Colliding Traditions.* New York: Greenwood, 1990.

Mitford, Jessica. *Poison Penmanship: The Gentle Art of Muckraking.* New York: Alfred A. Knopf, 1979.

Mollenhoff, Clark R. *Investigative Reporting: From Courthouse to White House.* New York: Macmillan Publishing, 1981.

Newhall, Beaumont. *The History of Photography*. 4th ed. New York: Museum of Modern Art, 1978.

Patterson, Margaret Jones, and Robert H. Russell. *Behind the Lines: Case Studies in Investigative Reporting*. New York: Columbia University Press, 1986.

Peck, Abe. *Uncovering the Sixties: The Life and Times of the Underground Press*. New York: Pantheon, 1985.

Phelan, James. *Scandals, Scamps, and Scoundrels: The Casebook of an Investigative Reporter*. New York: Random House, 1982.

Protess, David L., Fay Lomax Cook, Jack C. Doppelt, James S. Ettema, Margaret T. Gordon, Donna R. Leff, Peter Miller. *The Journalism of Outrage: Investigative Reporting and Agenda Building in America*. New York: Guilford Press, 1991.

Rabban, David M. *Free Speech in Its Forgotten Years*. Cambridge, England: Cambridge University Press, 1997.

Regier, C. C. *The Era of the Muckrakers*. Chapel Hill: University of North Carolina Press, 1932.

Reston, James. *Deadline: A Memoir*. New York: Random House, 1991.

Rivers, William L. *The Other Government: Power and the Washington Media*. New York: Universe Books, 1982.

Rosten, Leo. *The Washington Correspondents*. New York: Harcourt, Brace, 1937.

Salisbury, Harrison. *Without Fear or Favor: An Uncompromising Look at the* New York Times. New York: Times Books, 1980.

Schudson, Michael. *Discovering the News: A Social History of American Newspapers*. New York: Basic, 1978.

——. *The Power of News*. Cambridge, Mass.: Harvard University Press, 1995.

——. *Watergate in American Memory: How We Remember, Forget, and Reconstruct the Past*. New York: Basic, 1992.

Shapiro, Bruce, ed. *Shaking the Foundations: 200 Years of Investigative Journalism in America*. New York: Thunder's Mouth, 2003.

Sinclair, Upton. *The Brass Check*. Self-published, 1919.

Sloan, William David, and Cheryl S. Wray, eds. *Masterpieces of Reporting*. Vol. 1. Northport, Ala.: Vision Press, 1997.

Smith, Zay N., and Pamela Zekman. *The Mirage Bar*. New York: Random House, 1979.

Steffens, Lincoln. *The Autobiography of Lincoln Steffens*. Vol. 1. New York: Harcourt Brace Jovanovich, 1958.

Streitmatter, Rodger. *Mightier than the Sword: How the News Media*

Have Shaped American History. Boulder, Colo.: Westview Press, 1997.

Summers, Mark Wahlgren. *The Press Gang: Newspapers and Politics, 1865–1878.* Chapel Hill: University of North Carolina Press, 1994.

Tucker, Andie. *Froth and Scum: Truth, Beauty, Goodness, and the Ax Murder in America's First Mass Medium.* Chapel Hill: University of North Carolina Press, 1994.

Turner, Kathleen J. *Lyndon Johnson's Dual War: Vietnam and the Press.* Chicago: University of Chicago Press, 1985.

Ungar, Sanford J. *The Papers and the Papers: An Account of the Legal and Political Battle over the Pentagon Papers.* New York: E. P. Dutton, 1975.

Viorst, Milton. *Fire in the Streets: America in the 1960's.* New York: Simon and Schuster, 1979.

Weaver, David H., and G. Cleveland Wilhoit. *American Journalist: A Portrait of U.S. News People and Their Work.* 2d ed. Bloomington: Indiana University Press, 1991.

Weinberg, Steve. *Telling the Untold Story: How Investigative Reporters Are Changing the Craft of Biography.* Columbia: University of Missouri Press, 1992.

Wendland, Michael F. *The Arizona Project.* Mesa, Ariz.: Blue Sky Press, 1988.

Wendt, Lloyd. *Chicago Tribune: The Rise of a Great American Newspaper.* Chicago: Rand McNally, 1979.

Williams, Paul. *Investigative Reporting and Editing.* Englewood Cliffs, N.J.: Prentice-Hall, 1978.

Wilson, Harold. *McClure's Magazine and the Muckrakers.* Princeton, N.J.: Princeton University Press, 1970.

Wolseley, R. E., and Laurence R. Campbell. *Exploring Journalism.* New York: Prentice-Hall, 1946.

Wyatt, Clarence R. *Paper Soldiers: The American Press and the Vietnam War.* New York: Norton, 1993.

Articles, Book Chapters, Theses and Dissertations

"Investigative Reporters Form Own Service Association." *Editor and Publisher,* March 8, 1975, 10.

"Investigative Reporting Has Broad Public Support." *Gallup Report* 196 (1982): 31–37.

"More Investigative Expertise Urged." *Publishers Auxiliary*, December 21, 1974, 1.

Abbott, Stan. "A Study of the Status of Investigative Reporting in the 1980s." Master's thesis, University of Missouri–Columbia, 1987.

———. "National Survey Charts Growth of Investigative Reporting." *IRE Journal*, Summer 1986, 5–7.

Alterman, Eric. "The Ironies of Izzymania." *Mother Jones*, June 1988, 34–37.

Anderson, D. A. "Libel and Press Self-Censorship." *Texas Law Review* 53 (1975): 422–81.

Anderson, Douglas A., and Marianne Murdock. "Effects of Communication Law Decisions on Daily Newspaper Editors." *Journalism Quarterly* 58, no. 4 (Winter 1981): 525–28, 534.

Ashmore, Harry S. "The Story Behind Little Rock." In Louis M. Lyons, ed., *Reporting the News: Selections from Nieman Reports* (New York: Atheneum, 1968), 132–40.

Bagdikian, Ben H. "The Press and Its Crisis of Identity." In Warren K. Agee, ed., *Mass Media in a Free Society* (Lawrence: University Press of Kansas, 1969), 2–14.

Baldasty, Gerald J. "The Nineteenth-Century Origins of Modern American Journalism." In John B. Hench, ed., *Three Hundred Years of the American Newspaper* (Worcester: American Antiquarian Society, 1991), 407–19.

Bent, Silas. "Journalism and Morality." *Atlantic Monthly*, June 1926, 761.

Blanchard, Margaret. "The Hutchins Commission: The Press and Responsibility Concept." *Journalism Monographs* 49 (May 1977).

Blasi, Vincent. "The Checking Value in First Amendment Theory." *American Bar Foundation Research Journal* (1977): 521–649.

———. "The Newsman's Privilege: An Empirical Study." *Michigan Law Review* 70 (1970–71): 229–84.

Blevens, Fred. "The Hutchins Commission Turns 50: Recurring Themes in Today's Public and Civic Journalism." Paper presented at the third annual Conference on Intellectual Freedom, Montana State University–Northern, April 1997.

———. "Introduction: Shifting Paradigms of Investigative Journalism." *American Journalism* 3–4 (Summer-Fall 1997): 257–61.

Boylan, James. "Declarations of Independence: A Historian Reflects on an Era in Which Reporters Rose Up to Challenge — and Change — the Rules of the Game." *Columbia Journalism Review*, November-December 1986, 30–41.

———. "Reconstructing I. F. Stone." *Columbia Journalism Review*, September/October 1989, 46–47.

Cater, Douglass. "The Captive Press." *The Reporter*, June 1950, 17.

Christianson, K. Scott. "The New Muckraking." *Quill*, July 1972, 10–15.

Clark, Charles E. "The Newspapers of Provincial America." In John B. Hench, ed., *Three Hundred Years of the American Newspaper* (Worcester: American Antiquarian Society, 1991), 367–89.

Collins, Tom. "Uniting Journalists for a Common Cause." In Walter M. Brasch, ed., *Forerunners of Revolution: Muckrakers and the American Social Conscience* (Lanham, Md.: University Press of America, 1990), 170–74.

Coonradt, Frederic C. "The Law of Libel Has Been All but Repealed." *Quill*, February 1972, 316–19.

Daniel, Douglass K. "Best of Times and Worst of Times: Investigative Reporting in Post-Watergate America." In Marilyn Greenwald and Joseph Bernt, eds., *The Big Chill: Investigative Reporting in the Current Media Environment* (Ames: Iowa State University Press, 2000), 11–33.

Diamond, Edwin. "Reporter Power Takes Root." In David J. Leroy and Christopher H. Sterling, eds., *Mass News: Practices, Controversies, and Alternatives* (Englewood Cliffs, N.J.: Prentice-Hall, 1973), 241–49.

Dotinga, Randy. "News Probes Face Obstacles." *Editor and Publisher*, June 10, 2002, 9.

Ehrlich, Matthew C. "Not Ready for Prime Time: Tabloid and Investigative TV Journalism." In Marilyn Greenwald and Joseph Bernt, eds., *The Big Chill: Investigative Reporting in the Current Media Environment* (Ames: Iowa State University Press, 2000), 103–20.

Ettema, James. "Discourse That Is Closer to Silence Than to Talk: The Politics and Possibilities of Reporting on Victims of War." *Critical Studies in Mass Communication* 11, no. 1 (March 1994): 1–21.

———, and Theodore L. Glasser. "Narrative Form and Moral Force: The Realization of Innocence and Guilt through Investigative Journalism." *Journal of Communication* 38, no. 3 (1988): 8–26.

Ferguson, O. J. "Ideals and Duties of Journalism." In Frank Luther Mott, ed., *Journalism in Wartime: A Symposium of the School of Journalism, the University of Missouri* (Washington, D.C.: American Council on Public Affairs, 1943), 191–93.

Fielder, Virginia Dodge, and David H. Weaver. "Public Opinion on Investigative Reporting." *Newspaper Research Journal* 3, no. 57 (1982): 54–62.

Gieber, Walter. "News Is What Newspapermen Make It." In Lewis A. Dexter and David Manning White, eds., *People, Society, and Mass Communications* (New York: Free Press, 1964), 173–80.

Glasser, Theodore L., and James S. Ettema. "Investigative Journalism and the Moral Order." *Critical Studies in Mass Communication* 6, no. 1 (March 1989): 1–20.

Gopnik, Adam. "Read All About It." *New Yorker,* December 12, 1994, 84–102.

Hallin, Daniel C. "The Media, the War in Vietnam, and Political Support: A Critique of the Thesis of an Oppositional Media." *Journal of Politics* 46 (1984): 2–24.

Hamill, Pete. Foreword to Bruce Shapiro, ed., *Shaking the Foundations: 200 Years of Investigative Journalism in America* (New York: Thunder Mouth Press, 2003).

Hamilton, Mary Allienne. "J. W. Gitt: The Cold War's Voice in the Wilderness." *Journalism Monographs* 91 (February 1985).

Hartgen, Stephen. "Investigative Reporting: There's More Here Than Meets a Dragon's Eye." *Quill,* April 1975, 13.

Herbers, John. "The Reporter in the Deep South." In Louis M. Lyons, ed., *Reporting the News: Selections from Nieman Reports* (New York: Atheneum, 1968), 221–27.

Hindman, Elizabeth Blanks. "First Amendment Theories and Press Responsibility: The Work of Zechariah Chafee, Thomas Emerson, Vincent Blasi and Edwin Baker." *Journalism Quarterly* 69, no. 1 (Spring 1992): 48–64.

Hohenberg, John. "New Patterns in Public Service." *Columbia Journalism Review,* Summer 1962, 14–17.

———. "Public Service: A 1964 Honor Roll." *Columbia Journalism Review,* Summer 1964, 11.

Hough, Lory. "Truth Be Told." *Kennedy School Bulletin* (Autumn 2002). http://www.southernct.edu/~seymour/cases/invest.htm.

Ireland, Alleyne. "Joseph Pulitzer on Practical Newspaper Ethics." In Frank Luther Mott and Ralph D. Casey, eds., *Interpretations of Journalism: A Book of Readings* (New York: F. S. Crofts, 1937), 462–63.

Just, Marion, Rosalind Levine, and Kathleen Regan. "Investigative Journalism Despite the Odds." *Columbia Journalism Review*, November-December 2002, 102–5.

Karnow, Stanley. "The Newsmen's War in Vietnam." In Louis M. Lyons, ed., *Reporting the News: Selections from Nieman Reports* (New York: Atheneum, 1968), 356–66.

Kennedy, George. "Advocates of Openness: The Freedom of Information Movement." Ph.D. diss., University of Missouri, August 1978.

Klaven, Harry, Jr. "The New York Times Case: A Note on 'The Central Meaning of the First Amendment.'" *Supreme Court Review* (1964): 191–221.

Kraslow, David J. "National Security Fibs." In Louis M. Lyons, ed., *Reporting the News: Selections from Nieman Reports* (New York: Atheneum, 1968), 346–48.

Labunski, Richard E., and John V. Pavlik. "The Legal Environment of Investigative Reporters: A Pilot Study." *Newspaper Research Journal* 5, no. 3 (1985): 13–19.

Lambeth, Edmund. "The Lost Career of Paul Y. Anderson." *Journalism Quarterly* 60, no. 3 (Fall 1983): 401–6.

———. "Waiting for a New St. Benedict: Alasdair MacIntyre and the Theory and Practice of Journalism." *Business and Professional Ethics Journal* 9, no. 1–2 (1990): 97–108.

Lapham, Lewis H. "The Temptation of a Sacred Cow." *Harper's Magazine*, August 1973, 43–44.

Locklin, Bruce. "Digging Without a Shovel." *Nieman Reports*, Spring 1985, 51–52.

Lyons, Louis M. "Introduction: *Nieman Reports* and Nieman Fellowships." In Louis M. Lyons, ed., *Reporting the News: Selections from Nieman Reports* (New York: Atheneum, 1968), 1–51.

McWilliams, Carey. "Is Muckraking Coming Back?" *Columbia Journalism Review*, Fall 1970, 8–15.

Mencken, H. L. "Newspaper Morals." *Atlantic Monthly*, March 1914, 280–93.

Mollenhoff, Clark. "Investigative Reporting: The Precarious Profession." *Nieman Reports*, Summer 1976, 37.

Moyers, Bill D. "The Press and the Government: Who's Telling the

Truth?" In Warren K. Agee, ed., *Mass Media in a Free Society* (Lawrence: University Press of Kansas, 1969), 17–36.

Nord, David Paul. "Newspapers and American Nationhood, 1776–1826." In John B. Hench, ed., *Three Hundred Years of the American Newspaper* (Worcester: American Antiquarian Society, 1991), 391–419.

Opt, Susan K., and Timothy A. Delaney. "Public Perceptions of Investigative Reporting." In Marilyn Greenwald and Joseph Bernt, eds., *The Big Chill: Investigative Reporting in the Current Media Environment* (Ames: Iowa State University Press, 2000), 81–102.

Rowan, Carl T. "The Mass Media in an Era of Explosive Social Change." In Warren K. Agee, ed., *Mass Media in a Free Society* (Lawrence: University Press of Kansas, 1969), 39–48.

Rubin, David M. "The Perils of Muckraking." *[MORE]*, September 1974, 5–9, 21.

Schudson, Michael. "Watergate: A Study in Mythology." *Columbia Journalism Review*, May/June 1992, 28–33.

Smith, Robert M. "Why So Little Investigative Reporting?" *[MORE]*, August 1975, 7–9.

Stein, M. I. "Investigative Journalism Is Alive and Well." *Editor and Publisher*, June 13, 1998, 21.

———. "IRE Continues to Help Teach Investigative Reporters." *Editor and Publisher*, July 4, 1987, 11.

Weaver, David, and LeAnne Daniels. "Public Opinion on Investigative Reporting in the 1980s." *Journalism Quarterly* 69, no. 1 (Spring 1992): 146–55.

Weinberg, Steve. "Avenging Angel or Deceitful Devil?: The Evolution of Drew Pearson, a New Kind of Investigative Journalist." *American Journalism* 14, nos. 3–4 (Summer-Fall 1997): 283–302.

Whitney, D. Charles. "The Media and the People: Americans' Experience with the News Media: A Fifty-Year Review." Gannett Center for Media Studies (1985): 1–14.

Wood, Gordon S. "Intellectual History and the Social Sciences." In John Higham and Paul Conkin, eds., *New Directions in American Intellectual History* (Baltimore: Johns Hopkins University Press, 1979), 27–41.

Index

About the Author

Peggy Hanse

J ames L. Aucoin is Associate Professor of Communications at the University of South Alabama in Mobile. He is the author of *Water in Nebraska: Uses, Politics, Policies.*